DEEP IN THE BLUE

DEEP IN THE BLUE

A Life of Diving

*

REG VALLINTINE

A free diver is in the blue when he has lost sight of the surface,
cannot yet see the bottom, and his eye does
not lighten on any point of reference.
He finds nothing around him, but the deep blue of the sea.

ROBERT GRUSS, *The Art of the Aqualung*, 1953

ACHILLES PRESS

Published by Achilles Press
Craster Tower North, Craster, Alnwick, Northumberland NE66 3SS
London Office: Room 28, 53 Davies Street, London W1K 5JH
Reg Vallintine © 2007

ISBN 978 0 9547654 1 5

OTHER BOOKS BY REG VALLINTINE
Divers and Diving, (Blandford) 1981
The Pocket Guide to Underwater Diving, (Bell & Hyman) 1985
Learn to Scuba Dive in a Weekend, (Dorling Kindersley) 1993
The Club – a Celebration of the British Sub-Aqua Club, 1953-2003
(Circle Books) 2003

FRONTISPIECE:
Reg teaching at the London Underwater Centre, 1984
Photo by Keith Morris

Iain Bain *Typographer*
Newnham, Hertfordshire
Printed in Great Britain by
St Edmundsbury Press, Bury St Edmunds

CONTENTS

LIST OF ILLUSTRATIONS

LIST OF MAPS

Drawn by Reginald Piggott

ACKNOWLEDGEMENTS

Thanks are due to my friend Frank Sharratt who made the publication of this book possible and to my brother, John for his proof-reading skills. I am thankful to other friends who supplied suggestions, corrections and reminders. They include Elfie and Tom Baum, John Bevan, Trudy Brizzi, Roger Hale, Vernon Knapper, Peter Robyns, John and Jane Selby, Sam Selby, Seth Sethna, Bill Smith and Loran Waite. Finally to Iain Bain who designed and produced the book.

To friends and lovers –
may they forgive what I have written

INTRODUCTION

Just over 40 years ago, I was sitting in Giglio Porto with Alexander McKee, an established author, and discoverer of the wreck of the *Mary Rose*. I told him that I had been commissioned to write a diving autobiography. 'Do it now!' he urged, 'before you forget – you've got more material than any of us'.

My contract was passed from publisher to publisher as they gobbled each other up like hungry sharks, but I never produced 'the goods'. Now that I've reached my three-quarter century and am still diving, in spite of a few gadgets in my heart, the time must be right.

Memory sometimes plays tricks when you look back over 70 years and so I apologise for any unintentional inaccuracy or exaggeration. I do stand by the accuracy of the accounts of dives, as I have a log of all of them beside me as I write.

REG VALLINTINE

PROLOGUE

Using every ounce of energy I had, I fought my way up towards the surface. Breaking through, I swam round to our boat bobbling gently in the distance. I tore out my mouthpiece. 'Get me a line and another bottle', I shouted. They began to move as I swam in.

I knew that Ron Blake's life was ebbing away, trapped in the blackness a hundred feet below me. I grabbed the spare air cylinder, holding it against my stomach and changed mouthpieces. They passed down the thin coil of line into my other hand. No time to take the other set off my back. I swam down.

After what seemed an eternity, the black mouth of the cave, swirling with silt appeared before me. Linden helped me tie on the line and had to leave, her air exhausted. I started into the darkness. One hand on the line and the other feeling ahead for Ron. My air cylinder was floating away from me in the darkness only attached by the soft rubber mouthpiece which I was biting into to keep my supply going. I could see nothing through my mask but blackness and swirling silt. I desperately moved further in, sweeping my arm in front of me.

Suddenly I felt something soft in the darkness. It was an ankle. There was no sign of movement …

The date was the 7th September 1966 and it was probably the worst moment of my life …

CHAPTER ONE

First Dives

LIKE MANY BRITONS, I have always been drawn to the sea. My first swimming experiences as a young boy were, however, in the warm waters of the Caribbean where my father had been stationed in the army before World War Two.

We used to spend our summer holidays high in the Blue Mountains in the interior of Jamaica. This was known as the 'cockpit country' where the 'maroons', descendants of escaped slaves, lived, out of sight in the forest. It was cooler up there in the summer and we hired a small bungalow in the hills near Newcastle. It was there that my younger brother, John, and I learnt to swim in the Hope River in a quiet pool surrounded by floating watercress beds.

My mother had been a competitive swimmer in Dover in her youth, but my father's efforts consisted of walking carefully into the sea until it was up to his neck and then 'swimming like hell for the shore'. My parent's marriage had been an improbable love-match. Mother's aunts were among the first women doctors, teachers, graduates and suffragettes, but my father came from humbler stock. My maternal grandfather's thoughts on hearing that his eldest daughter was to marry a mere soldier in the Buffs whose father had been an unsuccessful house painter is not recorded. Forty years later when my father became a colonel, I think he was finally accepted by mother's family.

We spent four years in Jamaica during which my brother and I took turns in trying to kill each other, fortunately without success. The only time we combined our efforts, we set fire to the family bungalow while our parents were enjoying their afternoon siesta. They awoke to find smoke coming up from between the floorboards and the local fire-fighters were called in. By this time, my brother and I, who had been smoking out ants' nests, had left for an urgent appointment elsewhere. Retribution inevitably followed.

Looking back, it was an idyllic childhood, climbing our mango trees, collecting the ripe fruit and being put into the bath to preserve our clothes while we ate them (the mangoes that is). We explored Fern Gully an underground green world with fronds closing out the sky, and Dunn's River Falls where you could climb up to pools of gushing cool water as it came down on to the beach. Special friends were the Dickinsons, a black doctor and his family who ranged through all the variations from black to white. Helen Dickinson who was our age, had golden hair and blue

15

eyes. The story went that my brother and I were 'chased in by barracudas' while swimming with my mother. I certainly remember her having to have sea egg spines cut out of her foot.

We survived two hurricanes, one on board the *Ettrick*, a small passenger ship that was bringing us back to England. That was in 1939 and I was nine. We returned to our house in North Kent, which backed on to a large park, soon the scene of more youthful adventures.

The war brought excitement in the shape of German and British aircraft dog-fighting across the skies and we became experts at aircraft recognition. We collected the cases of incendiary bombs that landed in the park and, after filing them down, mixed the magnesium with potassium permanganate to make an explosive mixture. We set our 'bombs' off on a mound in the park. The bombs got bigger and bigger until one of my school friends, who had a real talent, managed to explode a charge of nitrogen iodide on his desk at school. He narrowly survived.

By the early 40s I was at Dartford Grammar School, four miles down the road and cycled there every day. Sometimes school hours were interrupted by air raids and we spent hours in tunnel-like shelters under the playground. School work suffered from this and the absence of younger teachers fighting the war.

New interests were raising their heads: Girls, table tennis and swimming. My first girl friend was called Olive and was slim and darkly elegant. I was painfully shy and she soon tired of me and I went on to a longer relationship with a county school girl called Joyce, whose powerful kisses took my breath away.

Table tennis became all consuming. We played at a youth club vaguely attached to a church. It was called the Guild of St Peter. We followed the international stars of the sport, Vana, Bergmann and later, the Americans, Miles and Reismann. By the time we were old enough to migrate into the Guild of St Andrew, we were playing in the local table tennis league.

At the other side of Danson Park stood Danson Lido, an open air pool where I spent hours practising my crawl until I couldn't open my chlorine-burnt eyes. We were in awe of a wild young man who high-dived from the top boards and was known as 'Tarzan'. Many years later I discovered that another young lad who shared our experiences there at the time, was David Bellamy, later a professor, botanist and diver.

Summer holidays were spent in Dover with father's sister, 'Auntie Doll' who had a flat at East Cliff next to the beach. I was enthused by the idea of swimming the channel and used to practice with a 16-year old boy from Ossett in Yorkshire called Philip Mickman, who was a serious contender. He successfully completed the swim taking longer than anyone before: 23 hours and 59 minutes, an incredible time to spend in the channel without protective clothing. 'Tell yourself it's warm', he used to say to me, as we swam to and fro between the groins in the harbour. Good advice for the future.

At the height of the German blitz on London, my mother took us to Barnstable in North Devon where we spent a year at the local Grammar School. We returned in time to experience the German secret weapons, V1 and V2. I remember watching the flying bombs speed along, and waiting for their engines to cut out, which meant they would be on their way down. We spent the nights at home in a Morrison Shelter, a kind of huge iron table in the front room. It all seemed tremendous fun to my brother and me at the time.

By 1946 I had scraped through School Certificate and an intermediate piano award and entered the Lower Sixth Form (Arts) at Dartford. Two teachers became an inspiration, Mr Mackerith, who had just returned from the war, in English and Mr Ratcliffe, a quirky old bird, in History. One of my sixth form friends, Alan Simmonds, introduced me to jazz and we went to see George Webb and his Dixielanders, probably the first British jazz band, at the Red Barn in Barnhurst nearby.

Father returned from the war and imposed a new set of rules, which I initially rebelled against. Then he was posted to Aldershot, so we saw him less often for a while. Mother held the family together as she always had, devoting herself to her sons unconditionally.

My brother left school to become articled to mother's brother, Fred, who had his own firm of chartered accountants in the City, and I stayed on in the sixth form, failing exams and enjoying life until it was time for the call-up for national service. The call came on the 3rd of January 1950.

It seemed natural at the time to choose the RAF, as I had admired 'the few' who had won the Battle of Britain and could recognise aircraft while they were still only dots in the sky. After square bashing, I was sent to Hornchurch for aircrew testing, but failed on the sight of one eye which was not quite the 100% needed to be a pilot. I was then posted to Prestwick Air Traffic Control Centre where I worked under the RAF air traffic controllers, giving instruction to RAF pilots and sitting next to a civilian controller who tried to keep the newly created airways clear of our maverick flights.

The first jet fighter, the Meteor had just been introduced into the RAF. They could only stay up for 30 minutes before running short of fuel and I remember the desperate Mayday calls as they tried to find emergency landing fields. Pilot Officer Griffin from Canada was wilder than the others. He would rev up his Meteor at the end of the runway until it was quivering and then, ignoring the correct procedure, would shout:

'Give me the woid and I'll make like a boid.'

'Cleared to take off', call again at 10,000 feet'.

There was a moment's pause and he would answer 'Roger, 10,000'. We presumed that he was then starting to climb until we knew him better. He was already there, having climbed vertically at full throttle.

We chased after girls and planes and I made new friends. Mike Pollard from Newhaven was a poet and potential teacher who fulminated against the primitive football sub-culture that we were surrounded by. 'Micky' Rogers, more philosophical, and from Carluke in Lanarkshire, was bound for a career in the civil service and Mike Sheeran from Yorkshire for the motor trade. I still had no idea where I was bound. When asked, I apparently replied, 'possibly a swimming pool attendant'.

The sea at Prestwick was freezing in the spring and I waded for a quarter of a mile to get enough depth to swim. I had bought my first 'Hurricane' fins and a large pair of swimming goggles and was determined to use them. 'Tell yourself it's warm', I repeated to myself as my extremities began to change colour.

We ticked off the days to demob on charts and were devastated when the government decided to extend national service to two years, so we had to do an extra half year. Demob finally came in January 1952 and I left Southampton on board the Union Castle liner *Dunnotter Castle* to join my parents who by then were stationed in Gibraltar. The plan was to spend my month's demob leave there. Gibraltar was a military town, full of friendly locals and less predictable visiting sailors. We had to reinforce the doors of our ancient house in Town Range when the colony was visited by the Canadian Navy.

The Mediterranean was a revelation. Warm, crystal clear, with mysterious depths and circling fish. I swam every day, usually from the officers' swimming club at Rosia Bay. I marvelled at the colours of the fish I saw below me through my misty goggles and peered down into the darker depths.

It was while swimming off Rosia that I had an encounter that was to change my life. One day when the sea was rougher than usual, I was enjoying swimming far out letting the waves carry me. Suddenly two strange figures swam up from nowhere. They wore masks and fins, but also snorkel tubes and harpoon guns – the first I had seen.

'What are you doing here?' they asked.

'Just swimming.'

'You look like you might make a good spearfisherman.'

I followed them back to Rosia.

Peter Robyns came from a family of Royal Marines and his father had been an officer involved with frogman operations in Gib during the war. Peter was still at school in Gibraltar, as was Tim Nicoll, who later became an RAF Group Captain. Peter had a slow drawl from the time he had spent in France as a boy. It was decided that they would teach me to hunt fish.

After some initial trouble with the snorkel, I was diving happily down to 30 feet or so and transfixing fish with my newly acquired Hurricane arbalette spear gun. We learnt a lot about fish and the sea and became fit enough to swim our way out of most difficulties. We became inseparable and, to the horror of other officers' families, came back day after day with a succession of bleeding fish which caused havoc when dumped on the roof of the club where their daughters would sunbathe.

One day, Peter tried to harpoon a tuna, which took off like a submarine, towing him through the water and downwards. Luckily he had a knife to cut the line. Groupers were our main quarry and good eating. In those days they were plentiful and we explored The Seven Sisters, a series of rocks between Rosia and Gibraltar harbour.

Peter, Tim and I next acquired canoes and paddled around the bay into Spain and to Algeciras. We took them on to Tarifa, the point that jutted out at the Southern tip of Spain, dividing the Med from the Atlantic. Here the fish were even bigger and monster groupers, over six feet long, rose from the depths and goggled at us before flipping their tails and disappearing again. Peter harpooned his first shark.

I became engrossed in the Spanish scene and took Spanish lessons. Spanish songs and the poetry of Lorca followed. I saw my first bullfight and was hooked on the courage, grace and skill of the matadors. My guides were the books of Hemingway and Kenneth Tynan: *Death in the Afternoon* and *Bull Fever*, reading about the opposite styles of Joselito and Belmonte and the grace of Manolete. I was not so happy with the cruelty involved, not to the bulls who were normally furious to the end, but to the unfortunate horses who were padded, but, none the less, punished by the bulls as the Picadors rode them close to the horns.

I loved flamenco, the passionate laments and exuberant excitement of the swirling Spanish girls and the syncopated *zapateado* stamping of the men. In those, now far-off, days, you could wander into a little bar, as I did one day, high in the mountains near the village of Ronda, and a gypsy would come in with a guitar and start to strum as you drank. He would be joined by a young girl, probably not more than 15, who would begin to dance. Flashing eyes, thighs and nipples produced an unforgettable scene.

Across the border from Gib lay the Spanish frontier town of La Linea. It had a sleazy appeal as it was full of dance halls and bars with hostesses and cheap liquor. We danced endless *pasodobles* with the hostesses and at midnight, bought boxes of unwanted matches from a tiny, thin 8-year-old waif of a girl, whose huge appealing dark eyes haunted us.

I could not bear the thought of leaving this life behind, and got a part-time job as an assistant surveyor, or general dogsbody with John Howard & Co., civil engineers, who were blasting huge storage chambers out of the Rock. Most of the tunnellers were local Spaniards, supervised by ex-miners from Wales. The civil engineers were from England, Scotland, and one from Spain. I measured the progress daily for them. The drilling face, deep inside the Rock, was a massive 50 feet by 60 feet, with Spaniards perched at all levels drilling holes for the explosives. One day the face collapsed burying numbers of them in rock and spoil. We had to dig out the survivors – the grizzliest task I've ever had to do.

The next year, when my parents left for another posting, I stayed on and transferred to the John Howard single accommodation down by the harbour. I taught the young engineers to snorkel dive and spearfish and our expeditions frequently took us across the border into Spain. One weekend, I harpooned a huge sting ray and hung it in the showers to clean. Unfortunately, I then forgot it until the senior engineer, one Claude Hoskins, popped in for a quick shower before bed. He walked in looking for the light switch, and was enveloped in the clammy arms of the ray. Horrified cries followed. They said that his hair had changed colour.

We visited Tangier, then an 'international city', several times, by ferry and also by the baby Dragon Rapide passenger biplanes of Gibraltar Airways. The old quarter was full of bazaars and brothels. I got an Arab boy to take us right to the centre of the Casbah. After traversing endless narrow passages, we arrived at a tiny courtyard. 'This is the centre', he said. The only thing there was a poster hanging on the wall. It read: 'Drink Coca Cola'.

The spoil from our tunnelling was dumped into Gibraltar harbour to form a new reclamation area. They took advantage of my newly acquired skills and I swam down and placed a pole at the base of the tip so that they could plot progress each day. The spoil hung in the water, making it opaque. I used a light weight belt to help me down until the day when, coming up after leaving the pole, I was surrounded by the white cloud and was suddenly unsure of the direction I was going. There's not much time to make up your mind when you're holding your breath. I didn't use the weight belt again.

Another, even more frightening, snorkel dive happened when we were exploring a small wreck at the end of the Gib runway which ran across the isthmus into Spain, projecting into the sea at each end. I took a deep breath and swam down to the shallow wreck. There was a large hole in the deck and I swam through into a cabin. There was light inside and a door to a second cabin. 'Just a quick look', I thought, and swam through the door into a second cabin. 'Time to get back.' Through the door and upwards. To my horror I saw that there was no hole in the deck. Luckily, before panic finally set in, I guessed that there must have been two doors in the second cabin and I had exited through the wrong one into a third cabin. With bursting lungs I swam back and found the hole. I was never so happy to see the sun again.

There were no aqualungs or Scuba sets of any kind available in Gibraltar in 1952, but I snapped up the first book by Hans Hass, *Diving to Adventure* in that year. I revelled in his descriptions of the Mediterranean and his first tropical dives in Curaçao. The next year, another book arrived in the local bookshop. It was called *The Silent World* by a Commander Cousteau, and told of the invention of the aqualung.

The main phase of Howard's tunnelling operation was now over and it was time for me to return to England. By that time, my father was stationed in Wiltshire and my parents had a 'hiring' occupying most of the first floor of a stately house, Prince Hill at Worton. It belonged to the Hon. Mrs Ivy Brassey. She lived there with her companion, Ruth Westlake-Wood who took one look at my new beard and christened me 'Rajah'. I settled into a country life, exploring the surrounding countryside, but soon became unsettled and anxious about my future. Finally I decided to follow father into the Army as the Royal Army Service Corps were being supplied with helicopters and would need pilots.

More inevitable weeks of square-bashing followed before I was posted to Willems Barracks in Aldershot where all the artistic misfits finished up. Artists became 'tactical sketchers', musicians, bandsmen and authors, clerks. We ran a lively newsletter called *The Willems Weekley*, which boasted some talented literary figures who were temporarily with us. I engaged in a 'paper battle' with one of them, Roy Wilkie, who had already travelled to China, making him subversive in the Army's eyes. He wrote that I had 'an air of infinite regression, like a mirror looking into a mirror'.

I remember another recruit with a nervous twitch who was obviously finding life hard. When we descended on a huge, barn-like hall for NAAFI break between drilling periods, he would creep on to the stage, open the grand piano and start to play the 2nd Rachmaninoff Piano Concerto. I was transfixed. He only had a few minutes before they drowned him out with pop music from the radio.

While at Willems, I saw a news item about the formation of the British Sub-Aqua Club and sent a postal order for 30 shillings for membership. I then got a personal letter from one Oscar Gugen which told me that they had 'already hired Chelsea swimming pool every Wednesday evening' and that branches had already been formed in Manchester, Blackpool and Bristol. The first AGM was scheduled for the 15th December 1953. I also got a membership card stating that I was member No. 74.

I was more interested in getting practical experience of the aqualung as soon as possible and few months later, my brother helpfully wrote from his office in Kinnear Webb & Co., my uncle's firm, enclosing details of various diving holidays and courses including a 3-day course at The British Underwater Centre at Dartmouth. The price was five guineas for the three dives necessary to qualify. Unfortunately, army courses and training got in the way, and it was not till early 1955 that I finally managed to book the course. My joining instructions included the request 'Bring an old rugger shirt'. 'What for?', I thought. Get-fit sessions beforehand? Emergency boat signal?

The Great Western train puffed its way down the valley of the Exe and I got views of a calm sea with red cliffs instead of the white ones I was used to from Dover. There were boats galore, with sails, oars and motors, all full of happy-looking people hanging over the sides.

When I arrived at the idyllic Warfleet Creek headquarters, the cottage owned by Captain Trevor Hampton AFC and his attractive young wife, Gwyn, he made the reason for the rugger shirt clear. 'That's what you're going to dive in, young man', he said with a smile.

We started with a series of lectures on the dangers of diving, breath-holding, bends and 'the narcs'. Trevor was patient but firm. He smiled often and his authority was unquestioned. He made sure that we understood the workings of the aqualung and the problems that could arise. We were in awe of his obvious experience and knowledge. It wasn't until much later that I discovered that he had been a test pilot and war time flier in Wellington bombers and, of course, the holder of an Air Force Cross.

There were two or three other beginners with me. One was a huge man, called Adrian Hayden from East London. He had long black hair covering his body. Perhaps this is what all divers need I thought. Would I be able to survive?

We boarded the Captain's sturdy-looking boat from the steps outside his home and headed seawards past the twin castles, which guard the Dart Estuary. Mercifully, it was a fine warm day in early summer as we bobbed along over the green sunlit surface. Our newly prepared aqualungs were near us, small grey cylinders with huge demand valves with their twin canvas-coloured hoses, through which we would take our first breaths underwater. I felt a sense of elation and well-being. After all, I had had two years experience in the Med breath-hold diving every day. The temperature of the water was the last thing on my mind.

We reached a small rocky island and weighed anchor in 35 feet of water in a natural lagoon. This was the big moment. I donned my school rugger shirt and strapped on the 'lung'. I fixed the 14 lb weight belt round my hips, adjusted the face mask and began going down the steps of the ladder which the Captain had hung over the bow. Icy water crept up over my knees and thighs. I quickly put my mouthpiece in and started to breathe the air from the 'bottle'. Suddenly I was in a tranquil, cold world with the surface above me. I stopped for a moment to catch my breath and to find my bearings in this unfamiliar territory. The air seemed to arrive with a hiss and there were bubbling noises when I breathed out. I moved from the last rung of the ladder on to the anchor chain, as I had been instructed before leaving, and started hand-over-hand for the bottom.

My ears began to hurt and I blew hard against the nose clip I had fixed on my nose until the pain stopped. Suddenly I saw hundreds of tiny minnows lying motionless. their tails twitching in the current. The bottom rushed up to meet me and I lay on the sand revelling in the new sensation of being able to breathe underwater. I checked my air gauge and calculated I had at least 25 minutes more at that depth. I took a deep breath and found I rose easily off the bottom. I swam slowly up toward the surface.

The colour of the water changed from deep to light green, interlaced with shafts of yellow light. I broke through into the daylight, climbed up the ladder and lay in the sun shivering to dry off. My first dive was over and I felt exhilarated. I would never have guessed that this would be the first of thousands of dives and the start of a new career.

'Skipper', as he liked to be called, had lots of tricks up his sleeve. On my second dive, he told me that I would not wear flippers. He put a heavy weight belt round me and I was ordered to slide down the shot line, walk around the bottom on the sand and then pull myself up again. I went sailing down without any trouble … into a clump of weeds about six feet high. I carefully detached myself, walked around and pulled my way up again.

'Good', said Skipper.

'By the way', I said, 'There's a thick patch of weed below us'.

No', said Skipper firmly, 'there's flat sand'.

'I've just been down there.'

'Must be your imagination, dear boy.' He smiled.

Skipper taught his pupils in the same way that he had learnt at the Siebe Gorman works where the diving equipment was constructed. Diving alone, self-contained, but with a life-jacket and boat cover. He also put a lifeline on the beginners for their first two lessons.

As we sipped mugs of coffee provided by Gwyn back at Boat Cottage, we slowly learnt more about this astonishing man who had started from very humble beginnings and become a racing motorcyclist, works manager, record-breaking canoeist and solo sailor. He had flown over 70 types of planes as a test pilot besides his sorties with Wellingtons in the war. I managed to persuade him to let me have a copy of his first book *Alone at Sea*, the story of a solo voyage to Spain, which he dedicated for me. His conversation was peppered with good diving advice, and he frequently emphasised how unforgiving the sea could be.

On the third day I received my certificate as a compressed air diver, registered as British Manfish No 143. Two summers before, Oscar Gugen and Peter Small, the founders of the British Sub-Aqua Club, had been down to take the same training course. Peter was Manfish No 91. There was no membership fee for the British Underwater Centre, but our names, addresses and qualifications were published in a professional-looking handbook.

At the end of Summer 1955, I decided to try spearfishing in British waters and with Bill Hemsley, an Army friend, spent a few days at Looe in Cornwall with the Spearfishing Club of Great Britain. Looe was also the headquarters of the Shark Angling Club and while we were there, a petite lady called Hetty Eathorne caught a porbeagle shark weighing 352 lb. I only caught two wrasse weighing 3 lb each, but it was a beginning and my first catch in England's icy waters.

My father had now taken up an appointment as Regimental Paymaster at Ashton-under-Lyne in Lancashire and he, and mother, were living at The Farmhouse, Little Moss Camp near Droylsden. I spent leaves there with my brother who was now doing his national service in the Coldstream Guards. He looked down his nose at those of us serving in the more effete Corps (RASC and RAPC) and regaled us with hilarious accounts of surviving 'St Trinian' schoolgirls' attempts to turn a fire hydrant on him while he was guarding the Tower of London, and of his solo march with fixed bayonet down the Mall when he mistook his transport and finished up at Buckingham Palace when he should have been guarding the Palace of St James.

I was by now deeply involved in a series of selection boards in an attempt to become an officer cadet. There were practical initiative tests in which we had to use pieces of plank, which were inevitably too short, to cross imaginary rivers. Team work was all important and it was essential to shout 'Follow me', and smile as the others in the group trod on your fingers. The most fearsome event for me was the agility test on an outdoor commando course. I had always been terrified of physical training as a schoolboy. Crawling through a pipe with a bend in the middle that was half full of water, although daunting for some, did not bother me, but climbing up rungs set in a tall tree and then jumping from a platform to catch a rope was another matter. I eventually managed to launch my quaking body, but in my terror, jumped down, rather than directly out. I've no idea how my arms managed to stay in their sockets as I made contact with the rope and clambered down to earth. I made some good friends though. Frank Sharratt was small and roundish and always cheerful in adversity. We were to meet again unexpectedly many years later.

Eventually I struggled through my cadet training at Mons Officer Cadet School and Buller Barracks in Aldershot and was commissioned as a Second Lieutenant in Her Majesty's Land Forces.

Now, I thought, for those helicopters. The Army had other ideas, and I was posted to BSE, 317 Tk Tptr Unit MSO at BFPO 20. This turned out to be at Hamm in Western Germany where I was to take over a platoon of Polish ex-servicemen in the Mixed Services Organisation tank transporter unit of the RASC. The British Supervisory Element consisted of a Major in command, a Captain who was second in command, myself and a number of national service subalterns with one or two wily regular sergeants.

Our huge Diamond T transporters were each capable of carrying a Centurion tank that their drivers drove up on to the trailer where they were secured by chains. Even larger transporters called Mighty Antars were on their way and took the bigger Conqueror tanks. The Poles wore blue uniforms and had ranks such as Superintendent, Foreman and Charge-hand. They were all drivers and many, ex-partisans from wartime. The oldest driver in my platoon was 62, held a pilot's licence and boasted that he had fought in three defeated armies. They had a lot more experience than we did. Our job was to transport the tank regiments when they moved from barracks to Luneburg Heath where they could exercise.

My fellow subalterns were Jerry Prynne, an aesthete and poet destined for an ivory tower in Cambridge, Nigel Goodman, who would become a head of English at Eton and Bill Witts, who had a quiet sense of humour doubtless inherited from his father who was a professor of surgery at Oxford. There was also Dickie Penn who aimed to become a 'legal eagle'. We shared a number of adventures for the next two years.

I looked forward to my first convoy but was somewhat alarmed to hear that I would be in command. Our OC, Major Archer and his 2 i/c apparently never left their desks. They assured me that the Poles had done it all before and knew every inch of the route. I set out my plan in all the required detail and then briefed the unit on the parade ground, waiting while each sentence was translated into Polish. After picking up the tanks at their barracks in Münster, we set off with me in my jeep in the front of the transporters, which stretched behind me for five miles. Our official speed limit was 12 mph, so you can imagine the frustration of German motorists trying to overtake. I did pretty well, but I did make one mistake. I took them into a cul-de-sac. A tank transporter with a hundred tons of tank on the back is not designed for reversing. It took us three days to get out again.

On another occasion, some of my merry men managed to collide with a railway train on an unguarded crossing. The transporter derailed the train, but no one was hurt, except my driver who got a headache. I had the No Smoking boards from the train in my office as souvenirs.

Some of the drivers were quite mad though. Bored with the speed limits, one of them on a solo transportation task, threw his engine out of gear at the top of a hill so that he could coast down. His speed increased alarmingly and his 'trailer man' jumped off before he tried to take the bend at the bottom of the hill. He didn't make it, and the whole transporter with 100 tons of tank attached, began to roll sideways off the road and down a hill. It went through a wood, smashing it to matchwood and straight through a farm building as well. Generally the convoys were less eventful and I slowly gained experience. We were also now accompanied by German traffic police who ensured our clear passage through villages and bottle-necks.

On one convoy in midsummer, the technical adjutant of one of the tank regiments insisted on being off-loaded on a normal road. I advised against it but he would not listen. It was August and the weather was decidedly warm. We stopped and the first tank trundled back off the transporter on to the soft surface. It sank six inches into the tarmac and then operating its tractors, took the whole surface off the immaculate road. The German police got extremely excited.

We generally dropped the tanks on to the heath land and then corralled our transporters in a huge area called Rheinsehlen Camp. A number of drivers then went into 'partisan-mode' and disappeared, to return with chickens and anything else that they thought would make life pleasant. Their chief superintendant suggested a party 'in honour of the convoy' and a high time was had by all. We drank toasts in vodka to Poland and Great Britain, chased down with beers before returning, duly rested, the next day.

A month later, the rather gruff Major Archer was replaced by a very different figure in the elegant shape of Major Patrick Terence O'Kelly de Conejera whose grandfather, so we were told, had fought for the King of Spain and been awarded the isle of Conejera in the Balearics. We joked that it only contained a couple of sheep, but Patrick spoke of a ruined castle that he intended to renovate when Juan Carlos became king. Patrick proved a charming OC who was apparently a member of a foreign order of knighthood. He wore a medallion round his neck on formal occasions. He was married to an ex-Major in the Women's Royal Army Corps and actually visited my convoys on location.

The army in Germany in those years was a very different world from Aldershot. It was only some ten years since the war had ended, and we lived a very comfortable life, waited on by elegant German staff, in an ex-German Officers' Club off the local park. It was our Mess or home. There were tennis courts at the back and it had a magnificent ballroom with stage, grand pianos and even a musicians' gallery.

The more senior officers in the Mess generally distanced themselves from the local Germans, but we were keen to make friends with the young Germans in Hamm. I seemed to get more entangled than most with a number of frauleins, who sometimes caused havoc among the young married officers too. We were allowed to invite German friends into the Mess for social events. The arrival of a team of British lady teachers added to the fun and we enthusiastically took to Scottish dancing.

Somehow, word got around that I was 'artistically inclined' and a new Major who had become President of the Mess Committee had decided that he would put us on the map with a series of unforgettable social events. The first of these was to be a South Sea Island fancy dress party. I was instructed to turn the ballroom into a South Sea Island with no expense spared. My driver took me to the local Ordnance Depot some miles away where I commandeered huge rolls of expensive cartridge paper on which to paint the background. Some huge vats of poster colour were located, and then I was off to the local Kurpark, where I borrowed some palm trees and several hundredweight of sand. A team of Polish carpenters and painters fixed the paper to the walls up to a height of 15 feet and began painting the scenes. We wore white 'Navy' uniforms and the girls were in grass skirts. It was a good party until one of the grass skirts was set alight. Parties on the themes of St Patrick, Scorpio, Shipwreck and St Andrew followed. The cost to the tax-payer was unknown.

I acquired an old Opel Olympia car that was pressed into service on numerous occasions. It would sway slightly when cornering and if I reached 60 mph, the small orange indicators would slowly rise on both sides, as though it was trying to fly. We called it 'George'. We decided to try it on longer trips and Nigel and I took camping equipment and visited the German island of Sylt off the Frisian coast, which was known for its nude beaches. The sight of large nude Germans playing with beach balls caused us some consternation, but we recovered amid the smiles of Copenhagen and then the cool beauties of Sweden.

Later I pointed 'George' in the other direction and Jerry Prynne and I drove down to Spain. We visited bullfights, Columbus's ship at Barcelona and linked up with Peter Robyns, who had just finished his national service in the Royal Marines, for some more spearfishing near Gibraltar.

Back in Germany the unit moved to Münster and I fell in with some serious drinking companions. The cavalry regiment's RC padre came from Ireland and used to order 36 small beers with his fellow carouser. They drank them straight down, and ordered another 36. In his cups he pronounced his verdict on me: 'Reg, for a dirty Protestant, you're not a bad chap'.

We continued to move the tank regiments and cavalry who were now also mechanised. It was raining when we moved The Greys. Their platoon officers were detailed to travel in their tanks on the back of our transporters. Their batmen meantime drove their Jaguars ahead to Soltau. One young officer asked one of my disreputable-looking Polish drivers if he could travel in the cab of the transporter and was told 'No'. He complied and endured the rain for two days. It didn't dampen his spirits, as when we arrived in the woods near Soltau, he brought out a bottle of Kummel which we shared. The officer was the Duke of Kent.

Our next OC was an even friendlier fellow, Major 'Tiny' Seymour was quite tall when he unwrapped himself and took a friendly interest in the welfare of his subalterns.

In 1958, I decided it was time to dive again and booked a few weeks holiday in August with the Club Méditerranée at their new 'village' in Santa Giulia in Corsica.There were a number of other English people on holiday there including an experienced BSAC diver called Harry Gould who was a chartered accountant and rising star of London's political life. Harry had brought a selection of Siebe Gorman helmet diver's knives as gifts to the French instructors, or *moniteurs*. I thought this unusually generous until I got to know them better. Then I knew it was a prudent insurance policy. I met an English girl called Astrid Cooper.

My practical technique was a little rusty, as I had not been down with an aqualung since my brief solo dives at Dartmouth in 1955. 'Those who've dived before attend the afternoon session on the boat for tests', we were told.

I watched the first 'experienced' divers go in and then come to the surface, many in distress, to be jeered at by the unsympathetic Frenchmen on board. I didn't know what awaited me, but was determined not to surface in that state. I donned the heavy equipment, checked my air and swam down to the shallow floor of the bay.

Sitting in a large clump of weed a short distance away was a huge French *moniteur* called Jacques, known as 'le phoque' (seal) because of his large moustache. He looked like a big ugly spider in a web. He beckoned me over to him. I made the 'OK' signal and swam across.

'Come closer', he indicated until I was within arms reach of him. Then, without any warning, he grabbed my mask and pulled it off! Although I had cleared my mask on my own at Dartmouth, I momentarily lost the knack and began to swallow the Mediterranean in through my nose. I rolled about and then blew a huge blast of air out into the leaky mask. It began to clear. I controlled my coughing and finally got it free of water. 'OK', indicated Jacques, 'go up'. I rose triumphantly to the surface to be accepted by the cognoscenti.

That year was the first time the Club had operated at this location and the village had some growing pains. There was a fire, which destroyed many of the straw huts we lived in. On Sundays there was no diving as the *moniteurs* went out with their girl friends to dive and picnic. One Sunday, they were bound offshore with the main diving launch and were all below, drinking wine with the Corsican skipper. The cabin boy who was alone at the wheel, ran the boat on to some submerged rocks. The skipper appeared, furious, and threw him into the sea. The *moniteurs* grabbed the life jackets. The boat sank. The only non-swimmer was the skipper who was borne ashore supported on a raft of life-jackets. No one was hurt, and the next day, they dived to recover the diving equipment.

The Club Med programme, after initial exercises, consisted of consecutive dives to 20, 30 and 40 metres depth. I received my Brevet de Plongeur Autonome from them after my first dive to 40 metres on 4th September 1958.

The next year, I followed the same team of moniteurs to Paleokastriza, a 'baby' village on the west coast of Corfu. The *Chef du Plongée* was Bernard Arnould and besides the 'evil' Jacques, there was a patient professor of sport called Guy Poulet.

I met up with a young Englishman and we booked on a bivouac trip which involved sleeping in sleeping bags on deserted islets and eating fish brought up by the *moniteurs* in an evening barbecue. The first night they built a huge bonfire above the beach. We sang songs, ate freshly caught grouper, and drank rough Greek red wine. Much later, someone swung their torch behind us to check on where to pitch his sleeping bag. Everywhere eyes flashed at us out of the darkness. We were surrounded by rats.

A discussion followed on whether it was better to sleep on high ground or on the beach. I opted for the beach and dug my large diver's knife into the sand beside my head to give me dutch courage as I dozed off. In the small hours, I felt a rat scamper over my arm. One of the girls higher up woke up in the morning with a rat in her sleeping bag beside her.

The next day we found a healthier island. My new-found friend and I had secreted a number of beers in our haversacks. We kept them cool by hanging them in the sea during the day. The weather grew hotter and the *moniteurs* coveted our secret beer supply. I woke in the moonlight one night to see one of them doing a leopard crawl up the hillside towards my haversack. I waited till he was about to pounce and sat up suddenly. Unabashed he whispered loudly: 'Reg, 'ave you some be-ere?' 'Non, c'est fini'. He slunk away disappointed.

The *moniteurs* were treated as Gods. They spoke only to the prettiest girls or the *Chef du Plongée*. Presumably the Chef spoke only to the *Chef du Village* or God. After a couple of weeks, my friend and I decided to try to reach the other side of Corfu where there was a larger Club Med village where we knew an English hostess. Nobody saw us leave. We hired two small donkeys and began the ascent over the mountain. I had the smallest donkey and after my beer drinking activities must have weighed a good 14 stone. The unfortunate beast developed what sounded like 'big end knock'. We finally arrived at Ipsos and happily slept on the beach for a few days, enjoying the more extensive social life before returning as silently as we had left.

Back at Paleo, we found a revolution was in the air. The Club Med brochure had promised weekly night dives but these were never organised. One of the more militant French divers led a deputation to the Chef du Village to complain about the lack of action by his *Chef du Plongée* – an unprecedented act. A message suddenly appeared on the notice board. 'Those wanting to night dive assemble for special tests tomorrow afternoon'.

We dived nervously into the bay at the stated time and were surrounded by the moniteurs and assistant diving staff. At a prearranged signal, they struck. One pulled my mask off, while another detached one of my fins. A third elbowed me in the stomach. Some got their night dive – 30 seconds at a depth of 6 feet.

On my return to Münster it was time to make the decision whether to extend my short service commission. My Colonel had written on my last confidential report 'Far too friendly with his Sergeants'. I felt the army while providing a great life, was not perhaps for me.

Before leaving, the PMC asked me if I would take care of his niece, who was due to arrive for a few weeks holiday. She turned out to be a painter called Gill Levin, and we got on well. My escort duties included banging on the doors of German mineworkers cottages at dead of night and trying to to ask in halting German, if we could stand in their back gardens while Gill painted the distant smelting works. She invited me to stay at her mother's home in Chelsea when I got back

On my last convoy, we laagered up at Rheinsehlen as usual, but this time the Poles arranged a special party for me in a disused school hall. We drank innumerable toasts. I remember them throwing me up in a blanket and seeing the ceiling getting nearer each time. I remember little else. I announced to the other subalterns that I intended to run a diving school. They bet me a case of champagne I would be back with them within six months.

I never collected my winnings.

CHAPTER TWO

A New Beginning

Back in London, I lodged with Gill and her mother, Eve, who was also an artist, at Mulberry Cottage in Smith Terrace, SW3. We lived with an owl called Lulu and a parrot called Sid. Lulu would fly freely about the house and perch on water pipes near the ceiling. If someone ran the hot water, she could be seen lifting and shaking each claw in turn; her way of dealing with the alarming change in temperature. Latterly she took to staring endlessly through the back window into the eyes of a visiting male owl, and went into a decline. Gill played double bass in a jazz band run by Dick Williams, then a struggling animator, but later the creator of 'Roger Rabbit.' One day she announced that someone important would be working in the sitting room and I was not to disturb him. I became curious and made the acquaintance of Stan Hayward, a quirky character who wrote brilliant experimental cartoon films that were admired throughout the world. Stan was interested to hear of my plans and was keen to learn to dive, especially if I finished up in the Med.

I spent a weekend with Astrid and her family at Seaford in Sussex and distinguished myself by harpooning a number of king-size plaice. Astrid's kisses were as soft as a Mediterranean breeze and I fell heavily in love again.

I wrote to all the diving holiday organisations asking for a job, without success. After a brief spell teaching at junior schools in Dover and Folkestone, I struck lucky. David Ross MC, an ex-Guards Officer and Olympic sprinter, who ran the World Sport and Travel Service in Sloane Street, asked me for lunch. He was 'not happy' with the man who was running his diving school, and felt that I might be a suitable person to take it over. It was clear that I had little experience though, and he suggested that I went out with the existing chief instructor to their base on the Costa Brava to learn from him. We would also sail the dive boat to a new location they had discovered in Italy.

I was over the moon until I met Jack Atkinson a few days later. He was an ex-RAF Flight Sergeant with a mean look about him and the pouches under his eyes of a heavy drinker. He was anything but friendly. I was the first instructor that he had not appointed himself from the ranks of the BSAC. He was their National Diving Officer and ran his courses like military operations. We were to leave in a couple of months' time to sail the dive boat, called *Sea Laird*, after David Ross's holding company, Lairdways, from San Feliu in the Spanish Costa Brava to Italy, where Alan

Williams, his second in command, had found a new location for the school on an island called Giglio off the West coast.

My brother, John was now based at Dover, still training as an accountant, and was a very popular member of the Royal Cinque Ports Yacht Club. I took the opportunity to volunteer as crew on their regular summer jaunts across the Channel to Calais and Boulogne. I was taken on by a pleasant enough yacht skipper, but unfortunately, he turned into a Jekyll and Hyde-like 'Captain Bligh' once we were at sea. His boat was the smallest ever to cross – a 14-foot gaff-rigged sloop. Once we were blown up as far as the Goodwin Sands by contrary winds. I suppose the experience did me some good.

In May 1960, Jack and I left for San Feliu. The atmosphere was frosty to say the least as he had become aware of the plan for me to take over his job with the Company. On arrival, I met Pat Harrison, a quiet diving pioneer, who had also set up a dive school in the town. I soon understood why David Ross wanted to get rid of Jack. The local Spaniards were not enthusiastic about his attacking their sons with freshly broken bottles when they dared to ask one of 'his' English girls to dance!

Sea Laird was a thirty-foot ex-Liberty ship's lifeboat built during the war. She was open to the elements and built of steel. Jack had fixed a large Ingersoll-Rand compressor on board that ran off the boat's motor. There was no shelter for passengers or crew and Jack told me that he had removed the buoyancy tanks to make more room. 'If she ships a green 'un, she'll go down', he muttered menacingly.

It had been planned that we shipped Sea Laird as deck cargo on the SS Augustus, an emigrant ship that would arrive at Barcelona from New York en route to Naples. We would be unloaded there and sail up the coast to Giglio. While we waited, Jack spent most of his time drinking with 'friends', while I scraped the boat free of barnacles in the sun. He became morbidly jealous that I spoke some Spanish and so could communicate with the locals.

The evening before we were due to sail down the coast to Barcelona, Jack warned me that we would be leaving at 6 a.m. He then left to meet drinking friends in town.

I was up at 5 a.m., but he had already left an hour earlier and was out of sight. I had no money, but talked my way on to a bus, and after arriving in Barcelona, put myself up at a cheap hotel to await his arrival. I had decided that I would put up with him until I saw the school in operation in Giglio and knew that I could manage it. I was on the yacht club jetty when he sailed in. 'Where the hell were you?' he demanded.

The Augustus duly arrived, full of steerage class Italians wearing cowboy hats, and returning to their home-towns. Sea Laird was craned on to the deck. It seemed no time at all before we were being lifted off again, this time clinging to the boat as it swung through the air and landed in the black and stinking water of inner Naples Harbour. Jack manoeuvred her into a mooring, and we prepared to spend the night on board in sleeping bags.

The next morning we discovered that someone had crept on board after dark and stolen all our tools. Jack also discovered that there was a line jammed around our propeller. 'Job for the Junior diver', he said, with satisfaction, 'You'll only need mask and tube'. The blackness closed over my head as I worked by feel to cut off the line. When it was free, Jack said 'You stink. When we get out to sea, you can jump overboard to clean off'.

Jack had run out of the money advanced by the agency. He was also responsible for paying me a nominal wage. We lived on spaghetti and oranges as we sailed northwards up the Italian coast. It was beautiful with little white-walled ports and villages. We left Civita Vecchia, the port for Rome, at dawn, as Jack had decided that instead of continuing up the coast until we were opposite the island which lay twelve miles off, we would set course north-west and sail direct for the island.

By 11 a.m. we were virtually out of sight of land and a Mediterranean storm was brewing. Jack reminded me about the buoyancy tanks he had removed. The wind and seas increased until we were fighting our way forward through waves and spray. We battled on all day and into the evening. It was dark when we sailed into the tiny harbour of Giglio Porto. I was never so glad to arrive anywhere in my life. The sea-water was almost up to waist level in the boat and our bags were floating. Friendly Italians ran down to help us moor. 'Don't speak to the bastards', ordered Jack, 'they're all thieves'. We were welcomed ashore at the old Vecchia Pergola hotel by Ido and Maria Cavero, and slept the sleep of the dead.

In the following days, we beached *Sea Laird* in the harbour and it was again my job to scrape and paint her, while Jack introduced himself to the locals. The sun burnt down and I rapidly changed colour watching attractive girl tourists sitting on the harbour wall above me, waving their legs and smiling as I worked. 'Well', I thought, 'there might be some compensations when I eventually take over'. The boat prepared to his satisfaction, Jack took us out 'for a run'. Returning to the stone jetty, bow first, he ordered me to go forward and fend off. At the last minute he accelerated and we struck the quay with a resounding clang. Luckily, I had withdrawn my arm in the nick of time.

On another occasion, we sailed out to a *secca* or underwater island far from the coast. The top of the *secca* was about ten feet below the surface. 'Let's see how well you can snorkel', said Jack. I jumped over and started snorkel diving. When I looked up again some time later, he had driven off! After about 30 minutes he came back.

At the end of May, the first holiday-maker arrived. I dived with him at Capel Rosso, the southern point of the island, and then off the village of Campese on the west coast. The Med was as beautiful as ever, with up to 60 feet underwater visibility. By the 15th June, I had been allowed to dive six times and was operating the compressor. We visited the neighbouring island of Giannutri eight miles away and dived below the remains of an extensive Roman villa that had belonged to Domizio Enobarbus, a cousin of Nero. At 140 feet the bottom was littered with Campanian plates and pieces of Roman amphoras. The only inhabitants of the island were the *guardiano* and his family. He was initially suspicious, and carried a rifle, but we soon made friends and explored the villa and surrounding countryside. We had to keep an eye on the weather as it took us an hour or so to get back and we didn't want to get caught in another storm.

I felt that I now knew enough, and the next time Jack erupted, I told him a few home truths. 'You're confined to your quarters', he roared, 'I'm cabling London about you.' His cable was followed by a long letter in which he detailed all my short-comings, real and imaginary, but by that time, David Ross knew what to expect. Alan Williams arrived on the island and, when his attempts at mediation were firmly rebuffed by Jack, he took me back to London where they suggested I spent the winter running their CCPR Ski Scheme before taking over the school the following summer. This gave me the opportunity to learn to ski at Geilo in Norway, but meantime I decided to gather more experience and, if possible, raise my profile with the company.

I signed up to a seamanship course for beginners, which was run on board the *Cutty Sark* at Greenwich, a wonderful location to learn in. Spearfishing was still a popular and accepted pastime, and Peter and I cobbled together a 'Gibraltar team' to enter the National Spearfishing Championships being held at Looe in Cornwall at the end of July. With the help of a member of the British team who was available, we managed to win the event and I was given the opportunity of a trial for the British team in the forthcoming World Championships.

With permission from the Royal Navy, the potential team members were training at the 100-foot submarine escape tank at HMS *Dolphin* at Gosport. It was with some trepidation that I went up in the lift to the top of the tower to be met by the Submarine Escape Officer, Lieutenant Commander 'Jimmy' Hamlyn and the other, already practiced, spearfishermen, who eyed me darkly. The tank was 'gin-clear', warm, and you could see the bottom 100 feet below quite clearly. It was very inviting.

I slipped over with my mask, fins and snorkel and a light weight-belt. The depths were conveniently marked on the walls of the tank. There were escape locks at 30, 60 and 100 feet. I took a deep breath, watched closely by a number of pairs of eyes, and duck-dived down. The depth marks seemed to flash by effortlessly. I was already deeper than I had ever been before. 'Better stop now', I thought and turned upwards. I soon realised that this was the first time I had snorkelled in fresh water. I desperately missed the natural buoyancy that normally helped me back up. I arrived, slightly purple, and gasping for air. My efforts seemed to impress the team manager, Ted Wells, and I was invited to take part in future training sessions.

Soon I managed to get to the bottom at 100 feet. My time down and up was just over 2 minutes. Jimmy Hamlyn spared no efforts to make the training as realistic as possible. A foam rubber 'fish' was fixed in the 60-foot lock and we practised 'double takes' – swimming down, harpooning the 'fish' and bringing it up, together with 8 lb of lead to simulate its weight. A few moments of deep breathing on the surface and we had to return to the lock and replace the weight belt. By the time we left England for the World Championship, we were all capable of bring up 8 lb of lead from 100 feet on a breath.

The World Championship was to be held that year in the Aeolian Islands, north of Sicily, for two days at the end of August. The provisional team that had been chosen was Major Derrick Baynham, Laurie Emberson and Dr Bob Stephens. Jack Wright, Mike Davies, David Griffiths and myself would travel as reserves. Jimmy Hamlyn came with us as team manager. We appeared on cinema screens in the *Look at Life* current affairs slot and then embarked on the long rail journey to Sicily.

One of the many problems of running world championships was that the home teams often knew the terrain well and had practised in the exact locations for many months. We had only two or three days to visit some of the sites. We saw groupers in 60 to 100 feet of water but few fish in the shallows. Italian aqualung divers had seen to that! Following re-assessments, conducted by all of us, the final team of three was selected: Derrick Baynham, a former team captain, Jack Wright, an experienced Mediterranean spearfisherman and myself.

We paraded through the streets of Palermo for the inaugural ceremony and the raising of national flags before a civic reception. The next day we set sail on a huge motor yacht *Caralis* of some 5,400 tons which would be our accommodation and the base for the small flotilla of smaller boats. Each team was allocated a motor launch and each competitor a rowing boat. The first day of the championship, we were off the island of Lipari and Jack did well, shooting a grouper, a yellowtail and several wrasse. Derrick and I had less success over the black volcanic underwater cliffs. Our groupers kept well below 100 feet. One of the other competitors reported swimming to shore and noticing an ice-packed grouper in a box among the rocks. He thought nothing of it until he saw it being weighed in later!

The next morning *Caralis* had arrived in Ustica, the northern-most island of the group. We all got stuck into groupers, but some wedged themselves into crevices and refused to budge. The team prize went, hardly surprisingly, to Italy. We were

14th out of 21 nations. The individual champion was a quiet young millionaire from Brazil, Bruno Hermanny. We enjoyed the open-air prize-giving by Jacques Cousteau, who was not at that time opposed to spearfishing. Sadly, Jack Wright was killed shortly after the championships by a local speed- boat which ran him down in the water near Palermo.

Before leaving Sicily, we were hosted by the Club Med at their village at Cefalu and I took the opportunity to meet up with Barry Blair who had been a most successful British underwater photographer and instructor and was then teaching at the Club Med dive school there. He had also been an assistant to Jack Atkinson at Le Trayas in the early days, and sympathised with me over my experiences with him. 'He used to come down in the mornings when a new group of beginners arrived, hung-over and red-eyed, muttering 'Now let's separate the men from the boys', he remembered. I asked Barry whether he thought it would be a good idea for me to get some more training with the BSAC before I left for Giglio and, to my surprise, he said, 'If I were you, I'd have nothing whatsoever to do with them'. I did a dive with him and he took some underwater publicity shots for me.

Soon after returning from Sicily, I came across a book about the history of the Eddystone lighthouses, and couldn't get the idea of seeing and diving at this lonely rock out of my head. It was the first lighthouse to be built on an isolated rock, 14 miles out from Plymouth. Peter agreed, and so did Bob Stephens and Laurie Emberson, friends from the team. Clustered around pints of bitter in the Fisherman's Arms at Looe, we listened to stories of 'the stone'. 'Congers? –ah – never seen the like – eyes as big as saucers' 'Sharks? – you could step across their backs to reach the light'.

One Saturday morning in late September, we were on our way over a gently heaving sea. Down below was the usual confusion of rubber, neoprene, chalk and metal: knives, spears, harpoons and cameras. Carefully stowed, was a reserve of battered grey and white air cylinders. Straining our eyes on the horizon, to catch a first glimpse of the lighthouse, we talked of past Eddystones with the skipper.

The first man to challenge the full force of the Atlantic gales to build a lighthouse on this slippery, sloping rock was a showman, illusionist, inventor and conjurer. His name was Henry Winstanley. There were no precedents and he spent the whole of the first summer drilling 12 holes in the steel-hard rock to anchor the iron bars which would hold it securely in place. Three years later, in 1699, it was finished. A somewhat ornate affair, many feared it would not survive the winter gales, but Henry had great faith, frequently boasting that his 'one great wish would to be in it during the greatest storm'.

In 1703, the biggest recorded storm in British history climaxed a fortnight of the wildest gales. Its final fury was concentrated into the few hours between midnight and dawn on the 26th November when it became a whirlwind of terrifying force. Early in the morning of the 26th, there had been a lull and Winstanley had set out for the Eddystone with a party of workmen to repair the damage. He landed on the reef in the early afternoon. The pale yellow light was last seen from Plymouth just before midnight. The next morning there was no sign that the lighthouse had ever existed, except for 12 warped and torn stumps of iron. Henry's wish had been granted.

The next man to design and build a lighthouse on the Eddystone was a silk merchant with a shop on Ludgate Hill in London. He believed that his tower should be built of seasoned Devon oak like the great ships. His theory was not unsound, because his lighthouse stood for 50 years until a night in December 1755. That night, the oldest of the keepers, Henry Hall, who was 94, was on the middle watch. Waking from a doze, he found the gallery full of smoke – the candles of the light had caught a crust of soot and the lighthouse was on fire. He roused the other keepers and they began the hopeless task of carrying buckets of water up from the sea far below and throwing them upwards on to the burning light. Henry, mouth agape, was staring upwards when there was a crash and he was showered with molten lead. He felt a searing pain in his throat and stomach. He screamed and moaned that he had swallowed some of the lead.

As the fire burned lower, the keepers became desperate. The only place to give some shelter from the heat was a tiny rock cleft on one side of the rock, but this was covered by the tide which seemed to recede with terrifying slowness. When the rescue boats finally arrived from Plymouth some eight hours later, it was too rough to think of landing on the rock, so the half-frozen keepers were pulled through the icy seas on a rope. After four hours of buffeting, they were landed and Henry Hall was still mumbling about the lead. It was a miracle that a man of 94 should have survived such an experience which, they thought, had clearly unhinged his mind.

Eleven days later, Henry seemed better, then, suddenly, on the twelfth day, he sweated feverishly and within a few hours was dead. Curiosity possessed the local doctor. Could Henry's story have been true? There was only one way to find out – an autopsy. Moulded into the bottom of the old man's stomach he found a piece of lead four inches long and weighing just over seven ounces!

Our talk was interrupted by a shout from Laurie. Straight ahead a tall fin stood motionless above the water. We rushed to the side. Through the water we could see the outline of a huge basking shark. Before we could do anything, it sensed our presence and slid lazily down and out of sight. A few minutes later the Eddystone was in sight on the horizon. Beside it was the remains of a previous tower, 'the Smeaton stump', Although the sea was calm, there was a swell running across the reefs. We paired off and with mask, fins, snorkels and guns, jumped overboard.

The water was magnificently clear with no bottom in sight. I took a deep breath and paddled down to 60 feet – still no bottom in sight, just sun-flecked greenness stretching into the distance. I wondered if the shark was still about.

We joined the others and together swam towards the rock. Suddenly the bottom appeared, rising steeply from the depths. Great rocks and masses of dark brown seaweed. Huge wrasse swam through the fronds and hundreds of large sea urchins decorated the rocks. A vast shoal of pollack appeared out of the distance, Hundreds of unblinking eyes bulged and passed on. We began to fish.

I followed a narrow valley of sand that wound between the rocks 40 feet down and came across the square metal framework of a kite. Kite fishing is thought to have originated at Eddystone where the sea is seldom calm enough to use a line. The tail of these kites is as long as the lighthouse is tall and large hooks are fixed to the last few feet. The wind tears it out from the top of the tower and it finally hovers a few feet above the sea with the hooks sweeping through the water. When a fish bites, the keeper pulls in the kite, line and fish.

Cruising along the bottom, I saw two eyes peering up at me from a patch of sand. 'Plaice', I thought, but when I poked the bottom, the sand flew apart and a very angry cuttlefish swept out of sight, pouring ink like a thick vapour trail. Peter swam across to me and we decided to take a breather and try to land at the base of the lighthouse. Clutching rock and scraping our knees, we were finally out and looked up. Far above a figure started to climb down. The keepers had never seen divers before and were pleased to talk. Back in the boat, we found that Bob had taken a pollack that weighed fourteen and a half pounds. It was a British record.

I had finally decided that it would be wise to go through the BSAC training before I left for Giglio, and had duly presented myself to London Branch at Seymour Hall baths for the test. This controversial introduction involved various exercises without any equipment, such as supporting weights, floating, and recovering weights from the bottom. No problems. Then there was the Primary Equipment Test with mask, fins and tube. Now I was thoroughly at home after years of experience. To my surprise my examiner, Ted Blackett, said I had passed, but that if I 'finned like that, I would scare all the fish for miles'. His friend told him that I had just returned from the World Championships, but Ted was not impressed. I then went on to perform a variety of gymnastics with the aqualung, artificially respirating 'bodies' and listened to numbers of lectures stressing the dangers.

During this time, I began to hear stories about the Diving Officer of the branch. Jim Phoenix was a very conscientious holder of the office and felt his responsibility for the safety of large numbers of divers keenly. He had become something of a disciplinarian as a result.

My first dive with the branch was on the 1st October 1960. In a long 'crocodile' we strained under our gear down the cliff to Stare Hole at Lulworth. In those days, boats were few and far between, and divers swam out to the dive site and back to the beach. In the afternoon, a young doctor called John Betts, was also performing on his first branch dive.

We swam out through one of the rock arches surrounding the beach. The visibility was not more than 4 or 5 feet on the bottom, but I enjoyed the dive. Swimming back afterwards, I became separated from the others, but was faithfully shadowed by my 'snorkel cover', Larry Ketley. Suddenly, all hell was let loose in the distance, inflated lifejackets, splashing swimmers and hoarse shouts. It looked as though John was trying out the branch's safety system. 'I'm fine', I told Larry, 'Go over and see if you can help'. Larry hesitated. He had orders to stay with me, but here was someone who really might need help. 'I'm fine, I repeated, 'I'll swim on in.' He left for the distant disturbance. I paddled gently on, feeling exhilarated after the successful dive. I began to look towards the arches. Which one had we come through? I swam a little further out for a better look.

Suddenly I noticed a ripple coming towards me from the distance. It turned into a large mass of flailing swimmers advancing in line abreast. As they got near, I recognised the familiar faces of branch members. 'I'm OK', I shouted, giving the OK signal. 'No, you're NOT', came the sharp reply 'You're alone and in trouble'. I was surrounded and hauled back to the beach protesting. Jim, the DO, towered above me and waved his finger in my face. 'Don't you ever do that again', he stuttered, 'or you'll never dive with us again'. I promised. John bought me a drink in the pub (a fairly rare occurrence at the time).

After some nil visibility dives at Chapman's Pool and a brief excursion to Laughing Waters, a shallow pond in North Kent, I was awarded 3rd Class Diver at the end of October. I pressed straight on with my 2nd Class tests and dived in Swithland Quarry in Leicestershire, Black Park lake near Northolt and in Chichester Harbour, enduring temperatures down to 4 degrees centigrade.

By March 1961, I was accepted on an expedition run by Leo Zanelli and George Beretta of the branch's Italian group to check the deepest soundings of lakes in Snowdonia. Snowdonia was a different world. I looked into mysterious Welsh forests in the early morning. There was the sound of waterfalls and the smell of smoke and peat. We climbed up rocky paths and over springy damp turf carrying our aqualungs on our backs.

Lake Llydaw was estimated to be 200 feet deep. We put a shot line down from the surface with a heavy weight on the end. Leo and Pat Healey would plummet to the bottom. In view of my lesser experience, I was to stop on the line at 100 feet and wait for them to return up the line. The snow gleamed on the mountains under the watery March sun. The lake temperature was 4 degrees. All went according to

39

plan. I seemed to fly downwards through a great green cathedral. I felt pretty lonely surrounded by green emptiness at 100 feet, but conserved my air until I saw the familiar black figures rising out of the murk again. They had apparently reached 200 feet.

By the end of April, after a few more Eddystone dives, I had completed all my tests and needed just one more dive for 2nd Class. The new DO, Brian Hesketh, agreed to my going to the bottom of Swithland Wood Quarry. Swithland was a sobering sight. Huge rock cliffs surrounded dark water. Suicides had been reported and no birds sang there. In fact there was just a solitary stunted tree bent out over the still, deep water. A shot line was was tied to the tree. The line dropped straight down to 165 feet.

There was a branch story that a confused beginner, doing a snorkel test on the surface had released his weight belt. Thirty feet below Jim, then the DO, was gently floating, checking that his brood of trainees were all in order. Like a thunderbolt, the weight belt arrived from above, wrapped around Jim's neck and he disappeared from the amazed view of his class. He surfaced some time later and there was hell to pay. The unfortunate beginner allegedly banned from the branch for life.

I was paired off with Pat Healey again. We sank, feet first, down the line, clearing our ears as we went. At 20 feet all light disappeared and we switched on our torches. All I could see was Pat's face in the light of my torch. He looked apprehensive. The luminous needles of our depth gauges moved slowly round the dials. There was only the sound of our breathing in the blackness. Suddenly I felt a sucking feeling round my legs. We had sunk into the mud bottom. My torch illuminated a field of debris, discarded weight belts and odd fins and even masks. We stayed close to the line and, after a few minutes, Pat signalled 'Up' and we gently rose, letting the line run through our hands. We spent the rest of the weekend reliving the experience.

I was awarded 2nd Class on 13th May. I now felt that I had at least some sort of dive leading qualification to count for running a diving school. In those days, there was only one qualification beyond 2nd Class, but the 1st Class diver was a very rare beast indeed. The award involved long experience and a national exam. Diving instructor qualifications were a long way in the future.

CHAPTER THREE

Giglio: Dramas and Discoveries

I ARRIVED BACK ON GIGLIO early in May 1961. This time I took the daily island ferry, the *Aegilium*, operated by Navigazione Toscana. It was named *Aegilium* from the Greek name for the island which meant, island of rabbits. The Porto looked like a village of coloured dolls houses as we approached. The ferry roared between the tiny automatic lighthouses at the entrance, swung round a huge buoy and edged up to the quay. Below us was a sea of welcoming Gigliesi faces.

Some changes had been made over the winter. The *Sea Laird* had been sold to a local, Filippo Fanciulli, who had promised to maintain it for use by our diving school and to provide a crew. He had decked in the bow and provided a 'portaloo'. Filippo was not on Giglio at the time, as, like many of the locals, he was *embarcato* or working on board ship to save enough to finance future projects and live comfortably back on his island home. Filippo was an enterprising young man who had become the chief steward of an American cruise liner plying between New York and the Bahamas. He doubtless saved his tips, and intended to earn enough to build an hotel on his family land, on the hill immediately behind the port.

Ido and Maria made me welcome at the Pergola. It was a pink painted two story building at the end of the port and was the oldest hotel on Giglio. Its grape vine spread over the large terrace and restaurant with a view over the harbour. Ido's father, Demo Cavero had been mayor of Giglio and a *Commendatore*, a title bestowed on distinguished citizens in Italy.

Ido's older brother, Renato, had a slightly raffish air. He was a *Cavaliere* and owned the new hotel called Demo's, after his father. It was a large, square building standing high up at the very end of the port beyond the Pergola and the nearest thing to luxury accommodation on the island in 1961. I was happy to settle into a small room in the cave-like warren of the Pergola.

Filippo had delegated his brother, Gennaro, to deal with the boat in his absence. He suggested that I took two local lads as my boatmen. They were Costanso Rossi (then 18) and Valdivio Baccalat (16). They made a lively crew. It wasn't long before we had a good working relationship and found we shared a similar sense of humour. They knew the local waters like the back of their hands. Their main struggle was in starting the engine of the boat and the compressor, which Jack had left in poor condition. I learned all my Italian swear words from them in the first few days.

We explored with the boat as far as Giannutri, the island 8 miles away to the

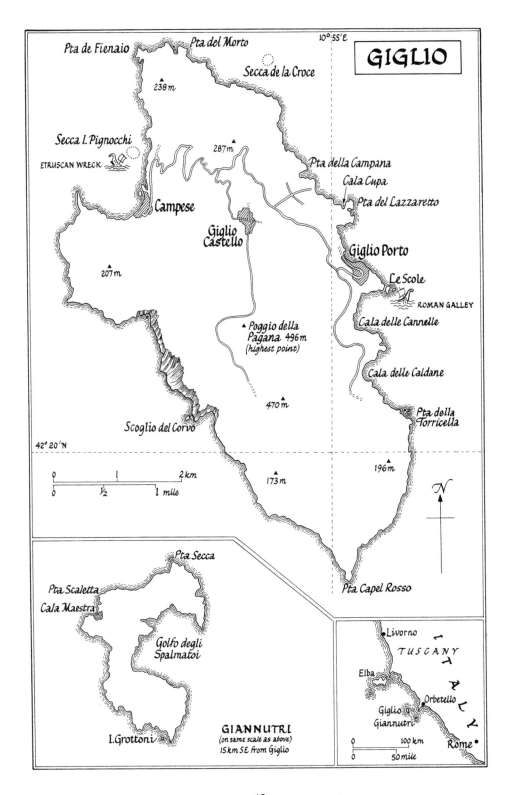

GIGLIO

Pta de Fienaio
Pta del Morto
10° 55′E

Secca de la Croce

238 m

Secca I. Pignocchi

287 m

ETRUSCAN WRECK

Pta della Campana
Cala Cupa
Pta del Lazzaretto

Campese

Giglio Castello

Giglio Porto

Le Scole

ROMAN GALLEY

207 m

Cala delle Cannelle

Poggio della Pagana 496 m
(highest point)

Cala delle Caldane

470 m

Pta della Torricella

Scoglio del Corvo

42° 20′N

196 m

N

0   1   2 km
0   ½   1 mile

173 m

Pta Capel Rosso

Pta Secca

Pta Scaletta
Cala Maestra

Golfo degli Spalmatoi

Livorno

TUSCANY

Elba

Orbetello

Giglio
Giannutri

I. Grottoni

GIANNUTRI
(on same scale as above)
15 km SE from Giglio

Rome

0   100 km
0   50 mile

42

south-east. They ran into a cave where we found no space to turn round. A lot of pushing with oars on the roof and side of the cave eventually got us round and we shot out again. Luckily the *Sea Laird* was made of steel and drew only about 18 inches, so the odd scrape on the rocks only bent the bottom slightly.

Giglio measured 15 miles from north to south and was about 3 miles wide. On top of the mountain, 400 metres up, was the small medieval town of Giglio Castello. It was surrounded by high walls and towers, dating from the twelfth century, that had protected the inhabitants from Saracen and Corsair attacks over the centuries. A tablet just inside the drawbridge-like entrance commemorated the successful repulse of the last attempted invasion by 2,000 Tunisians as recently as 1799. It looked like a film-set with its winding narrow stepped streets and alleys. Hens poked their heads out of grating in the walls of the houses as we passed. At the top of the little town was an old restaurant Da Maria, which, I decided, would make an ideal location for dinner. No cars could enter Castello. It was the centre of the island's administration, although it had less inhabitants than Porto. In fact, the whole island population was only some 2,000 souls, the smallest number at the village of Campese on a bay on the west coast that had the only reasonably-sized beach. They were the friendliest people I had ever met.

In May, the island was beautiful, with flowering shrubs, and lizards sunning themselves by the paths as I walked to the first beach south of the port, called Cannelle. A rambling house spread behind it that I was to get to know better as time went on.

I encouraged Peter Robyns to come out at the beginning of the season as an assistant instructor and to help me explore to find the best sites underwater. He brought his new girlfriend, Coral Shawland along to keep him company. Soon an enterprising member of the BSAC, Lloyd Poulton, arrived. Lloyd was an expert parachutist, glider pilot, commercial pilot and ex-works manager of Rolls Royce. Together we discovered a great field of broken amphoras off Lazzaretto, the old site of a leper hospital. These were Roman or Greek two-handled jars that the ancients used to carry wine, oil, grain or even water, if necessary, digging their pointed bases into the sand ballast of their galleys.

We also found a Second World War mine on the bottom at a little inlet called Cala Cupa. We reported this, and Peter offered to blow it up as he had been trained to do in the Marines. We had an official visit from a warrant officer in the Italian Army. He took us for dinner at Castello and afterwards told us that it was too dangerous to handle and advised us to just warn local fishermen to keep their nets away. It was later blown up by Italian Navy. I dived deep with Lloyd, who was a BSAC First Class Diver, off the rocks just south of the port which were called Le Scole and we were circled by two huge amberjacks, each between four and five feet long.

Each morning I would look at the chart and tell Costanso where we wanted to dive. There were deep soundings indicated close to the coast off the west of the island at a rocky islet called the Scoglio del Corvo or Rock of the Crow. Each time I wanted to go there, Costanso gave a reason why it would not be suitable that day. Finally I insisted, and he then told me that two German divers had disappeared off this rock two years before. There were stories of deep currents, rip tides and large underwater beasts. We left for Corvo at once.

Lloyd, Peter and I dived down the rock faces to 180 feet through a strong surface current and found Mediterranean lobsters, bushes of black gorgonia, and the fragile coral-like structures that the French called *rose de mer*.

On the 18th of May, my first beginners arrived. I gave them their initial lessons in the shallows off the tiny beach at Caldane, a small bay beyond Cannelle.

Lloyd, Peter and I broke the '200-foot barrier' for the first time on the 25th, north of the sinister sounding Punta del Morto, and I cautiously spent 25 minutes decompressing in the shallows.

At the end of the month I did my first dive with 'Sigi' Koster, a brilliant underwater photographer and member of the Munich underwater group who regularly visited the island. At the beginning of June, I had to deal with my first panic-stricken beginner, an Italian who clung to a rock just below the surface and wouldn't be moved until I took his weight belt off. I was learning fast and from that moment, seldom took my eyes off a pupil.

I began to love the excitement of diving alone without responsibility for others though. Swallow diving down through the cool, sunlit Mediterranean was exhilarating, and the chance of discovering ancient wrecks became a secret passion. On the 11th June I did a solo dive beyond the Le Scole rocks where a great amphora wreck was said to lie. I arrived on the sloping sand bottom at 160 feet and swam on down to 260 feet, recording that I 'felt no narcosis symptoms'. I was only vaguely conscious of the risks I ran, but, using the French Navy decompression tables from the Cousteau manual, decompressed for 14 minutes to avoid the bends.

Five days later Sigi and his diving companion, Franz Dobler, took me to the wreck. It was difficult to anchor in the deep water, immediately over it, so we swam out from the main islet until there was nothing but mysterious blueness below us. We dived 'into the blue' with our columns of exhaust bubbles our only reference to where we were. Visibility must have been close on a 100 feet, and suddenly rock cliffs appeared below us. Clouds of black sea bream (*Chromis*) parted and Sars slid down into the clefts as we passed. The bottom dropped down in vertical reefs. We followed a ledge to 140 feet where the sand began. We left trails in the sand as we swam on down to 160 feet. At 160 feet most sea life began to disappear leaving only isolated shells and sponges. Suddenly in the distance I became conscious of something unnatural. A huge mound with what looked like a mass of tiny tubes sticking out of it. We swam closer and I suddenly realised that we were looking at the wreck of a great Roman ship and the 'tubes' were the necks of hundreds of amphoras sticking out of the sand. I shall never forget that first sight. Squeaking wildly into our breathing tubes, we thrashed around the wreck. It must have been over 100 feet long. Every amphora was complete and encrusted with red, white and brown sea growths. In between them swam tiny pink and blue fish. Out of one a moray eel poked its head. Euphoria possessed me, and I felt as though we had found Atlantis. Sigi photographed and we carried on down to 240 feet. It was the last day of their stay that year.

Stan Hayward arrived in mid-June and took to the diving like a duck to water. He was also an ex-quartermaster in the merchant marine with a wealth of knowledge about knots and other nautical matters, most of which were beyond me. I asked him about his experiences as a merchant seaman who had steered cargo ships through the oceans of the world.

Stan had a strong sense of right and wrong. Once when he had the misfortune to be working on a particularly disreputable tramp steamer, he had led a 'mutiny'. It consisted of an attempt to complain to the Captain about the lack of soap and the standard of food on board. Stan agreed to be spokesman and led a long crocodile of indignant seamen across the deck and up the ladder to the bridge. The Captain, known for his fierceness, stuck his head out and shouted:

'What the hell do you want?'

Stan prepared his brief and glanced round for support. All the others were melting away and he was left alone. After that things became very difficult for him. He jumped ship when they got to Australia and made his way up country.

He met a farmer and asked him for a job.

'Can you shoot?', he asked.

'Of course' lied Stan glibly.

'Here take this rifle. See how close you can get to that crow on the top branch of the far tree'.

Stan gingerly took the gun and uncertainly held it to his shoulder. He squinted along the top and aimed in the direction of the tree. He was dazed by the report and recoil, but, the crow fell to the ground.

The farmer was amazed. So was Stan. He got the job

I became interested in the octopuses that had their lairs among the rocks. At first, I would wrestle them out of their holes and deliver them to the Pergola kitchen for dinner. The largest we found we hung from the grape vine above us and its legs trailed on the floor.

Stan hated us taking them and would try to go down first and 'warn them that we were coming'. Slowly, we came to appreciate their intelligence and sensitivity. I read all the books I could find on their habits, learning that they saw as clearly as we did through a mask and that their mating habits were legendary. The last time I tried to pull one out of a hole, I felt a sharp cut on my hand. Looking in, I saw that the octopus was pushing out a broken beer bottle at me. This was followed by two sharp shells. I watched them change colour – white when alarmed – red when angry. They could match their backgrounds perfectly when they wanted to be less visible. They jet propelled themselves, blowing out water in emergency and then blew out clouds of black ink to confuse attackers.

We did an experiment. After taking a lobster, the octopus's natural prey, we put it on a rock close to the octopus. The octopus flicked out a leg and seized it in its suckers. We then took the lobster away again and repeated the procedure. The octopus blushed red with anger. Small octopuses had the habit of crawling under your air bottles, after handling. They obviously felt safe there – until you 'broke the rules', by climbing out into the air. You could almost see the reproachful look in their eyes. I once thought my exhaust valve had jammed, as I couldn't breathe out. I discovered that an octopus that I had been playing with, had wrapped itself around my regulator.

A photo of me with an octopus appeared in the *Daily Telegraph*, and I got a letter from Dr Martin Wells of Cambridge, one of the world's leading experts on the beast, asking if I could collect some specimens for him.

At the end of June, a group from my BSAC branch in London arrived. It's not easy to impress your own club, especially if you've only recently gone through their training course. I prepared everything for their arrival, checking their rooms, planning outings and picnics and booking dinners at Castello.

The ferry arrived from Santo Stefano on the mainland. Familiar faces under unfamiliar headgear, were pointing excitedly as the ferry swept in. The gangway descended and I waited for the first hairy figure to come down.

I extended my hand. 'Welcome to Giglio, Bill'

'Don't just stand there with your mouth open, where's the diving boat?' the first face replied.

I kept them happy during the following days and learnt that divers will forgive you most things if you show them good diving and, at least reasonable, food. We dived at Corvo and on the Secca at Campese. After dives off the north and west coasts, we would run the *Sea Laird* up on to the beach at Campese, wander up to the only bar and eat our picnics. We would drink campari sodas and dance in the sand with the girls who had come out for the day, to the music from the jukebox.

Once a week, we would head out for Giannutri. As the *Sea Laird* only made about 8 knots, it took us an hour to get there. We found fabulous diving at the Grottoni, tall cliffs that surrounded a hidden deep cave full of precious red coral. After the dive, we returned to the baby harbour at Cala Maestra where we went ashore to explore the Roman villa. There were mosaics, partly covered by gorse bushes, including one of Theseus, the maze and the minotaur. As you walked along the main approach to the villa, where columns still rose above you in the distance, you could see the Roman underfloor heating arrangements and the remains of passages for the slaves. We ate our picnics back near the boat, and kept an eye on the weather, anticipating our voyage back.

Costanso and Valdivio were a frequent source of fun. *Sea Laird*, being still registered at Lloyds, boasted a red ensign that we flew proudly when out at sea. Bill Butland of London branch was particularly patriotic. When we were safely anchored at Giannutri, at a signal from me, Costanso grinned and pulled our flag out of its fixing and flung it in the sea, shouting 'Inglese bandera – merda!' We chased him round the deck and finally threw him overboard to retrieve it.

On the 4th of July, 'rapture of the depth gauge', as it became known, struck again and I sailed down to 270 feet at Corvo looking for any evidence of the missing Germans. I became aware of nitrogen narcosis for the first time. Above the islet loomed a tall forbidding cliff, and Costanso told me that in ancient times, the Gigliesi would run their old and inform donkeys off the top.

London branch wanted to take an amphora back for their club room. I told them that Italian law was that they belonged to the government, but if recovered, they would receive a quarter of the value. Only snag was that this never made it through the official channels. They also requested a dive to 200 feet and reluctantly I agreed, warning them that they must follow my instructions exactly and stay close to the shotline. A young diver called Mike Busuttili, together with John Cottrell and Brian Hall dived successfully to 220 feet on the 6th of July and departed happy.

In mid-July another group from the branch arrived including Jim Phoenix, the ex-Diving Officer and Ted Derrick, an unassuming Second Class diver. We visited the great Roman wreck at Le Scole regularly and I usually did a bounce dive to anchor the boat there first, toured with the group, and then did another quick dive to untie the line. We discovered that the amphoras were late Roman, dating from about 300 A.D.

I gave diving lessons to Valdivio, and we collected the wild thorny oysters that grew on the Le Scole reefs. We ate them, with a squeeze of lemon, washed down with Campari, at Nilo's bar back in the port. The Italians swore that they held the secret of endless sexual feats.

On the 21st July, we were at Corvo. This time I was taking Ted, and we went deep looking for lobsters. I stopped on top of the deepest rocks and glanced down at the sand far below. There were two white patches there. They intrigued me. I signalled to Ted, to check that he had no narcosis symptoms, and we sank deeper to 180 feet. Now I could see bones! My first thought was that we had found the remains of one of the old Giglio donkeys.We swam on down and suddenly became aware of two aqualung twin-sets amid the remains. We had found the skeletons of the lost Germans!

I tried to lift one of the twin sets, but it was heavy – central European sets always seemed to weigh a ton. I checked my depth gauge. It was reading 230 feet. The remains of the two divers were distinct and I had the impression that one had been following the other when disaster struck. The torsos were preserved and there was a still loaded harpoon gun locked in the remains of one diver's hand. I had no sense of horror, but just excitement at what we had found. In my naivety, I thought I ought to bring up some evidence, and picked up a leg bone and a flipper (still with the remains of a foot inside) and paddled up with Ted. Back at the boat, our female passengers recoiled in horror, and the grizzly remains were hung on a line from the stern, as I went down again to do some extra decompression.

Back at Campese for lunch, I telephoned the *carabinieri* in the port, as I thought they might be interested in our finds. Both *brigadieris* (sergeants), Antonio of the *carabinieri* (criminal police) and Silvio of the *Guardia de Finanza* (customs police) arrived by boat at once. Their first question was 'Would I be prepared to recover the bodies?'

By this time, I had a number of divers, including Mike and Beryl Brooshooft booked from England and also casual pupils from Italy, Germany and even USA and Australia, who were passing through. I decided to set aside the following Monday and Tuesday for the recovery operation. I didn't realise that news of our discovery was leaking out to the Italian national press.

Three days later,we were back at Corvo as *La Nazione* the Italian daily, headlined an account with 'Today a diver goes down 70 metres to recover bodies'. This time we were at the head of a flotilla of boats containing Georgio, the Mayor (or *Sindico*), numbers of police, and various helpers. Also in a separate rowing boat a reminder of the task, two coffins newly prepared. The plan was that we went down, taking two sacks attached to 80 metres of line, one painted with a red cross to contain the shallower of the two bodies. Loose ends of line beyond the sacks would be used to tie on the respective breathing sets for identification. Once we had packed the bodies, they would pull them up.

Then our problems began. By this time, I had been joined by Roger Hale, a stalwart member of Southsea BSAC and a talented underwater photographer. He had applied to help me as an instructor for the busy holiday period, and David Ross had agreed. Roger was quiet, competent and experienced, someone I felt I could rely on. He was happy to help with the recovery. We started down carrying all the equipment and looking for the site at 1 o'clock. Strong currents swept us away from the position and we lost it. Diving again at tea-time, we found the site, but were unable to get the sacks there, due to the lines being stuck in the rocks on the way down. I brought up another fin with a foot inside.

The next morning, the papers trumpeted the news that we had 'Failed in [our] first attempt'. We dived at 11.30, concentrating on getting the sacks and lines down on to the sand at 220 feet. We searched unsuccessfully for the bodies and both agreed that we had suffered greatly from narcosis. Once we had got rid of the excess nitrogen, we dived again in the afternoon and finally found the Germans. We struggled to get the sacks to the bodies and then left them buoyed for the night.

The next morning was my birthday. The locals were excited by the press coverage which was now headed 'Vallintine has failed in the second attempt'. To Roger's dismay, I insisted that on the bottom, he should hover thirty feet above me, ready for action if I succumbed to narcosis as I worked. I untied the sack marked with a cross and then couldn't remember which body was supposed to go into it – narcosis again! I finally packed in the shallower body and Roger came down and tied on the respective cylinders. I moved to the deeper body and managed to get half of the remains in before my air was getting short and nitrogen building up. In the afternoon, Roger stayed at 150 feet to keep the lines clear while I completed packing the second body and tied the line to the remaining bottle. I noticed some small bones down the slope and went to 250 feet to collect them, together with a German Drager depth gauge with its needle stuck at 75 metres.

I was now anxious to get back to teaching. Pupils and holiday divers had been waiting patiently for the operation to end so that they could dive. I decompressed and then ordered the boatmen to pull up the lines. They pulled away and I took off my twin-set and prepared to relax. The lines were caught again. Frustrated, I grabbed the nearest single set, reserved for any extra decompression, fitted it on, and plunged down alone to 150 feet to clear the line from under one of the huge rocks. Fifteen minutes later the second stuck. Exasperated, I took the single set again, expecting that this time the problem would be shallower, but the sack had stuck at the bottom of a deep rock at 200 feet. At 150 feet, the air in my already-used cylinder was becoming low and hard to breathe, but I pressed on to 200 feet, relying on my reserve. I pulled the line out and dislodged the sack. I pulled the reserve lever at the side of my cylinder, but got no more air. I suddenly realised that it had already been pulled on the surface when it was filled. I was at 200 feet with no air at all!

I steeled myself not to panic and started up holding my breath. I knew that if I continued like that, I would suffer a burst lung, even if I avoided an explosive decompression accident. I became conscious of my lungs filling as the residual air, from my last breath, began to expand. I started to breathe out and blew a steady stream of bubbles. It was quite comfortable, but there was still a long way to go. I was amazed at the amount of air that bubbled out of my mouth. As I approached 30 feet, I decided to breathe out more strongly. I arrived on the surface in a mass of bubbles, gasping for air. Back at the boat, I called for another cylinder, knowing that I might have two minutes before bubbles formed in my body. Down again to 100 feet and a long inactive decompression time as I watched the sacks being pulled up past me. I climbed back in the boat, cold and exhausted but having gained in confidence, knowing that I could make it back in emergency even from the deepest depths. The papers celebrated the successful recovery, and I was interviewed by Italian TV.

I was told that I should attend the autopsy in the local churchyard. It was a burning July afternoon and the sun beat down on us. A police surgeon picked up pieces of body with forceps as his assistant squirted lemon air freshener around. I began to feel dizzy, sat down on a tombstone and accepted a cigarette, even though I didn't smoke! Following the autopsy, it was clear that neither body had a head. This gave rise to some macabre jokes between the experienced divers about head-eating monsters that lurked at 300 feet.

The dead diver's aqualungs still had some air in them, and they were eventually sent back to Germany for analysis. Some time later I received a nice letter from the President of the German Underwater Federation, Jens-Peter Paulsen, thanking me for my 'fantastical work', but giving no news of the results of the analysis. Members of the families of the divers arrived from Germany, and the brother of one said he believed that his brother had died shallower, and then sunk to the bottom. I had a distinct impression that their positions indicated that one had been following the other along the bottom. Clues to the tragedy after two years were slight and it is extremely doubtful that anyone will ever know what had happened on that sunny afternoon in 1959.

In the days that followed, we were plied with free drinks by the Gigliesi. We were just happy to get on with the diving and instruction. I taught my youngest pupil to date, Nicky Tovey, aged 13, from England, and his father. The youngster was a natural in the water. Lloyd came back for another session, hoping to shoot a big moray. He practised 'cake hole shots', hanging upside down under his bed at the Demos.

Whenever we had girls in the group, Renato owner of the Demos, was hospitality itself, inviting us back to the hotel for late night drinks and sandwiches. He asked the girls to join him in the kitchen to help cut the bread. We couldn't understand why they always seemed to cut themselves, until one of them divulged that while their hands were engaged, the bold *cavaliere* made an advance from behind …

After every excursion for dinner at Castello, we visited a bar run by an ex-opera singer called Paletto, who often then invited us into his wine cellar to try 'special vino del Giglio'. It had some amazing effects. On one occasion, Lloyd, dressed in a tie and blazer, returned without incident to the port, but then uttered a loud cry and ran like a mad thing down the breakwater and leapt off the end into the blackness. He was last seen breast stroking out into the night. He was always back ready for the dive next morning.

I had another close call in August when an Italian Navy tanker called *Ticino*, put into port with a cargo of much needed water for the island. The Captain came to see me and told me that he had a cable wound round his prop shaft. Would I clear it in return for a bottle of duty free whisky? I said 'Yes'. The *Ticino* was large but the prop shaft was only about ten or fifteen feet below the surface. I could see the heads of onlookers peering down through my exhaust bubbles as I worked. I edged between the prop shaft and its support to get more purchase, and found myself stuck in the narrow space. What a way to end my career, I thought, 15 feet down in full view of a non-comprehending audience. I eventually managed to wriggle out, sweating with fear. I'd learnt another lesson.

Mike Brooshooft was an ex-Spitfire pilot, and with his attractive wife, Beryl formed a charming couple. We picnicked with them on Giannutri and various deserted beaches. A slim quiet American girl called Day Lanier arrived from the mainland. Her blue eyes softened when she looked at me and my knees turned to jelly. I desired her more than anything I had ever seen, but she seemed to be accompanied by an American boy friend, so my love remained unrequited.

On the 2nd August, I dived again at the Secca Pignocchi off Campese with Mike and Beryl. The top of the *secca* was only ten feet below the surface. It was a wonderful place to see fish. Ombrine, sar, corvine and huge shoals of salpe (*Boops salpa*) were flitting through the rocks. We swam down passed a cleft that was the home of a wily old grouper. I followed him into the cleft until my shoulders were touching the rocks on either side. He was illuminated in a patch of light from above, turned and gazed at me lugubriously and slipped away into the darkness beyond.

We followed the rocks down to 150 feet. They opened into broad sand valleys. Over a dividing ridge we went, and suddenly, in the valley beneath, were scattered objects, blocks and amphoras. Each pot, amphora and bowl was a different shape – so different from the uniformity of the Le Scole wreck. We didn't know at the time, but we had found the oldest and most significant wreck on the island, an Etruscan ship dating from 700 B.C.! The Etruscans had predated the Romans, with their own civilisation that was rich in art, music, sport and architecture. Women enjoyed high positions in their society and they were known as 'the lords of the sea'.

We began finding ancient wrecks off nearly all the headlands. Punta Fennaio, the northern point had round amphoras and the Punta del Morto, further south, a trail of broken pieces cemented into the bottom. Other London stalwarts, Colin Robinson, Mary Bruce and, the exotically named, Bougainvillea Jasmine Kane or 'Bogie', as she was known, who was a friendly marine biologist. She became fascinated with our discoveries and happily followed us into the depths.

Colin and Bogie asked if I would organise a night dive. I didn't dare tell them that I had never done one myself. We took the *Sea Laird* plus drinks and sausages out to Le Scole on a moonless,warm night in August. Phosphorescence sparkled from our bow as familiar landmarks disappeared and Costanso manoeuvred us between dark rocks to the chosen site. We anchored and the motor was turned off. All was silence for a moment, and I briefed Bogie and Colin about procedures and signals, that I had read up in my manual. I rinsed out my mask and was conscious of a flash of light as I nonchalantly jumped into the blackness with it clenched in my hand. I surfaced and waited for them to come in. With all torches on, we swam gently down to 50 feet. Signalling, 'OK?' I thought to myself how bad the underwater visibility was at night, the divers appeared blurred in my torch beam. Suddenly I realized that I was still holding my mask in my hand!   Putting it on and blowing out the water, I could suddenly see clearly.

After our return I was excited by my success. It was a beautiful, calm night and I still had a lot of air in my set. On impulse I slipped away alone while Roger took in the second group and swam out to the 'drop-off'. I had a depth gauge with a luminous face and as I sank, I turned my torch out. The darkness was absolute and I watched the dial creep round until it got to 200 feet and I grounded on the sand bottom. I turned it on again and illuminated an amazed little red scorpion fish.

I realised that this had not been good practice and that I was probably taking unacceptable risks. I swam up through the darkness, thinking of Odysseus and his 'wine dark sea'. I 'flattened out' for my first stop at 30 feet. As I drifted at 20 and 10 feet, decompressing, I wondered idly how close I was to the boat. Ten minutes later I surfaced and swung round to look. I could just pick out the masthead light in the distance! A night current had wafted me further out. It took me nearly half an hour to swim back, as the sound of drunken singing wafted across the surface from the boat. No one had noticed that I had gone. I learnt another lesson.

I got a letter from London. It was from Day, announcing that she was returning to Giglio with friends, 'Sandy' Jencks and his wife. I was now living in a room hired out by Stefanino, a fisherman, and booked a second room for her there. We began a passionate affair. I brought her warm doughnuts from the baker for breakfast and was completely infatuated. I remembered ruefully the remarks I had made to friends about avoiding American women. I never generalised about them again.

On the first day of August I was back at Corvo for a deep dive with Bogie and John Watson. At 240 feet, I indicated that they should return together while I pressed on to look for any more evidence at the body site. At that depth, Bogie, according to the Italian magazine *Mondo Sommerso* had become the 'deepest woman in the world'. I reached 280 feet and found a German snorkel tube and more pieces of bone and many lobsters.

In September I ate my first oyster underwater, a procedure not recommended by knowledgeable biologists, unless you had had a vaccination against typhoid. After levering the oyster off, you inserted the tip of your diving knife and cut the muscle that held it shut. You looked at the inside to make sure that all small fish, parasites and marine worms had left 'the sinking ship', then, we advised:

Take a deep breath
Think of England
Remove your mouthpiece.
Replace with oyster.
Chew and swallow oyster.
Think of England.
Replace aqualung mouthpiece
Breathe again.

The result was either ecstasy or an emergency ascent! *Diver* magazine in UK published an illustrated article on the subject.

Day ventured down to 30 feet for the first time and I guarded her like a precious jewel. We were visited by two well-known Italian underwater photographers, Maurizio Sarra and Victor de Sanctis, who would dive with us regularly, and we explored a wreck off the southern point of Giglio, where a mast stood provocatively upright in the sand. We found old metal plates and cannon balls. Victor was the inventor of a new gadget, the Automatic Decompression Meter or DCP which I was to use successfully on hundreds of occasions and which had been invaluable during the recovery of the bodies. Victor asked if I would be the British agent for it. I told him that I had no set-up for this, but he said that he was more interested in having someone who really believed in it and had had experience using it.

I began to regret the amount of ancient material that was disappearing from the Giglio seabed and suggested to Georgio, the mayor, that we set up a museum on the island. He agreed and initially set aside a room in Castello. I brought up a Roman anchor for the museum on 16th September together with some amphoras. We also gave some mysterious round objects which when scraped were blue-green in colour. It later turned out that they were copper ingots from the Etruscan wreck.

Tom Baum, an artist and courier for Ingham's Travel did his first dive with me on 20th September and was hooked. He was their representative on the Rome Express, bringing British holiday makers to Italy. He suggested that we hired a house between us the following season and he would bring out his girl friend to cook for us.

Near the end of the season we visited the tiny uninhabited islets to the north of Giglio called the Formiche di Grosseto, discovering amphoras, a Roman anchor and groupers. Roger left us in mid-September. Day left unwillingly at the end of the month, and then wrote that she wanted to come back. I cabled 'Don't move, I'll be back in ten days'.

I had done 298 dives during the season and taught 58 beginners, mostly Britons, but also visiting Italians, Americans, Germans, Australians, Swiss and one Irishman. It had been the most exciting summer of my life. I rushed back to London where Day was waiting.

CHAPTER FOUR

Life in the Porto

DAVID ROSS OF LAIRDWAYS welcomed me back, but broke the news that the number of clients he had attracted hardly justified his running the holiday any longer. After discussion, he agreed to act as my booking agent, and that I could still base myself at his offices in London.

I set about producing my first brochure. The school would continue to be known as the Club Aquatique and I wrote purple passages on Giannutri – 'populated only by butterflies and pheasants, with the ruins of a Roman villa to explore. Evenings at Giglio are spent open-air dancing and visiting Giglio Castello'. Not so very far from the truth, I thought. There were photos in the brochure of Roger with pots recovered from Campese, and his photo of the Giglio wreck 165 feet down. The price for 1962 would be £62.5.0, which included air travel to Pisa, Second Class rail and boat travel from there to the island, and 13 nights B&B. at the Pensione Bahamas, Filippo's embryo hotel, not to mention accommodation in Pisa 'when necessary'.

I set up a business name – SOS Diving Equipment and persuaded my old friend, 'Mickey' Rogers, ex-RAF Prestwick, and his new wife, Marion, to organise the sale of Victor de Sanctis's DCP and depth gauges for me. I handled the liaison with Victor's SOS factory in Turin, and started advertising regularly in *Triton*, the BSAC magazine.

In December, the Royal Navy Submarine Escape Officer, Jimmy Hamlyn, was in contact again. The Duke of Edinburgh was to inspect HMS *Dolphin* and there would, of course, be a demonstration of submarine escape by his instructors in the 100- foot tank. Rather than keep this to themselves, they had decided to invite the British Spearfishing Team to put on a performance for the Duke. We had a couple of practice dives, drilled by Ted Wells, and found we could still recover weight belts from 60 and 75 feet and get to the bottom at 100.

The visit took place on the 18th December, and we waited in the water for the Duke and various Admirals to arrive. Colin McLeod, the Chairman of BSAC, and sponsor of the spearfishing team, was also there. It had been decided that Derrick Baynham and I would be the ones to do the deepest dive to the bottom of the tank.

The Duke arrived with a large entourage of Navy officers. Team members began to demonstrate fish shooting and recovery. It was finally time for Derrick and me to do the deep dive. We coordinated our preparatory breathing and I took a last huge breath. Unfortunately, in the excitement, my snorkel dipped below the surface and I got a mouthful of water! It was too late to turn back, Derrick was already on his way. I followed him down, trying not to choke and swam once round the bottom. My surfacing must have been a sight to see. I had no air to blow out the snorkel, but the Duke seemed to enjoy the performance and wanted to get into the tank himself to try. Sadly, he was dissuaded by his accompanying aides.

I was now a regular member of London Branch and happily dived through the winter with them, surviving freezing temperatures and underwater visibility of 1 foot at Swithland, Swanage and the Eddystone. I made my first guest speech at Bournemouth Branch Dinner, which must have been excruciating to watch. I took Day with me to the dinner, although our affair was now ending as quickly as it had begun.

Tom and I drove back to Giglio in May '62 in his van, which he had named 'Hannibale', and picked up his girl friend on the way. We rented a small house on the Via Castello, a small road winding up behind the Pergola. We had to install a shower to make it liveable.

Tom's girl friend, Elfriede Maria Messerer, always known as 'Elfie', was a slim, lively, attractive Austrian blonde. She set about making the house into a home for us. She quickly became an expert in negotiating in the weekly market for salads and vegetables, and a regular at the butcher's shop in the Port. The butcher was called Angiolino. He was tall as a tree and made a fearsome sight, standing on a dais behind his counter, wielding a huge knife. His sister, who had an aristocratic look, and a fine facial bone structure, manned the cash register.

As I was now responsible for the finance of the diving school, I felt I could not afford to pay Roger a salary, so he regretfully stayed behind in Southsea, organising a holiday for his fellow Southsea BSAC members who came to Giglio later in the summer.

The house that we had rented had a number of large rooms with sea views and also a basement cellar. Poking about down there, Tom found that there was a freshwater spring below the floor. His imagination worked overtime. Why not tile the cellar and open it as a club for the divers? He began to work like a Trojan, only breaking off at weekends when he had to act as chief courier on the Rome Express.

It was wonderful to be back on Giglio. Costanso and Valdivio had left the island, and Filippo's wife, Wally was now supervising work on their new Pensione Bahamas. Wally was a personable English-speaking girl from Yugoslavia who had been purser on the cruise liner with Filippo. Filippo had recommended his cousin, Costantino Fanciulli to run the boat for us for the season. He was small, wiry and had the posture of an experienced sailor. He hesitantly asked if I approved his appointment. Feeling rather pompous, I asked him if he had any qualifications to do the job. He produced a battered document from the Italian Merchant Marine stating that he was qualified to drive 20,000 ton ships about the world! 'That would seem to be satisfactory', I said loftily, 'Why do you want the job?'

'I might get the chance to meet some nice English girls', he replied.

'Sounds a good reason to me. It's yours.'

Costantino had a generous and open personality and all the Gigliesi referred to him as 'molto bravo'. His brothers had been killed in sight of the port by one of the occasional waterspouts that frequented the Tyrrhenian Sea. His aging mother therefore kept a close eye on his activities.

At the end of May, Harry Gould, who I had first met in Corsica, arrived with his friend, Anthony Redmile. Harry was in his element and it was only a day or so before we were down on the Le Scole galley at 165 feet. Harry and Tom also dived the Etruscan wreck off the Secca Pignocchi near Campese, collecting bonus lobsters.

One afternoon, Harry took me aside. 'As you know, Reg, I'm currently Mayor of Holborn, and we have an international mayoral network. I've brought some gifts for the mayor of Giglio. Do you know him?'

'Yes,' I confirmed.

'Could you fix an appointment for me to meet him?'

'Of course. Anytime.'

'Anytime? You're sure?'

'Yes.'

'Well, what about this evening before dinner?'

'OK, Harry', I said`.

He returned to the Demos and changed into a smart blazer and tie. We walked along the harbour towards the bars at the end. The last, the Bar Sport, was the most disreputable-looking. Fishermen were shouting at each other as they slammed playing cards on tables. We approached the bar. Harry looked puzzled. Behind the bar was a large man, wearing a vest that had certainly seen better days. Black hairs sprang over the front of it. His florid face beamed goodwill. 'Eh! Valentino!', he shouted, thumping me in friendly fashion, 'Una, birra?' 'Grazie, Georgio'. I turned to Harry. 'This is Georgio, Mayor of Giglio'. 'What, him?', whispered Harry in astonishment.

I introduced them and translated for Harry, who had brought a mayoral sash and an official guide to Holborn. Georgio put the guide down upside down in a pool of beer and offered Harry a drink too. Harry asked me to enquire about the system of election for mayor of Giglio.

'No election', said Georgio firmly. 'Well, how did you become mayor?', persisted

Harry. Georgio reached across the bar and stubbed his index finger into Harry's shoulder, emphasing each of his words: 'Because, I'm the best man for the job'. That seemed to end the discussion.

Elfie did her first dive on the 9th of June and another group from London branch arrived. Tim Glover and Geoff Harwood were part of the research division of Kodak and expert underwater photographers. They intended to pay for their holiday by selling the photos that they took. I motored them round to Cala Cupa where we regularly fed the small wrasse. I broke open a sea urchin for the fish to eat from our hands.

Tim didn't mince his words: 'Right, Vallintine, that's all we want. Just bring us here every day'. He was small and slight but would jump in laden with a vast amount of equipment and weights. He landed like a bomb on the sand, 15 feet below. He then got up briskly, walked over the bottom and set up a tripod. They chummed the fish and the flash bulbs began to pop. They paid for their holiday as planned.

After a few days, Tim and Geoff joined Harry, Tom's brother, Frank, and me to dive the *secca* at Campese and Le Scole. Harry asked if he could dive where we had recovered the bodies, and I took him down there to 245 feet. He was as cool as a cucumber as we collected lobsters for dinner.

Tommy Wardle and Ian Unsworth also joined us from London. Ian was a doctor and came from a long line of physicians. He was destined to become President of the South Pacific Undersea Medical Society. Diving a new site with him, he found a small Roman pot that, according to archaeologists, may have been a personal cooking pot from a Roman galley. We were finding more and more ancient remains on nearly all our dives.

By now, Tom had finished tiling our cellar and had built a rustic bar. We fixed fairy lights in the trees outside. I called on the Giglio police chief to discuss getting a drinks licence. 'Valentino,' he said, 'You haven't got a chance. The application will go to Grosseto (the provincial capital) and a letter will come back telling you that Giglio has 2,000 inhabitants, and the number of bars on the island is sufficient.'

'But,' he added, 'as it's you, we won't make our inspection until October, and you'll be gone by then, won't you?' I thanked him for his help. 'No trouble, though', he warned.

We decided to call the bar The White Dolphin Club and the divers enthusiastically did their drinking there, with Elfie patrolling to and fro carrying cool lagers. The trouble was that, when visiting young Italians arrived, word got around that there was this club up the hill, run by an Englishman, that it was impossible to join. They were charming, promised to behave and we let them in. Elfie got busier and busier and, as we had no fridge, we imported blocks of ice that arrived on the ferry every morning. We hoped that we would make our fortunes.

Tom spent the rest of his time painting large and impressive expressionist canvases and found his portraits in great demand.

I began to learn more about Costantino. He was very unassuming and looked pretty scruffy. I noticed that when he filled *Sea Laird's* petrol tank from the local petrol pump, he didn't pay. I queried this and he told me that he owned the pump. It also soon materialised, that he owned his mother's flat and also the block of flats it was in. I always said that, although I was treated like a king, I was the poorest man on Giglio that summer.

Mondo Sommerso, the colourful Italian diving magazine produced an article about our school, illustrated with Maurizio Sarra's photos.

One day, a small luxury launch arrived in the port with a harpooned dolphin hanging, bleeding from the bow. I walked past in the evening, when the occupants were drinking their cocktails and said in italian: 'This is the boat of the murderers'. The owner was Ferdinando Schiavoni, an important Italian businessman and keen fisherman. He came to see me the next day, complaining about my remarks and explaining that he only harpooned dolphins because they did damage to fishermen's nets. I told him that the dolphin was a much more intelligent mammal than he was. This was apparently something of an insult in Italian, and he had to be restrained by his friends. I was proud to have him as an enemy on these grounds. The effect was spoilt a few years later, when a visiting Italian friend said to me 'I met up with a friend of yours in Milan, called Ferdinando Schiavoni. He told me about you and the dolphins and we had a good laugh about it.'

I always seemed to get on well with Italians and especially with the Gigliesi, who were endlessly helpful and friendly. Tita, the local mechanic, always seemed to be repairing our engine and seldom charging for it.

Stan arrived again in July, and one weekend, Maurizio brought Claudio Ripa, an Italian spearfishing champion whom I had first met in Sicily, when he had come third in the world championships. He was a quiet Neopolitan with an easy smile and, of course, was a brilliant diver. We took them to Giannutri with Elfie, Bill Butland and a student. We dived in the morning to 140 feet at La Scaletta where there was an amphora wreck. Maurizio and Claudio dived independently of us, calculating their own bottom times and decompression. At lunchtime, Claudio came with us on a shallow dive to photograph Elfie with an amphora they had found. Costantino also dived with us on one of his first underwater sorties. In the afternoon we dived again at the Grottoni and collected red coral from the cave at 170 feet. We returned to decompress and Maurizio and Claudio followed us some minutes later. During his decompression stop, Claudio made signs that he had problems with his legs and we sent further bottles down for him to extend his decompression. He finally surfaced, a very worried man, still with shooting pains in his leg. We took him as fast as possible to Porto Ercole on the mainland and he was then whisked off to Naples where he spent several days in the recompression chamber. For several months after treatment he walked with a limp, but finally recovered completely.

On 20th July I took Bill Butland, and Norman Simmonds from Chelsea branch, to 245 feet at the Scoglio del Corvo. We collected a large lobster and I came face to face with a big amberjack which looked at me over a rock pinnacle.

I was still enjoying diving alone, and on the 21st went down to 260 feet off Cala Cupa, but felt a tingling feeling from 200 feet onwards and had the impression that I might blackout. I was still unsure about the effects of nitrogen narcosis.

We enjoyed a lot of drinks at lunchtime on my birthday in July. Maurizio and I drunkenly agreed that we would go to collect some oysters. We seemed to have a lot of trouble putting on the diving gear, but the cool water partly revived us. It was a shallow dive. We collected the oysters and went to bed for a few hours. At tea time we woke, to find that half of what we had collected were rocks!

On the 28th, we were back on the Etruscan wreck at Pignocchi. This time I took David Stokoe and Heinz Olschar from Munich with another diver from Munich called Franz. We found small amphoras of different shapes and, sensationally, an ancient bronze Corinthian helmet with eyeholes and protective nose piece. After cleaning off some of the marine growth, we found it also had decorations of wild boars and serpents. Franz, who may, or may not, have first sighted it, carried it off back to Munich after my warning about the Italian law. I resolved to safeguard any future finds of that nature in the island museum in the safekeeping of the mayor. I also decided that when I returned to England, I would try to interest an established diving archaeologist in organising a proper expedition to excavate the wreck.

Gill, a popular young diver from London branch arrived and made an ideal diving partner for Lloyd who had considerable experience. He asked if he could take her to 150 feet and I said 'Yes, but no deeper'. After a few minutes, and on impulse, I followed them down. I caught up with them at 180 feet, still on the way down, and firmly signalled 'Go up' to Lloyd. I always remember his guilty look as their prior secret plan was discovered.

More and more holidaymakers arrived. We collected coral at Giannutri and oysters and amphoras at Giglio and met up with many more octopods. Dick Williams, the animator, had contacted me from London, asking if he could come out with his girlfriend, Angela, and two members of the band, 'Patch' Pierce and Pete Shade. 'If you play in our cellar each night, we'll give you free tuition and diving', I said. They agreed. Even more visitors flocked into The White Dolphin Club. Elfie seemed to move in three directions at once, and Tom and I were even surer we would make our fortunes.

Giglio has a magic of its own which draws you back. Later friends used to say that I had an invisible elastic band with one end attached to me and the other to the island. The tourists came and went usually having little long-term impact on the life of the island. One exception was when two lively young girls from Australia arrived. One had Austrian parents and was called Trudy. The next year, she met and married Carlo Brandaglia, who used to drive the local taxi. Sadly he died a few years later, but Trudy took over the taxi business and also the their real-estate business too. She met another Gigliesi, Gigi Brizzi, who, rather improbably, was an ex-World Champion cocktail shaker. They now live in a beautiful house overlooking the Port and Cannelle, with the ruins of a Roman lighthouse in their hilltop garden.

One of Trudy's friends was a delicate and sophisticated young lady from Rome called Franca Moscatelli-Gentillini. I came under her spell and she became a great comfort to me. Franca had a heart condition and had decorated her bedroom in Giglio with a freeze consisting of her heart echo trace. She was also to have a long-term affair with the island.

A professional author called Alexander McKee booked a diving holiday with me and later wrote about it in his books *History under the Sea* and *Tarquin's Ship*. He later became famous as the discoverer of King Henry VIII's warship, the *Mary Rose*.

On the 28th August, I dived to 230 feet at Corvo and on my return suffered pain in my left arm. It eventually subsided, and I was diving the next day with 'Mac' McKee, Angela, and Victor de Sanctis, who photographed us at 100 feet using his oxygen set! The pain recurred that evening, but I was still not sure that it was 'bends' and ignored it. I took my first holiday the following day, and that seemed to finally cure it. Although I knew that deep diving brought risks, I was careful not to encourage others to do the same.

Costantino was diving regularly, although with his pinched face, we could never find him a mask that didn't leak. Dick, Patch and Pete had now been with us for over a month and finally had to leave. Patch and Pete were last heard of diving through anacondas and piranhas in the Amazon as they recovered emeralds. True adventurers! Besides Tom and Elfie, I now gave Filippo, who had returned for a short stay, some lessons.

In September we heard the sad news that Maurizio had been killed by a shark off the isolated Secca of Circeo, near Naples. This was such an unusual occurrence in the Mediterranean, that doubts were expressed that it was the real cause of death. Claudio confirmed to me that he had found the shark's teeth marks on the holster of Maurizio's knife. It seemed that he had found and photographed a rare 'Alexandrine' grouper and had then returned to his boat to get a harpoon gun. The boatman reported that they had sighted a shark fin. Being an experienced diver, Maurizio was unconcerned, and returned to shoot the grouper. It lost a lot of blood, and he was engaged in trying to get it out of its hole when the shark came in behind him and bit a lump out of his calf. He surfaced, and his small boat started back for the mainland. It took an hour or so to get there and he was then taken to a cottage hospital. Instead of waiting for his shock to subside, they started to operate, giving him 300 stitches. The combination of shock and loss of blood caused heart failure. He was still only in his 20s when he died. He had enjoyed his weekends with us, teaching us his latest version of 'the twist' and had been a good friend.

My local reputation as a deep diver brought me more problems with the Gigliesi when their fishing nets got tangled on the bottom. 'It's only at 50 metres', they would say, 'that's nothing to you'. Arriving at that depth I could often see them stuck at 70 or so. I found that if I went down fast enough, I could arrive on the bottom with a completely clear head. A few moments to pull the net clear and then narcosis hit with a bang. Hopefully by then, I was already on the way back. In recovering the bodies the year before, Roger and I had found that we seemed to suffer less if we had a good breakfast before we left. Physiologists I spoke to believed there could be reasons for this.

Towards the end of the season, Tom got out his book of accounts to see how much we had made on The White Dolphin. The answer seemed to be 1,000 Lire (about 50p). What had happened? We looked disbelievingly at each other. More consultation furnished the reason. With the cost of the ice we had cheerfully ordered from the ferry, we would have had to sell over 50 beers each night to start to make any profit. It seemed we were not going to make our fortunes after all.

Tom was conscientious and extremely dedicated. On one of his courier trips on the Rome Express, they pulled in to a station and announced that there would be a half-hour stop. Tom advised his clients to get some refreshment from the station restaurant. A few minutes later, the train driver changed his mind, and announced that they were leaving at once. Tom pleaded that all his holiday makers were in the restaurant, to no avail. As a last resort, he lay down on the tracks in front of the train! The Italians had never seen such devotion to duty. They waited for the missing English to return.

It was October and the weather was changing. I needed another amphora for the museum. I dug it out 160 feet down, lifted it on to my shoulder and started to remove the rubble and mud inside, using a spare harpoon. Then I lifted it high again, took out my mouthpiece and put it, bubbling air, beneath the mouth of the amphora, so that the air gathering inside would make it more buoyant. I put my mouthpiece back and found that instead of air, I had a mouth full of mud and stones. A nasty moment!

I had done 357 dives since late May and it was time to go. Tom, Elfie and I drove back through Europe, enjoying stopping at little French bistros with remarkable food. Tom had invited me to spend the winter with them in Zermatt in Switzerland which was his winter courier and 'rep' job. I would be able to perfect my skiing and they would find a part-time job for me there.

The part-time job was in the Glacier Sport shop in the main street of the high Alpine village. It was run by a Mr and Mrs Perrin. He was charming, but she was definitely not, insisting that we kept on our feet every moment of the day. I only worked in the mornings, but we began very early and so I spent the afternoons dozing rather than skiing, before the inevitable 'après-ski' celebrations every evening. My skiing did eventually improve.

Tom and Elfie organised a Snowflake Club for Ingham's holiday makers and arranged a number of prizes for different races. They were very much at home, as Tom had ski-jumped for Austria in his youth and Elfie came from a family of ski manufacturers.

Zermatt had been run by the Perrin and Julen families for generations and was slow to change. The fresh water pipes under the main street had not been examined for very many years and ran alongside the waste disposal system. During the winter, sewage seeped between the pipes. Not surprisingly, there was an outbreak of typhoid that spread rapidly, but was kept quiet. Tom heard about it early on, and we got ourselves inoculated against the disease. When it became a national scandal, the Swiss army moved in and confiscated all passports while they tested everyone in the resort. Tom and I were 'negative', but Elfie tested 'positive'. 'That's because she has just had an inoculation', explained Tom, but they would have nothing of it. He had to threaten adverse publicity and dire consequences if she was not allowed to go. We got out on the last train feeling like refugees.

Back in London, Tom had arranged for a friend in travel to act as our agents for the summer and I renamed the school The Neptune Diving Club. Tom and Elfie would be elsewhere for most of the summer, and so I moved into the Pensione Bahamas which was now becoming the Albergo Bahamas, Filippo having built on a first story. Costantino was also not available, and our boatman was now Nuncio, a colourful island character who had spent many years in America and was nicknamed 'Briscola', because of his expertise at a card game of that name. I asked about the island museum. 'Sorry', the Mayor explained gently, 'but we had some important visitors during the winter and had to give the contents away as presents'.

Wally had employed a large statuesque female from the village as waitress and cleaner. She was always dressed conservatively in black. During the previous summer, a young lawyer from Rome, Ludovico Ceccacci had dived with us and came back at the end of May with his beautiful girlfriend, Marinella. Tony Moore, a diver from London branch arrived and we dived together. The evenings were very quiet in May, as few other tourists had arrived.

One evening, feeling bored after dining in the Bahamas, we decided to play cards. Someone suggested we played poker,and someone else, that we liven it up with strip poker. Half an hour later we were still sitting in the deserted dining room, but Tony and I were completely nude and Marinella was deciding whether to remove the last of her clothes, when the door opened and the serving woman stood with her mouth open and eyes bulging. She disappeared like a rabbit out of a hat, and we remembered that nudity was a crime in Italy and rapidly dressed. The next morning fingers were waving and we were teased unmercifully round the port. No charges were brought though!

I had first met Luciano, a visiting prince from Rome, at the end of May when I disentangled his fishing net from the Secca della Croce, north of the port. He was said to own 'half the stock exchange in Rome'. He was slim and slightly worn-looking. He came to Giglio for weekends always bringing a different beautiful model with him, usually French, English or German. Sadly for them, Luciano's real passion was fishing, and instead of the Riva gin palaces which were popular with his contemporaries, he had bought a small practical fishing boat, which he called, *Giglio Uno*. He went out in all weathers, sometimes becoming de-masted far from the coast in storms, but came back with the largest fish we had ever seen.

Most of his girl friends were not happy at being left in the Pergola for most of the weekend while he fished. One weekend he arrived with two Swedish girls, Anne and Katya. They came out for the first day on *Sea Laird* and then, to his astonishment, joined him on *Giglio Uno* while he fished. He brought them back again for an unprecedented second weekend. Unlike their predecessors, they did not expect presents or expensive dinners. He was captivated.

Luciano had a friend called Lorenzo Ricciardi, who was also passionate about the sea. He had been the head of an advertising agency, worked as an assistant to Federico Fellini, the film director, and had played the part of Christ in the film, *Ben Hur*. He had dived before, but had never taken a course. He enrolled with us.

I suggested that he should start by demonstrating his prowess by taking his mask off underwater.

'But,' explained Lorenzo carefully 'you're supposed to keep it on the head and with air in it'.

'Yes, I know', I said patiently, 'but the exercise is to get the water out in case you ever need to'.

'But, my mask never leaks'.

I eventually got him to try.

Regular English divers such as Tim, Geoff and Ian returned, as did the club from Munich. I dived with Sigi, Heinz and Erich Berghammer at the Formiche di Grosseto. They had asked me to teach Erich so that he could dive safely with them. He

1. Helping to keep brother afloat. Hope River, Blue Mountains, 1936.

2. Member of the Guild of St Peter, 1948.

3. Vallintines in Spain, 1952: Reg, John, mother and father.

4. First goggles and flippers.
Blackstrap Cove, Gibraltar, 1952.

5. First bass and first beard, Rosia Bay, 1953.

6. Author as a young soldier with my convoy of tank transporters, Rheinsehlen.

7. *Sea Laird* at San Feliu, before leaving for Italy, 1960.

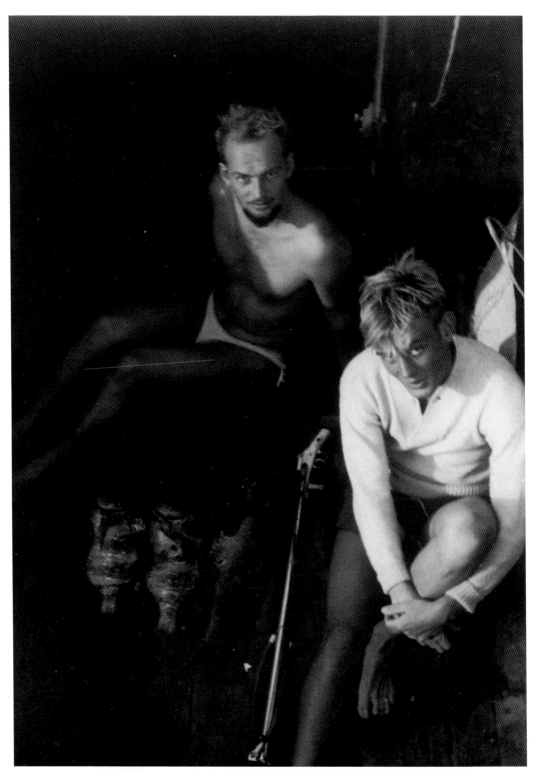

8. Spearfishing at Punta Carnero, 1953. Reg with Peter Robyns.

9. British Spearfishing team Palermo, 1960. L to R: Mike Davies, Reg, David Griffiths, Jimmy Hamlyn (with flag), Jack Wright and Derrick Baynham (with banner).

10. Giglio Porto looked like a village of dolls' houses.

11. On the Roman wreck at Le Scole, 1961.

12. Hundreds of amphoras lay in the wreck.

13. Reg 'eye to eye' with an octopus

14, Reg at Giglio. Further encounters of the clammy kind

Tre immersioni a 85 metri
Recuperati i due corpi al Giglio

L'eccezionale impresa del « sub » inglese Reginald Valentine - Si è immerso tre volte senza concedersi riposo - Per ogni discesa ha impiegato quasi un'ora - Altri

IL MACABRO RINVENIMENTO NELLE ACQUE DEL GIGLIO

Fallito il primo tentativo
di recuperare i resti dei «sub»

Il maltempo ha notevolmente ostacolato le operazioni - L'istruttore inglese ha compiuto un'immersione

ALL'ISOLA DEL GIGLIO

Fallito un tenta
di recuperare i
dei due "sub" ted

IL RECUPERO DEI RESTI DEI «SUBACQUEI» TEDESCHI

Valentine ha fallito
anche il secondo tentat

NELLE ACQUE DELL'ISOLA DEL GIGLIO

Recuperati gli scheletri
dei due "sub" tedeschi

15. Italian national headlines describe our body search and recovery, 1961. The photograph shows one of the two German aqualungs brought ashore.

16. *Sea Laird* approaching dive site. Reg on foredeck, Costanso at the wheel, Valdivio to his right.

17. Reg with Campanian plates from Giannutri.

18.Guarding a precious jewel: Reg and Day Lanier, 1961

19. 'Bogie' Kane and Roger Hale with amphora
from the Etruscan wreck at Campese.

20. Anne, Katya and Reg on the beach at Cannelle.

21. Mary Bruce holds ancient drinking goblets from the Campese wreck, 1961.

22. Elfie and amphora
at Giannutri, 1962.

23. Waiting for the Duke to arrive. Submarine Escape Tank at HMS *Dolphin*, December, 1961. L to R (*outside tank*): Colin McLeod, Ted Wells, 'Jimmy' Hamlyn; L to R (*in tank*): Petty Officer, Bob Stephens, ?, Reg, Derrick Baynham, Mike Davies, Cliff Lock, Laurie Emberson.

24. The Duke arrives. Derrick surfacing, Reg still below.

25. Giglio Porto in 1963.

26. Reg with 1962 skipper, Costantino.

27.. Victor Perrocino's house on the beach at Cannelle with *Sea Laird* next to the beach.

28. Zembra, 'Les Grands Bâtiments' and bay, 1964.

29. Loran, Reg (*left*) and, newly arrived, Vernon Knapper (*centre*) in restaurant at Zembra.

30. 'Sacapuces' and master on the *langoustier*.

31. Zembra taxi, 1965.

32. Reg and sting ray at Zembra.

was a young weight-lifter and on his first dive discovered that you can lift more underwater than on the surface. He was fascinated, and spent most of his time underwater lifting huge rocks. We were more interested in seeing what crawled out from underneath.

I dived with Tim, Geoff and Ian off Cala Cupa and found a huge angler fish. They have ugly ragged skins and large grey teeth, but are good eating. I returned to harpoon it, and pulled in the harpoon. It swam up the line towards me, snapping its huge mouth. I landed it with difficulty and generally gave them a wide berth thereafter. We also dived off Giannutri's northern point, the Punta Secca. It was an astonishing site. A flat sand bottom as you swam seawards and then ahead, a black line across the bottom. When you reached it, the bottom dropped vertically in a splendid rock reef with bushes of gorgonia, lobsters and many fish. At 180 feet at the bottom of the wall, I saw a huge head appear round a corner. This was followed by two more heads – but apparently no bodies! These were the strangely shaped, 'moon fish' (*Mola mola*) who rowed themselves along with their top and bottom fins. I looked them up in my large book of fish by Alwynne Wheeler of the Natural History Museum in London. He had written, 'Nothing is known of the depths to which these fish swim'. I reported back and he said he would amend the comment in any future editions.

During the summer we got to know Victor Perrocino, a well-known character who lived with his elegant wife in the sprawling house on the beach at Cannelle. Victor was now retired and told us that he had had a famous restaurant in London called Chez Victor. He also told us that he had introduced King Edward VIII to Wallis Simpson there. We took these stories with a pinch of salt until he pulled out a drawer in his sitting room and showed us letters from Lord Mountbatten and many members of the British aristocracy. Victor was sophisticated, funny and unconventional. He invited us to lunch with them and the food was delicious

We also got to know Federico Pardini, a civilised Swiss hotelier, who had a small honeymoon hotel on the coast further south, that served *haute cuisine* and could only be reached by sea. He made his own rules and guests were allowed to sunbathe in the nude from the rocks below the hotel. As a variation from the local food, we took our divers down there occasionally to enjoy his six-course dinners and then dance on one of the open-air balconies overlooking the sea far below. We sailed back on the *Sea Laird* at midnight. Sometimes, if it was calm and the company was good, we would stop for an impromptu swim off the beach at Cannelle on the way back. Victor would invite us into his home for coffee. Once we banged on his door after midnight and were invited in, to find two distinguished lady visitors from England. Their eyes widened as the collection of nude brown bodies came through the front door. Victor loved every moment.

By mid-summer, Filippo had returned to the island for good, and was planning to build a further storey on the Bahamas to officially make it an hotel. I came up from the boat one afternoon to find him in earnest conversation with the mayor, police chief and the priest from the church next door to the Bahamas. Filippo looked very concerned. I asked him what it was all about. 'The priest says that I have built the hotel two metres too close to the church and, according to the regulations, it will have to be demolished.' It transpired later that a suitable contribution by Filippo to church funds might solve the problem.

Franca was back on the island from Rome. She was now involved with a young Italian Navy Captain called Antonio. He commanded a sizeable survey vessel that was moored in the port and was charting the sea-bed around the island. He was extremely enamoured of Franca and she invited us on board, where we happily consumed his duty-free whisky. One beautiful, moonlit evening, relaxing on his quarter- deck, Franca looked up from her drink, and said,

'Wouldn't it be great to go to Montecristo for a midnight swim'.

Without hesitation, Antonio leant back and pulled the emergency 'action stations' alarm. His crew turned to, and they steamed out 40 miles to Montecristo for the swim. Sometimes the Italians deserve their success!

At the beginning of August I got a telegram from Gill back in London. 'Arriving in a week's time, will sleep anywhere – on the beach if necessary'. August was a difficult month to find rooms, and at one week's notice it was impossible. It was definitely against the Italian law for a single girl to sleep on any beach. She duly arrived. I had had a new double bed installed in my small room in the Bahamas. The only space seemed to be in one half of that. That seemed to present no problem to Gill. We became even closer friends.

One evening, a week or so later, I was sitting over a campari at Nilo's bar with Stan and Gill, when I suddenly remembered that I had not made arrangements for the group dinner at Castello. 'Look after Gill', I said to Stan, 'I'll be back soon'. When I returned they had gone. I had to speak to Stan about the numbers. His room was next to mine, so I just knocked and walked in. The rest you can imagine. I left rapidly.

My pride was slightly dented, but my heart was still intact. I went up on to the roof, where Filippo had installed a bar and some music, and stood at the edge, looking down, sipping another drink. Below me, Gill appeared out of the hotel back door, looking as if she had suffered a bereavement. She walked slowly down to the harbour. Next Stan appeared, nervously asking if anyone had seen me. He appeared on the roof, apologising and expecting a less-than-enthusiastic reception. 'It's OK', I said, 'that's life, but you can buy me another drink'. He was delighted. Gill moved next door.

Brian Hall from London was helping me out by mid-summer when we had large numbers of students and visiting divers. At the Punta della Campana, north of the port, we found some small caves and one with a dome-shaped top. We took our mouthpieces out and let air bubble into the small space. We then surfaced in it to speak to each other, and found that we had strange squeaky voices due to the pressure on the vocal chords. I taught my youngest pupil yet, 10-year old Michael Easter-Bruce who was like a fish in the water. Tom and Elfie were back on holiday as was Jim Phoenix, now engaged to Marisa whom he had met on Giglio the previous year.

One day at tea time, Gill told me that her 'fiancé', Eddie, who was half Italian and half Arab, would be arriving that evening, so she would not be able to go to Castello with us. The numbers had fluctuated several times and I persuaded her to come and leave a note for him, telling where she was. After dinner at Castello, we moved to Paletto's bar and cellar. At about 10 p.m, Gill was happily sitting on Stan's knee, when the bead curtains opened and Eddie walked in. I turned to Stan. 'Right, you and I are going back down on the first taxi right now'.

Eddie asked if he could speak to me outside. We walked in the moonlight through the battlements to a space by an old pump. It looked like a guillotine in the moonlight. He told me about his love for Gill. 'Yes,' I said, 'a fantastic girl'. We returned without incident. Stan and I left, leaving Eddie with Gill. After we went, they had an argument and blows were struck. Three Milanesi in the bar didn't like seeing a girl attacked, and gave him a black eye. The police were called. Meantime I was relaxing, looking out of my bedroom at the peaceful scene. Suddenly the door was flung open and Gill grabbed me. 'Don't let him get at me!' Eddie came through the door with blackened eye, apologising. I tried to sort things out. The police chief thought it was the funniest thing he had heard of, as at that time the image of the English was of stiff upper lips and bowler hats. 'Che passione', he smirked. Luckily no charges were brought.

There was little opportunity for the police sergeant to shine on Giglio, as there was virtually no crime. I remember only one time, when a red-headed Milanesi refused to stop playing the juke box when Nilo closed at 11 p.m. Georgio, the mayor was called. He had a certain gravitas on occasions like this. He arrived with one of the village policemen and listened while Nilo explained and the tourist argued. Georgio pointed at the Milanesi, 'Him', he said briefly to the policeman, 'to jail'. The tourist spent the night in the old Saracen watch-tower which was the nearest thing to a jail. He went off crestfallen on the morning ferry.

Towards the end of the season, Lorenzo, who had houses in London, Rome and Tunis, told me that the Tunisians wanted to start a diving school on an uninhabited island called Zembra. They had built a touristic village and he had suggested me for the job. I told him that I was quite happy on Giglio, but he persisted, extolling the virtues of diving from a new un-dived island. If they sent me an air ticket and invitation would I go and look at it? I agreed, wondering if I could organise holidays from both islands.

At the end of September, Filippo took me to Montecristo for the first time. It lay 45 miles to the West of Giglio and its mountain could be seen on a clear evening from the restaurant at Castello. It rose dramatically from the sea and was higher than Giglio at over 600 metres. The only inhabitants were a caretaker and his family. We delivered some urgently needed supplies. I dived off the Punta della Piana to 230 feet, finding many lobsters and scorpion fish. I was to see more of this strange island in the future.

I did my last dive of the season on 6th October. It was my 988th from Giglio.

CHAPTER FIVE

Zembra – Island of Mysteries and Monsters

B<small>ACK IN</small> L<small>ONDON</small>, my room at The Cottage was taken, and I moved into a small hotel in Earls Court – then known as 'Kangaroo Valley' because of the number of visiting Australians. It was called the Belmont Court Hotel and was run by two formidable old ladies. There were many rules pinned up on the notice boards, but we managed to break most of them. The hotel hosted a variety of exotic life from Australian accountants to Icelandic ballet dancers.

I met a bizarre and willowy young lady called Sandra Matthews, who originally hailed from Brighton. She had an amazing sense of humour and treated me rather as an exotic species she had acquired. She made the best apple crumble I had ever tasted and had some other less obvious talents as well. She promised to visit me in Zembra if I ever got there.

I had only been back a few weeks, when a letter arrived from the Société Tunisienne de Banque, enclosing an open air ticket and invitation to visit their country as their guest. As I was due to spend a quiet Christmas with the family, I thought it would be fun to fly out on New Year's Eve. Lorenzo was sure to be having a party. I sent him a cable, giving my arrival time.

I arrived in darkness. Tunis airport was full of strange figures in Arab robes and strange exotic smells. I looked around for Lorenzo. No sign. I waited, realising that I knew no one in the country or where I was supposed to go. After some time, a mafia-like figure detached itself from the crowd and approached.

'You Vallintine?' the figure enquired curtly, then, 'Come with me'. We walked out to a waiting armoured jeep and drove off in a cloud of dust under a sky full of stars. The driver was not talkative. I discovered that he spoke Italian.

'Are we going to Lorenzo's?' I ventured.

'No'.

'Well, where are we going?'

'To Beltran'.

I knew nobody of that name, but presumed I soon would. We drove up to some wrought iron gates. Behind them was a drive leading up to an impressive staircase and villa.

'You get out here'. He drove off into the night. I opened the gates and started

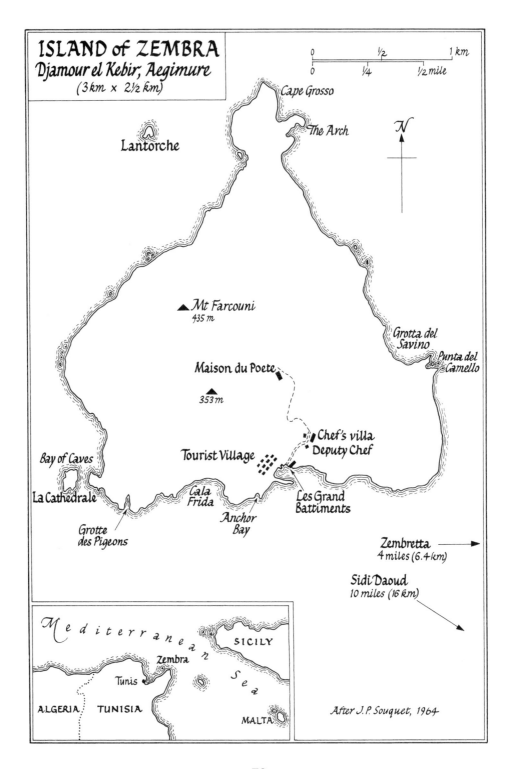

ISLAND of ZEMBRA
Djamour el Kebir, Aegimure
(3 km × 2½ km)

0   ½   1 km
0   ¼   ½ mile

Cape Grosso

The Arch

N

Lantorche

▲ Mt Farcouni
435 m

Grotta del
Savino

Punta del
Camello

Maison du Poete

▲
353 m

Chef's villa
Deputy Chef

Bay of Caves

Tourist Village

La Cathedrale

Cala
Frida

Anchor
Bay

Les Grand
Battiments

Grotte
des Pigeons

Zembretta
4 miles (6.4 km)

Sidi Daoud
10 miles (16 km)

Mediterranean Sea

SICILY

Zembra

Tunis

ALGERIA   TUNISIA

MALTA

After J.P. Souquet, 1964

70

walking up the drive carrying my bags. A figure came out on the steps of the villa. He had a gun! He fired twice in the air. I thought my last moment had come. Then I recognised Lorenzo's grin.

The villa belonged to Alberto Moravia, author of *A Woman of Rome*. It was packed with partygoers and a number of Alitalia air hostesses. I gratefully accepted a large drink.

After a day or so, Lorenzo took me to meet Azzous Mathari, the President of the STB, who were financing the new sailing and diving centre. The STB was the Tunisian equivalent of the Bank of England. They had set the new centre up under the name Centre Nautique International de Tunisie, or CNIT, for short. There was a separate office in Tunis, run by Rachid Driss, a bank employee.

One problem for most foreigners working in the country was that they could not export the money they earned. The charming Monsieur Mathari would make an exception for me, I learnt, and offered a very substantial salary as their *Chef du Plongée*. Meanwhile, as their guest, they would take me anywhere I wanted to go in Tunisia. My first priority was, of course, to see the island, which lay off the end of Cap Bon in the north-east tip of the country.

Zembra was 10 miles off the coast, but was quite different from Giglio. It was only 3 km long, 2 and-a half-wide and 454 metres high. The only habitations visible were the twelve new Arabic-style bungalows that they had built on the hillside for the already existing sailing school. There was also a large two-storey modern restaurant with kitchens, bar and storage areas which was known as Les Grands Bâtiments. A primitive jetty adjoined the small newly constructed harbour. Brand-new French compressors and diving equipment had already arrived. There was even a one-man recompression chamber. Money seemed to be little object.

Off the south-west corner of the island was a huge isolated rock, known as La Cathédrale. I dived there on the 3rd January on a calm, warm day, and to my delight found numbers of large groupers in residence. It certainly looked to be virgin territory.

They asked if there was anything else I wanted to see before I left, and on impulse, I told them that I had heard tales of a French diver who went down to 300 feet for coral everyday. I would like to meet him. After much discussion, we left for Tabarka, a town on the coast in the far west.

The coral diver was indeed French, and worked for the Tunisian Office National de Pêche or Fisheries Department. He was understandably suspicious of my motives and intentions at first, but mellowed after I explained that I was not there to coral dive, but to teach diving at the other end of the country. He had a French wife with him and several small children.

We discussed the coral I had seen in Giannutri and, after a few drinks, he took me up to a bedroom and pulled out a huge chest. 'You must not tell what I am going to show you'. In the chest was the most enormous tree of precious red coral I had ever seen. It was several feet long and probably a foot in diameter. 'At 100 metres', he said, 'the coral does not grow down from the roofs of caves, but up from the bottom looking like real trees'.

I asked about his solo diving and whether he had suffered from 'the bends'. 'Oh, yes – I've had it. Once I lost the feeling in both legs and one arm as I surfaced. I went down again with spare bottles for six hours of decompression alone before recovering.' The Tunisians had insisted that he took a Tunisian assistant. The assistant was dead within six weeks! Lorenzo took me hunting. Like most Italians, he was mad about shooting. They shot tiny woodcock-like birds, that we later ate. I took my leave a few days later.

In London, I made arrangements for Roger Hale to run Giglio for me during the forthcoming season, while I would be on Zembra. Dick Williams designed a new brochure for me, which featured a mermaid in a yashmak. I sailed into Zembra again early in May with Stan, my trusty companion.

I met André Nerisson, the chief of the sailing school, who was also responsible for the overall administration of the island. Both he, and his deputy, Jean-Pierre Souquet, were *anciennes* of Glenans, the famous French sailing school in Brittany.

André was quiet, serious and slightly distant. I had the feeling that he liked to keep himself apart. He was anxious though that the diving side, over which I would have complete jurisdiction, was successful. Jean-Pierre was friendlier and also a well-known French diving instructor. He had been a French Navy diver as long ago as 1935, and had produced a splendid map of the island. His wife, Francine, was charming and learnt to dive with us later in the season.

On the hillside, a few hundred metres from the bungalows, the bank had built a small palace-like house for the island chief and a smaller bungalow lower down for his deputy. I moved into one of the other bungalows. It had a balcony, bathroom, kitchen and spare room. It seemed ideal. The food at the communal restaurant left something to be desired after Giglio, but the wine was free. I soon got used to couscous, as there was little else to eat. It was due to improve when the main body of French sailing students arrived a few weeks later.

The builders were still clearing foundations by the tourist bungalows and were finding the walls of an ancient villa. Inside the walls they found human bones. The Carthaginians, the old inhabitants of the country, were known to have made human sacrifices to their God, Tanit, so perhaps this was some grim evidence of that. Like the Etruscans, they had been enemies of Rome, so much of their history had been obliterated. Even before the Carthaginians, those great sea traders, the Phoenicians, preferred to use offshore islands for watering and refuelling. I had high hopes that the waters around Zembra, which lay across their famous route to the silver mines of Spain, might conceal evidence of their passing.

We set about organising the diving equipment and were provided with a small (30-foot) *langoustier* fishing boat and a Tunisian fisherman to run it. I couldn't wait to get underwater and begin to explore.

Zembra had no indigenous inhabitants, although there was a mysterious ruin up on the mountain which was known as the *maison du poête*. Who the poet was, I never discovered, but he must have had a thin time. There was a Tunisian who was described as 'the farmer', but he had just been imported to grow useful vegetables for the centre. The nearest thing to a local inhabitant was the island dog, a splendid and fearless aquatic mongrel called 'Sacapuces' (flea-bag). The dog had a hard time scrounging food, and immediately adopted us. She became our mascot and came out on the diving boat with us every morning, leaping off to chase rabbits while we dived and then swimming back to the boat and hanging on to the diving ladder until being hoisted aboard. She was something of a canine swimming champion, and it was impossible to keep up with her without using fins.

Unlike my first year in Giglio, when we had little time to find the best underwater sites, there seemed to be no rush to book divers for me to teach and guide. My own brochure was, of course, now available in Britain, and a trickle of new clients arrived. The first was Dick Harris, a British European Airways Captain and leading member of the Silver Wing branch of BSAC. We explored the island and also the islet of Zembretta, 4 miles away, collecting slipper lobsters or *cigalles* (*Scyllarides latus*). We also found a number of Roman anchors and the occasional amphora.

The most magnificent dive was off a rock islet off the north-west coast of Zembra called the Lantorche or Lantorcho – old Italian for lantern. It was standing on three gigantic rock legs, through which huge bands of sunlight shone, illuminating the vertical walls, which were covered with yellow and orange cup corals. Swimming through the islet underwater was like being in a cathedral. Up in the top of the drowned arches were crawfish and corbs and tiny rock fish, (*Serranus scriba*) that swam upside down, in relation to the nearest rock surface

The narrow rock plateau surrounding Lantorcho attracted pelagic fish of all sizes. Huge amberjacks cruised past the striped groupers and circled curiously around us, their great eyes goggling.

Giant sting rays lay on the platform, huge and evil-looking with their spiracles, looking like eyes, moving in time to their breathing. Their tails stretched out like leather thongs for five feet or so straight out behind them. Half-way along the tail and almost invisible, was the six-inch dagger which gave the sting ray its name. It took a while for us to pluck up courage to the point where we took hold of the end of the tails. We felt sure that if you held the end of the tail, the ray could not operate its dagger defence, but we had no idea what they would do when we let go again! The tail itself was serrated and after suffering scratches, we found it better to use a sponge as a pad.

The first ray that I successfully gripped took off lazily from the bottom, pulling me effortlessly behind. He headed down the slope into deeper water. I dug my heels in, but could only stop him for a few seconds. He became more agitated as he realized I was still holding on and beat his wings furiously. At 150 feet I let go and the ray cruised on down into the distance. I relaxed as I saw that he had no intention of returning.

At the end of May, a handsome young newly wed couple, Nico and Vivienne, arrived from Belgium and I started teaching again. John Bowman, a British medical salesman based in Africa, also took lessons. He was something of a 'great white hunter' in the Hemingway tradition, and argued constantly with Stan whose credo in contrast, involved 'love, truth and beauty'.

A six-foot Hammerhead shark appeared at the surface after one of our dives and reminded us that we were in southern Mediterranean waters, with a tunny trap or *madrague* off Sidi Daoud, the village on the mainland opposite Zembra. Once the tuna were in the trap, fighting and losing blood, every large carnivore for miles was attracted to the area.

On 2nd June, I was diving with Stan at the Cathédrale when we saw an enormous lobster (*Hommarus*), which waved its claws menacingly in our direction as we approached. I had never seen a clawed lobster before. We finished the dive, and on our return passed its hole. I saw that the lobster was outside and got Stan to divert its attention from the front while I came down on it from behind, seizing it across the back with both hands. Its giant claws parted, but, to my relief, could not bend backwards behind its head. I brought it up, put it in the boat, and told John not to touch it while I returned to decompress. When I had gone, he hit it with an oar, breaking the shell. The lobster weighed eight and a half kilos. I have never seen another so large.

Zembra was becoming an isle of monsters and mysteries. We found a narrow cave, just three metres below the surface in the northern face of the Cathédrale. Edging in, I could see what looked like a carved stone table in the distance. Probably a natural feature, but who knows? In the shallow area between the rock and the coast, there seemed to be the remains of walls on the bottom. Perhaps the sea level had altered since classical times.

By the end of June my first French-speaking beginners were arriving. My 'fractured French' began to improve and I remembered my Club Med dives and the terms they used. Stan helped me by acting as guide for the more experienced. I taught Dominique Marchal, a mischievous, attractive, bubbly girl who turned out, most improbably, to be a commercial pilot, and guided Hugh Hennessy, an experi-enced diver from Belfast BSAC, who enjoyed seeing another shark and giant sting rays. I enjoyed teaching Randall Lemoine, an experienced yachtsman, who had worked with the French diving pioneer, Yves Le Prieur in the '40s, together with the son of the British ambassador to Tunis.

We used a shallow bay to the west of the Cathédrale for our beginner's dives. We found a series of shallow caves around the cliffs bordering it and so named it the Bay of Caves. There was one cave in which you could surface in air and with light from a high cleft in the rock face high above.

On a calm day at the end of July, I tried a deep snorkel dive in the Lantorcho grotto and managed to reach 32 metres, a record for me. On our first night dive we found the fish were so tame that we stroked them as they dozed with their eyes wide open. David Stokoe of London Branch who had been on Giglio with us, arrived and after a few days acted as dive guide for a party from the Tunisian National Guard. Jean, a French *moniteur* also came to help me. John Bowman came back with his Sudanese girlfriend, Lilly, who learnt with us too.

At the beginning of September, a party from the Tunisian Navy arrived to be taught. The party were commanded by a Chief Petty Officer whose name was 'Turki'. Turki had boundless energy and an air of command. He immediately took over the operation of our boat, shouting orders at the sailors. Turki, so the others told us, was an ex-helmet diver. During my introductory lecture, I mentioned pressure on the ears underwater and methods of clearing them. To my surprise a voice from the back said: 'Nonsense!' Turki, it seemed, had no ear problems – such difficulties he informed us, were all imagination. He would like to demonstrate a free dive to ten metres to prove it. I agreed to watch.

The next morning after our first session, we stopped at the Bay of Caves and Turki jumped in feet first without any equipment at all. Watching through my mask, I saw him descending motionless in the position of 'attention', except for strange whirling movements of his hands, which made him look rather like an overweight humming bird. After a few seconds, he arrived, still at attention, on the bottom, whereupon he commenced the whirling hand movements in the opposite direction and popped importantly back to the surface. 'Ears', he said, 'are no problem to the Navy'. Our doctor thrust his spy glass into Turki's ears and informed us that he had drums the size of a baby's.

Towards the end of their three-week course, we let the Navy men take it in turns to lead a dive under our watchful eyes. Turki swam off at enormous speed down-wards with scattered sailors trailing behind clutching their ears. Omer guided them back, as I went after Turki. He was resting by a rock at 160 feet eyeing me calmly as I approached and made thoughtful 'I am OK' signals at me. When we got back to the boat I told him in no uncertain terms how he might have caused the death of his companions. 'And a very good thing for the Navy if I had,' muttered Turki.

Their dive discipline was non-existent, and I had to constantly retrieve those who swam in the wrong direction, completely unaware of the position of the group they were supposed to be part of. After a few weeks, a Navy captain in a smart uniform arrived in a motor torpedo boat and asked me how the men were doing. 'Quite well,' I lied, 'but their underwater discipline leaves something to be desired.' The captain took Turki's hand and upbraided him gently while still holding it. They then walked off together talking and still holding hands. 'A different ethos,' I thought, and wondered what my colonel would have thought.

The next uniformed group to arrive were made up of Tunisian firemen. They were good students, and hung on my every word of instruction. I later heard that, with no training at all, they had been strapped into aqualungs to recover a number of bodies that had finished up in deep wells during the French occupation of the country. One told me that at first his ears had hurt in the well, but then there was a 'pop', and he felt them no more. Another unfortunate fireman had been sent down into a vat of petrol to remove the plug! His skin suffered, they said.

Before they left, the Fire Chief arrived. He was a perky, know-all sort. He decided that he wanted to dive.

'Have you done it before?', I asked.

'No, but I can do anything my men can do.'

'I'll take you down on the ladder', I agreed, and turning to his men, said 'You can get him kitted up'.

I went down the ladder and waited on the surface. Down he came.

'What are you going to breathe from?', I asked.

'The bottle, of course', he snapped.

'Well, wouldn't it be a good idea to have a demand valve on it?'

The firemen kept straight faces.

There were numbers of morays off the west coast of the island. I was standing on a rock on the bottom, directing the firemen's exercises, when an excited beginner snorkelled down and pointed behind me. I presumed that there was some sort of fish she wanted me to look at and carried on. She continued to come down and point. I finally turned to find a huge moray that looked like a python, rearing out of its hole with its teeth just a few inches from my bare leg.

In mid-October, at the end of the season, I travelled back to Giglio with John Bowman and Lilly, who wanted to see the island. Arriving at Santo Stefano, we found that there was now a second car ferry to the island. It was run by a private company. It was similar in size to the *Aegilium*, with a uniformed captain and crew. Arriving in Porto, I watched as the usual small rowing boat appeared beneath the bows. This time Costantino was in the boat. The captain bellowed orders at him as he grabbed the hawser and clipped it on before getting out of the way in the nick of time as the ferry swung round the buoy. We went ashore and Costantino offered us camparis at Nilo's.

'A splendid new ship', I said, 'Who owns this independent line?'

'Well', said Costantino hesitantly, 'Mainly me, and my cousin, Pepe. Little had changed on Giglio.

I met Luciano in the Port, who looked at me with tragic eyes.

'Reg, something terrible 'as 'appened'.

'What, has the *Giglio One* sunk?'

'No, worse!'

What could be worse than that?, I thought. He explained.

'I am MARRIED'.

'Oh, Congratulations. Anyone I know?'

'Ze Swedish girl', he said, rolling his eyes.

Franca was also on the island. She was organising her birthday party in Ruggiero's restaurant. I asked her about Antonio, the Italian Navy captain.

'Antonio?' she said dismissively, 'a thing of the past'.

It seemed he had departed with his ship to Corsica for more hydrographic work. He was evidently not part of her life any more.

The morning of the party, an Italian sailor in uniform arrived on the ferry. He caused some curiosity, but said nothing. In the evening, Franca sat at the head of a long table with 20 of us celebrating her birthday. At the end of dinner, the sailor marched smartly in through the door with a bouquet of flowers that stretched to the roof.

He saluted Franca and announced, 'I have been detailed by Lieutenant Alberto Tarantini, to bring you these flowers from Corsica.' He saluted again and went out. 'Give the man a drink!' we suggested, 'He's come all this way'. 'No, it is not necessary', declared Franca, 'Alberto is a thing of the past.'

Back in London again, I realised that we did not have enough bookings to continue to run both islands. I was loath to leave Zembra where we had made such a promising start, but always felt that Giglio was my second home.

Meantime, I decided that, apart from visiting branches and trying to stimulate interest in the holiday, I should try to find some part-time employment. One of the few useful skills the Army had taught me at Willems Barracks was touch-typing. I enrolled with the largest 'temps' agency. I was doubtless one of the strangest they had ever had on their books. After much cogitation, they despatched me to Philips Electrical in Shaftesbury Avenue where a new Economic Research Department had just been formed. It consisted of three young economists, and now, me. They told me that although I would be paid for the whole day, there was no need to arrive until 11 a.m. Before that, they read the *Financial Times*, and at 11, dictated a report to me, which had to be perfectly typed and correctly punctuated. It took me until 12 midday, and then we all went home!

During a subsequent winter, I asked to be sent back, but the Agency reported that the Economic Research Department had been disbanded. They sent me back to Philips though, where I operated in a huge room with some 200 girls. For my first job, I was given a ladder and asked to put up the Christmas decorations!

The Tunisians were anxious for me to get back in early April 1965, and Omer, a young Turkish diver who had been with us the year before, came across to help with the teaching. He was quick to learn and proved to be an excellent instructor. I arrived on the island before him.

By the 9th of April, Omer and I were already teaching and guiding a mixed group of English, French, Belgian and Guadeloupian divers. There seemed to be more clawed lobsters in the Spring and I also saw my first John Dory (*Zeus faber*) besides the huge amberjacks and great *Dasyatis* sting rays. One calm day the tiny Caravelle dinghy we were using was surrounded by lazily rolling dolphins who escorted us back to the village.

In May my doctor friend from the British Spearfishing Team, Bob Stephens, arrived and we took more slipper lobsters and admired a bevy of colourful sea slugs or nudibranchs.

The office in Tunis reported that they were sending me a group of traditional sponge divers who, the Fisheries Department wanted to convert to using compressed air aqualungs. When they arrived, they seemed to be quite young to be helmet divers and I asked what equipment they had used. 'We're not divers yet', they explained, 'We were unemployed and the officials visited our village and asked if we could swim and wanted to be divers'. 'We all volunteered at once.' Most could hardly swim and had never seen mask, fins or tube before, so it was an uphill struggle.

We dived off a huge rock arch to the east of Capo Grosso, and 'Sacapuces' caused concern by going missing after swimming ashore to hunt rabbits. I returned the next day, but there was no sign of the dog. I felt as though I had lost a diver. On the third day, we anchored there and suddenly spotted a tiny head swimming round the next headland toward us. She arrived exhausted and hungry at the boat. We were overjoyed.

In mid-May we had an incredible dive at the Cathédrale. Through huge clouds of fish, swam dentex, giltheads and, finally, twenty five or so amberjacks, each nearly six feet long. We also tried diving in mid-channel between Zembra and Zembretta, finding strange sponges and yellow gorgonians at 150 feet.

The sponge fishers were now in aqualungs, but they varied widely in competence. Those who listened to our instructions began to improve, but others adopted frog-like kicks when they suffered minor panics in the shallows. They needed careful watching and I was concerned at the idea of their harvesting sponges professionally. I stressed the danger of 'bends', and carefully explained the function of the decompression tables. After two weeks, I reported to Tunis that they needed another two weeks, at least, before I could declare any of them competent to dive together. They reluctantly agreed to their staying on. They eventually left, having enjoyed their first 'holiday' ever, and free food.

Later in the season, I asked the CNIT if there was any news of how they were getting on. Sadly, it seemed that several had died and many were suffering from the bends. Apparently the amount of sponges they had found at one location, represented untold wealth to them, and they just stayed down until they had collected them all. The same temptation had been the end of so many commercial coral and sponge divers in the Mediterranean over the centuries.

On the 17th of May, we took our *langoustier* fishing boat across to Sidi Daoud to see the *madrague* or tunny trap in operation. The general principle was that, as the tuna, usually mysteriously led by a sword fish, followed the same migration route along the coast every year, they laid a net out to sea across their path. The tunny turned to seaward, only to find another net at right angles, guiding them in until eventually they were in a huge *chambre de mort* where the net covered the bottom as well. After some days, the net was slowly pulled up by hundreds of chanting fishermen from a circle of fishing boats. Ten, specially chosen individuals were then allowed to jump down into the shallow net. By this time the sea had turned red with the blood of the tuna threshing against each other in their attempts to escape. They gaffed the giant fish and swung them out on to the deck to die. A grizzly sight. The Tunisian captain allowed us to dive in his nets before they were pulled up.

Bob Stephens and I swam down the huge net walls that stretched to the bottom at 75 feet. Entangled in the net were moribund sharks, turtles and ocean sunfish. Suddenly from the distance what looked like numbers of sleek submarines roared past us. The tuna were an astonishing sight, smooth, powerful and swimming perfectly in unison. After what seemed like only a few minutes, beating noises from the boat above brought us back to the surface. The captain was worried as we were causing fish to jump out of the net.

The next day, we dived again between Zembra and Zembretta finding huge rocks, large groupers and amberjacks. Looking up from 100 feet down, I saw a large fish approaching fast above us. It had the power and then the shape of a large shark. It came on and then, suddenly becoming aware of us, flipped round backwards and upwards to disappear from view.

We used an 'underwater sledge' for the first time, tilting it to 'fly' up and down, while being towed behind the boat. Another group of dolphins took an interest.

We had been provided with a new 'captain' for our *langoustier*. He was an adventurous young fisherman called Hasen El Bey, who was a good swimmer and snorkeller. I soon taught him to dive and he proved a reliable aide. At the Cathédrale we finally perfected the art of holding the tails of rays and using them as 'taxis'. Others held our ankles and were pulled down the slope until we let go. A photograph of the 'taxi service' later won a photographic prize.

At Anchor Bay on the south coast, we adopted a striped grouper, calling him 'Oscar' after the founder of BSAC. We took him tit-bits and he quickly became tame, swimming up to us to receive the remains of our picnics.

By June, Hasen was dive guiding in the absence of any other instructor. He proved very reliable. He had been to Zembra many years before and told me that there were three great island mysteries. They were La Maison du Poête, the Tombs of the Ancients and the Cemetery of the Birds. The Maison du Poête we knew about, although its history was still unknown. The old tombs were apparently on the eastern coast of the island and the cemetery we were to discover later.

I had a new idea to divert the experienced divers. On their first dive I took them into 'our' cave in the Bay of Caves and surfaced them in the pool inside. There were low rocks at water level and I had secreted a bottle of Martini and some glasses there. We each had an aperitif before replacing our mouthpieces and diving out again.

A young Englishman, Bill Smith, who was an air traffic controller, arrived in July and dived with us. On one of our visits to Zembretta, a young French group asked if they could sunbathe in the nude there. I decided that the best plan was to divide the isle in two with nudity permitted on the western side. I sometimes joined them.

One day we were lying digesting our picnic after diving when a rare cruise boat appeared over the horizon and it was soon clear that it would pass very close to us. We couldn't resist holding hands and doing a nude dance along the shore. There was a rush of passengers to the side of the vessel, which sailed, heeling, into the distance. We wondered what tales they told of the primitive natives of Zembretta.

Bill asked whether he could dive at dawn. I was not too enthusiastic, but promised that if he got me up, I would organise the boat and skipper. He did. We went out to the Cathédrale and discovered many more fish than usual and one or two groupers who were hunting far from their regular holes. They lay trembling in shallow hiding places as we reached in and stroked them. It felt wonderful to return with a giant appetite for breakfast, but we never repeated the experiment, although we did regular night dives.

Late in July, Marc Jasinski, a noted Belgian cave diver and underwater photographer, arrived with a television crew to make a film on the island. They brought an attractive news reader, Monique de Lannoy as star. We discovered fish that I had never found in Giglio, such as trigger fish (*Balistes*) and bristle worms. The trigger fish had dug a nest in the sand off Zembretta and was immovable as it guarded its eggs. We saw dolphins underwater for the first time. A French *moniteur*, Pierre Chaussend came to help with the increasing numbers of beginners and Stan was back in August acting as a dive guide.

Towards the end of the season, Stan and I dived into the centre of the grotto in the Lantorcho. Looking out through the main entrance, I saw a large shark moving across outside and attracted Stan's attention. It was obviously curious about us and turned into the grotto, looking very sinister in black silhouette against the blue outside. We flattened ourselves against the rock wall and it turned and left us. We surfaced briefly to discuss it, before going down again to be surrounded by amberjacks. We found an Angel Shark (*Squatina*) on the bottom. We thought it must be the start of a 'fish convention'.

For some time, I had been planning a small expedition to some tiny islands over the horizon to the west. One of them was called the Ile Cani or island of sharks. On 18th September we equipped our *langoustier* with provisions and camping gear and set sail. The crew, all divers, were Hasen as captain, our little Tunisian mechanic, Ayeddie, Stan, Mireille Andreas, who had agreed to act as cook for us and Yves Octors from the sailing school, acting as navigator.

A number of hours later, we arrived at a low island, the Ile Plane. It had a lighthouse and the keepers were shooting rabbits when we arrived. We moored and discovered the wreck of a Greek ship, the *Nerion*, only a few feet below the surface. She had been run ashore following a gale two years before.

The keepers took us to see the graves of four British sailors who had been wrecked on the island during the last war and then strafed by planes. There was no readable detail remaining on the simple wooden headboards, but we were told that the graves held the remains of a commander, an NCO and two sailors.

We dived on the ship the next day, exploring the wreckage of masts, rails, anchor chains and portholes. The keeper showed us boxes of ancient human bones, some of children, including skulls. There were also pieces of the amphora they had been buried in. We presumed they were Carthaginians.

We left for the next island, Ile Pilau just 30 minutes away, where there was said to be a Roman wreck. We found nothing there except rock and weeds, and left in the afternoon for the Ile Cani. It took another two hours to reach it. Here there were more friendly keepers, who offered us rooms in the lighthouse for the night. We gratefully accepted as we only had the bare boards of the *langoustier* to pitch our sleeping bags on. The next day I shot a grouper to swell our dwindling food supplies. We returned from diving to find the weather deteriorating and a Sicilian fishing boat moored close by. The skipper invited us aboard, and we shared their vermouth and vino and down in the hold, ate the most delicious fresh turtle stew by the light of hurricane lamps.

We were now blocked at the anchorage by the increasing seas. The lighthouse keeper made it clear that we could stay ashore as long as we supplied them with free vino! Luckily we still had some left. Hasen and Ayeddie elected to stay the night on board to care for the boat. I swam out to them the following morning through choppy seas, to find Ayeddie prostrate with sea sickness. We ferried him ashore together with tins of food and bottles of vino. The chief keeper made bread for us and we shared a dogfish in the evening.

By the 22nd, we were seriously short of provisions, however, the weather was improving, and we left for the nearest harbour at Port Farina. Arriving near the Ile Pilau, we changed our minds and set course back to Zembra. It was unnerving to see waterspouts all around the horizon when we were out of sight of land. There seemed to be no way of knowing which direction they were travelling in, so we just kept our course and hoped for the best. We sailed in to Zembra after 7 hours. The season was over.

Instead of travelling back to London, I was asked by the STB to accompany Rachid Driss, the manager of CNIT, on a European publicity tour that included a Conference of Youth Travel Organisations in Austria. We flew into Vienna, and I played truant from the conference when we got to Salzburg, to visit the fairytale castles in the hills around, returning in time to be taken to the Vienna State Opera.

While in Munich to see tour operators, we were taken to the Hoffbruh House during the Oktober Bier Fest. Rachid, being a strict Moslem, did not touch alcohol. The locals grudgingly accepted this, but when he refused to have 'water with bubbles in it', they nearly poured it over him. We zoomed through a number of capital cities before parting company, and I returned to London.

CHAPTER SIX

A Drop of Whisky & a Deadly Cave

BRITISH INSTRUCTORS WORKING ABROAD were now well established. Not only were they teaching at the Club Med's numerous 'villages', but also, like me, in individual locations, mostly in the Mediterranean.

As there were no diving instructor qualifications in Britain at this time, the Club Med insisted on Brits taking the French Federation's Moniteur Nationale exam in France and in French! There was some agitation for the creation of a British instructor exam, but the BSAC, the governing body, had difficulty in changing its standards immediately. It was decided therefore to set up a new organisation called the National Underwater Instructors' Association (NUIA) to run a suitable qualification. The BSAC took a close interest, providing finance and administration for the first year and sending observers. Jack Atkinson, ex-Giglio, acted as Honorary Secretary of the new body.

He phoned me up one afternoon in November '65. 'We're having another meeting tonight at Ironmonger Baths in the City. You should be there!'

'I'm meeting my brother for a drink', I said, 'I'll be along as soon as I can'.

We had several pints of Guinness. When I arrived, Jack said:

'Are you going to take it or not?'

'What?'

'The national exam – this is the first weekend and we're testing your pool work'.

Pat Harrison was lurking in the background, and whispered to me that I should not do so. 'We'll start our own professional organisation', he said.

Leo Zanelli, an observer from the BSAC, offered his swimming trunks. I decided to go ahead.

Twelve of us plunged in to swim 200 metres in less than 6 minutes, and to then dive for a heavy manikin and keep it above the surface for 2 minutes. Don Shiers of the Aquatic Club was fiercely competitive, and had doubtless been practising. To his delight, he beat me in the swim, but we were both well within the limit, as were Mike Busuttili and Ted Derrick from London Branch, Brian Booth, the BSAC National Coach, and John Davis of the Aquatic Club. We all managed to hold up the manikins and also run a beginner's aqualung lesson.

Because of potential jealousies among existing professionals, it had been decided that the Navy, who had advisors on the new Association's board, should run the first exam, basing it on the syllabus of the French event. Commander 'Jackie' Warner, the Deputy Superintendent of Diving, led the examining team.

The next weekend we were at Horsea Lake, near Portsmouth, the RN training centre. We each gave a lecture on some aspect of diving physiology then it was up to the diving boards built above the lake for jumps in snorkel gear and full kit.

From 10 metres, we hit the water like rockets. My mask disappeared, but I managed to retrieve it. Mike's fins were up to his knees after the impact. Then we were off for a 1500 metre swim which included snorkel dives. After another 100 metres on the surface in full gear, it was tests of underwater navigation with and without compass and a 'circular sweep search'. The underwater visibility was nil.

The third weekend we were at Stoney Cove, the flooded granite quarry in the Midlands, recovering 'lifeless' fully-equipped divers 'preferably without use of life jackets'. It was hard work. We also dived to 136 feet in a black hole in the middle to tie knots to order, before taking the gear off and snorkelling down again to 10 metres. Mike 'Bus'. demonstrated his new adjustable buoyancy 'Fenzy' jacket which caused the RN Petty Officers to christen the event 'Inflate yer Mate Week'. Then it was on to boat handling and seamanship.

The fourth weekend at HMS *Vernon* saw us doing arithmetic in the deep experimental chamber at 180 feet, and then it was into a classroom for written and oral exams.. It was finally announced that six of us had passed the exam at a high enough standard to act as examiners on the next. I was now National Instructor No. 6. (If my name had begun with an A, I would have been No. 1).

Before leaving Zembra, Bill Smith, the air traffic controller who had been based at Stornoway in the Hebrides, had invited me to come up there at Hogmanay to see-in the New Year and dive with his local friends. I couldn't resist his stories of wild ceilidhs and fabulous diving conditions and agreed to go.

Meantime, I had been invited by Don Shiers to go with him as his guest to the Royal Navy Divers' Dinner at Portsmouth. I had heard tell of this event too, where alcohol 'flowed like bathwater.' The details of the dinner are understandably vague in my mind, but I do remember finishing up at 3 a.m. on the morning of 10th December, talking about the Hebrides with a RN officer who had been the deepest helmet diver in the world back in 1956 when he had reached 600 feet on an experimental dive at midnight in a Norwegian fiord. I mentioned that I was due to go to the Hebrides shortly and Lt George Wookey then told me about his discovery of the wreck of the *Politician*, the 'whisky galore' ship there.

The 'Polly' had set sail from Liverpool in 1941, bound on a great circle route for the USA with a cargo of fur coats, brandy and 20,000 cases of the finest whisky. These were the dark days of World War Two, when whisky, that the islanders referred to as 'the water of life', was impossible to come by.

The ship was commanded by a Captain Beaconsfield-Worthington. Her route should have kept her clear of the islands. She was merrily steaming along at 18 knots into the night when she mysteriously struck a sand bank called Calvay between Eriskay and South Uist. To hit this bank, in a largish vessel would be extremely difficult even if you planned it! Captain Beaconsfield-Worthington was below at the time of striking. It is recorded that the Mate shouted 'Battleship on the port bow' before they hit. There was, of course, no battleship.

While the Captain was steadily (or unsteadily) making his way to the bridge, the mate ordered 'Abandon Ship' and one boat was away rowing bravely into the night before the captain could recall it. He then radioed his position as 100 miles south of Barra Head, an error in navigation of 100 miles. The local lifeboat was launched and spent many fruitless hours searching in vain.

Meantime, the rowing 'survivors' had arrived at an island. They managed to get ashore on the beach and, finding driftwood, built a fire. When dawn broke some hours later, they found they were on Eriskay surrounded by houses!

The locals came down and could see the *Politician* with a broken back on the sandbank in the distance. They offered help. 'What was your cargo?' one of them enquired. '20,000 cases of whisky' came the reply.

There must have been a moment of pregnant silence as the locals grasped the significance of this revelation. They didn't waste any time. They knew the excise men would be on to it. They 'rescued' or 'removed' the remaining crew and then set about hooking cases of whisky out of the flooded hold with gaffs, fishing rods and anything that came to hand. They got 7,000 cases ashore before the dreaded customs people arrived. The islands went on a six-month continuous happy booze. The whisky even got into the chicken food, so they were happily staggering about as well.

Compton McKenzie, the well-known author, was living on Barra at the time, and wrote a fictional version of the stranding called *Whisky Galore*. The book became famous and the subsequent film, even more so. Eventually the wreck slid off the sandbank into two halves and disappeared beneath the waves.

George and his RN diving team had been recovering guided missiles, which the Army shot towards the isles of St Kilda, 45 miles out. When they had spare time, they relocated the wreck and brought up some bottles.

At 3 a.m., after the Diver's Dinner, he was generous and expansive and pulled an old envelope out of his pocket and drew a map of Eriskay and South Uist to which he finally added the traditional cross to show the position of the wreck. I drunkenly thanked him and stuffed it into my own pocket for future use.

I arrived at Stornoway towards the end of December and settled into a small guest house. There was just one other guest for breakfast next morning – a young

English girl. I sat down opposite her. 'Have you seen Bill Smith?' were her first words. I would have been astonished if anyone had then told me that she would become my first wife. (Doubtless she would have been equally amazed).

Loran had been in Stornoway before as part of a British European Airways trainee course. She had spent a lot of happy hours carousing with friends, including Bill, in tiny Hebridian shelters called shielings. They were both enamoured of the local songs and history, performing a beautiful duet of a lament called 'Island Moon', when primed with a certain amount of the 'life-giving' liquor.

Bill introduced me to his diving friends. There was Horace Capaldi, whose grandfather had emigrated from Naples to Stornoway and opened an ice-cream parlour. Horace was an equally improbable character who was still running the local café. He was softly spoken, incredibly hospitable, and enormously enterprising, with a capacity for whisky that was mind-blowing. He was married to a charming and supportive Scottish girl called Annetta.

The other divers were Ian Davidson, who owned the impressive County Hotel (and who later sadly 'died of the drink') and 'English Roddy' MacLeod who was the local police sergeant. How he got his nickname, I've no idea, as the Hebrides were the traditional home of the MacLeods.

We used to assemble at Ian's hotel to change into our wet suits in the warmth of his boiler room. He would then produce a bottle to make sure we were warm inside as well.

I did my first dive with Bill and Roddy on the 28th December in heavy swell and freezing seas off Bayble Pier on the Eye peninsula. We then dived daily, finding wrecks and collecting enormous sea urchins for souvenirs. On the 30th, I saw my first grey seal while on the way to the wreck of the *Holm* off Eilean nan Uan and on New Year's Eve we dived into a wild sea there with the wind gusting to 35 knots.

I remember little of the Hogmanay celebrations except that they were the wildest I had ever known. We needed two days to recover before starting to dive again on the 3rd of January. The sea had now calmed, but was frozen over in the shallows. We 'cracked' our way in, before crashing through the light covering of ice. On the bottom, I waited apprehensively for the first trickle of icy water to penetrate my ill-fitting wet suit. 'Tell yourself it's warm', I repeated again.

Ian filled our cylinders from a compressor in his boiler room. One evening he forgot to take my twin-set off when it reached working pressure. His relief valve failed, and so in the morning he presented me with a set filled to well over 350 atmospheres pressure – a potential bomb. Instead of sensibly letting some air out, I decided to use it up underwater.

We had a long trek to the dive site and wore our sets as we walked. Reaching the low summit before our dive site, I slipped and fell backwards onto the big twin cylinders. I was like a beetle turned on its back, and felt momentarily incapable of movement. I looked up for help, but the others seemed to be legging it as fast as they could in a number of different directions. I managed to roll over and stagger upright. The cylinders were still in one piece and the air seemed to last forever once I got underwater.

On one of our last dives, we decided to paddle out to the site using a home-made canoe. We brought it alongside the harbour wall. We had a lot of weight, but the canoe had a decent freeboard. I was the last to step gingerly into it carrying my heavy twin-set. Before I could sit down, water poured over the gunwale, and the canoe sank beneath us with all our equipment. After floundering ashore, the others turned to me. 'We've heard you're a champion snorkeller – it's a shallow bottom, off you go!' They passed me a line. Each time I surfaced having tied it on to something, and blew out my snorkel, Ian poured whisky into it to revive me. We eventually got everything up.

I spoke to the others about my encounter with George Wookey and diving the *Politician*, but discovered that the wreck was 100 miles further south. They suggested that we meet again on Benbecula in the south in February which would be the 25th anniversary of the sinking. We agreed to do so.

Back in London, I got a temporary job at Kings Beam House, the headquarters of Her Majesty's Customs and Excise. The work was boring but the girls exciting. I took the opportunity to look up the files on the *Politician* and its cargo. A useful exercise.

By February both Horace and Bill were in London and we flew together to Benbecula to meet up with Roddy and Ian. I was not too hopeful that we would immediately find the wreck, as George had described the hours he took to find 'a quite unrecognisable ship … completely grown over with thick kelp.' Horace knew better. He had chartered a local boat run by John MacIsaac, who quietly assured us that he would put us on the wreck.

The weather was kind for February and, unbelievably, 20 minutes after leaving, John confidently anchored in 30 feet of calm water, so clear that we could see the white ripples on the sand below as they reflected the sunlight. A dark mass was obviously the remains of a ship. We went straight in and found an incredibly beautiful wreck with huge girders covered in multi-coloured anemones and a school of pollack swimming lazily between the broken beams.

Although I had been told that we would only find the remains of No.5 hold and the engine room, the wreckage stretched for at least 30 metres along the bottom. To our delight, after only a few minutes, we unearthed the first bottle of whisky. Not, as I had expected, from some dark corner of the hold, but from the sand under the distorted plating of the wreck. It was like a dream come true. Clutching our bottles, we swam over the wreck taking photographs and trying to forget the temperature of the water.

The next day we were back again collecting a lobster from a ventilator and more bottles with corks still firmly in place. The local BBC radio journalist, Donnie B. McLeod, a friend of Horace's, of course, had been alerted and interviewed us. As part of his recording, he got us to open and sample the whisky. He pushed his microphone forward to record each sound as we opened the first bottle. It smelt like a mixture of bad eggs and camembert. We poured out a glass full, which looked normal enough and each took a swig. It was revolting! Five minutes later one of us noticed that the remains in the glass had turned black, and we looked at each other, realising that that was probably happening inside each of us too. By then we had had some reviving drafts of a more recent vintage. There were no after effects. We contacted the Customs people, but they were no longer interested in undrinkable bottles of whisky from the wreck.

'Donnie B' also interviewed a selection of the old locals and, as he was a local man himself, they 'opened up' as they had never done before.

'What was the atmosphere like when you were fishing the whisky?', he asked.

'It was very quiet, rather like a shrine', one softly spoken old man said.

'And what did you do with it then?'

'We dug a hole in the peat. Rather like a grave, but with a little more care.'

A retired schoolmistress told how when the excise men came round to search the houses, they hid the bottles everywhere, even emptying the balance into lavatory cisterns. At the last moment she found that she'd forgotten one bottle in the bedroom. She pulled out an empty 'jerry' from under the bed and poured it in. 'Then', she said, 'just to make sure they wouldn't test it, I popped a string of sausages in as well.'

To the locals it had been an almost mystical experience. Another old man said: 'Our need was great and she came. It's time we had another.'

One islander wrote a poem in Gaelic called 'The Song of the Politician' It was translated into English by Arthur Swinson who wrote the first book on the stranding, *Scotch on the Rocks*.

> Don't ask me why I'm feeling sad,
> My thoughts are melancholy
> The truth is that I've had a dram
> Of whisky from the Polly.
> For that's the ship that came ashore
> And you never saw her like before
> She'd whisky in the hold galore
> And it's led me into folly.

When they brought the news that she was there
I took my boat to board her;
Found silk and cotton, sherry, stout
And fine goods ranged in order.
But down there in the flooded end
Was every kind of brand or blend
That God or kindly fate could send –
And me the first marauder!

'Twas clear to me and clear to all
That ship was wrecked for ever;
And if we left the whisky there
It would be tasted never.
But soon the Customs men came around
And though I'd hid it underground
My stock of good 'Spey Royal' they found
And I thought I'd been so clever.

So to Lochmaddy Court I went
Bewildered and outwitted
The Fiscal stood and read the charge
But I would not admit it.
The policemen stood around there tense
While the Customs gave their evidence
But the sheriff said it didn't make sense
And so I was acquitted.

So here's a health to the Captain bold
Of the good ship Politician
And here's to the rock she struck that night
A-sailing on her mission!
What's left of her can still be found
Off Calvay Isle in Eriskay Sound,
Of all great ships she is renowned –
The Polly!
The Polly!
We shall not see her like again
Though we live from now to a hundred and ten,
The good ship Politician!

After three days diving on the wreck, we had amassed 30 bottles between us and decided it was time to go. There was a ceilidh at the Lochboisdale Hotel nearby where I remember dancing with one of the most provocative local lassies. As I recovered the remains of my body, I asked her what she did when she wasn't driving men mad. 'I'm a physical education mistress', she replied, with a knowing smile.

We met a group of commercial divers who told us they had been hired to recover whisky and then blow up the wreck. They were not happy that we had got there first.

At the airport, we were having a last drink. As we walked out, Roddy clapped me on the shoulder and pushed a large brown paper parcel into my hand: 'Just a wee present to remind you of the Hebrides. Come back soon!' We walked up into the aircraft and I pushed the parcel under my seat. Somewhere abeam of Glasgow there was a tap on my shoulder. A distinguished, white-haired Scotsman sitting behind spoke:

'Excuse me Sir, but your parcel's bleeding over my foot'.

'Roddy's a police sergeant', I thought. 'He's given us a severed hand'.

We peered into the parcel. There was a beautiful salmon with a neat harpoon hole through it. We ordered another dram from the hostess.

We changed planes at Glasgow and I carried the parcel with a salmon's head sticking out, through the airport, blissfully unaware that in Scotland it was practically a capital offence to be in possession of three scales of a salmon in that month.

I gave a bottle to Harry Gould and also to a beautiful blonde model called Elise who was learning to dive at London Branch for the next James Bond film. Elise was half Norwegian and half Welsh. One evening when I was due to take her for dinner, I met up first with a young businessman called Brian May. He was a branch member too, and was anxious to give up his business in the City and buy a boat to cruise the Med. I introduced him to Elise and they got on like a house on fire. I think it was love at first sight.

* * *

News of our activities in Zembra was spreading, and the CNIT were getting enquiries from France and Belgium. We had more from England, and then the Tunisian services were interested in more courses too.

It was clear that I would need more help and equipment for the 1966 season. There were also vacancies for other Europeans. I met up again with Loran in London and somehow persuaded her to give up her job with BEA to run the Zembra bar. I was also approached by a young member of Bournemouth Branch, Vernon Knapper. He told me glibly that he was an experienced instructor, linguist and chef. He was as keen as mustard and I agreed that we should probably need another instructor. I alerted Mike 'Bus' and John Davis my fellow candidates in the first NUIA exam and they agreed to come out in late summer.

The Belgian end of the organisation was run by an ebullient and friendly lady called Lulu Gewelt. She and her husband, Louckie, became good friends and I went across to their reunion in Brussels. They organised a *moniteur fédéral* from Belgium called Georges Barbier for me.

Meantime it was time for the second NUIA exam that would be run by the successful candidates on the first. This time those we were to examine included Dick Harris from BEA, Jerry Hazzard, later BSAC National Coach, John Towse, who had dived on Giglio, and my old assistant, Roger Hale. The examiners decided that we should give the candidates some 'real' experience by acting as incompetent beginners during some of their practical teaching sessions.

In the deep pool at Crystal Palace, I acted as a panic stricken beginner while Roger was teaching. I rolled my eyes, pulled off my mask and clawed my way up towards the surface. Roger tried to control me, and I attacked him, but he successfully resisted. On the surface, I clawed on to him, holding him under. He eventually successfully 'landed' me over the side. A watching Crystal Palace pool attendant came up to help. 'Is that bloke going to join your Club?' he asked. 'I wouldn't ever let him in the pool again after that.' I felt I had missed my vocation as an actor.

Early in 1966, I was invited to Broadcasting House to be interviewed on a BBC radio programme called *It Takes all Sorts*. The other 'sort' was the distinguished RN underwater hero, Commander Ian Fraser VC. We chatted happily about our respective diving careers and Ian promised to send his son out to Zembra to learn to dive. I also gave pool lessons to the assistant director and others who were due to leave for the West Indies to make the James Bond film *Thunderball*.

On 6th May I was back on Zembra, diving with Hasen at the Cathédrale. We were surrounded by bottle-nosed dolphins, on our return from the dive. A few days later, my dentist, Anne Putt from London Branch, was climbing into our Caravelle dinghy when she thought she saw the chief instructor surfacing some distance away. Large brown eyes looked lovingly at her, whiskers twitched and he was gone. The biggest seal she'd ever seen. Monk seals (*Monachus monachus*) are now rarely seen, but 2,000 years ago were plentiful throughout the Mediterranean. Aristotle, Plutarch and Homer described them, but they were decimated by the Newfoundlander Abraham Kean in the seventeenth century. He boasted that he had killed a million. One of their last breeding grounds was the wild and isolated Galite Islands off the Tunisian north coast. We christened our seal Boris, and were to see more of him in the future.

Bob Stephens, my doctor friend, and a colleague Keith Mortimer joined us. We collected slipper lobsters and langoustes (*Palinurus*). I dived in the *chambre de mort* of the *madrague* seeing huge tuna and many bonitos. Anne's dentist husband, John flew in with Jean Pears and Angus Loch of London Branch and we saw more dolphins.

At the end of June, Loran arrived to run the bar. We were pleased to see each other again, and it was some time before she mentioned that she had come out with Vernon, my new assistant. I had completely forgotten about him in the excitement, and returning to the port, found him sitting patiently on a bollard on the quay. After settling him into accommodation, I took him for a 'shake down' dive to get used to the equipment and conditions. I always used the oldest valve, that was a bit watery with a mouthpiece which was rotting away. Somehow Vernon got my DV by mistake. He thought it was some sort of test and rolled about, swallowing water until he managed to clear it. He had tremendous drive and was determined to learn all he could while he was with us. His friends in the branch had helpfully told him that he would not survive if he came out with me to Zembra, as I was diving to over 200 feet every day. In fact I was doing less deep diving since moving to Zembra, although I had done an experimental 230 feet the previous week to test out my instruments. He offered to cook English breakfasts for us each morning and we gratefully accepted. He went down to the main kitchens in the Grand Bâtiments for ingredients, but allegedly had to keep his back to the wall to prevent amorous advances from the cooks.

There was a new sailing supremo who was single and did not need the sole use of the large villa on the hill that had four or five bedrooms. I moved in with Loran and Vernon, with the spare rooms ready for other diving instructors to come. Sacapuces, of course, came too.

Divers and trainees were now appearing from Tunis, France, Belgium and England. Vernon and I were soon busy instructing, with Hasen dive guiding. I pinned the dive plan to the mast of the *langoustier* every day and duly signed it 'god'. Harry Gould arrived again with Anthony and enjoyed feeding 'Oscar', our pet grouper. I took Loran on her first dive on the 4th July and she continued to enjoy diving whenever possible in the following months. We were seeing more octopods, and I was bitten by one as I tried to pull it out of its hole. Their beak is like a parrot's, but they did not normally use it offensively.

The CNIT provided us with a young maid and cook called Latifa for our 'mini-palace' on the hill. On an afternoon dive, we caught a large cigalle lobster and stuffed it in the fridge. During the night it must have revived and was walking about in a dish of strawberry jam. When Latifa opened the fridge when she arrived in the morning, it jumped out flapping and scattering gobbets of jam. She fled out of the kitchen and down the path in such panic that we feared we would never see her again.

Our Belgian *moniteur*, Georges, was helping out by the end of July, by which time there was an increasing stream of 'debutants' or beginners. They came in all sizes, shapes, sexes and nationalities, and we encouraged them as much as we could. It was tempting to generalise on national traits.

Many of the greatest divers I know are Italians, but when an Italian beginner has trouble it can be a real *catastrofo*, flailing arms, legs and rolling eyeballs. The French are inclined to blame the equipment, and their reproachful eyes imply a fiendish plot on the part of 'les Anglais'. Englishmen on the whole are merely apologetic. Americans, always the most appreciative, are a very different proposition.

After a long talk in the bar one night, an ageing American journalist decided that he was 'akin to a dolphin' and I promised to take him just below the surface on the diving ladder the next morning. Next day we were surrounded as we made our way down the ladder by his young daughters, who snorkelled effortlessly down to 30 feet. The surface lapped calmly above us as we hung on to the bottom rung of the short ladder at a depth of 3ft 6in. White showed around the eyeballs of my companion and his clenched knuckles also showed white. Feeling disappointed, I motioned for him to climb back up the ladder. 'Anything wrong?', I inquired encouragingly. He looked at me a long time thinking deeply. 'I think', he said, 'what I feel is psychosomatic.'

The medical back-up on the island was organised by a student on vacation. I managed to gouge a deep hole in my leg turning too close to a rock on a dive. I felt nothing underwater but back on the surface the wound gushed blood. It needed stitching and I was prostrate for a couple of days and pumped full of penicillin. Vernon and Georges held the fort.

Mike 'Bus' and John Davis were in operation by late July and Omer shortly afterwards. This brought our instructor team up to full strength. John was a particular asset, as he was also dedicated to overhauling and checking the equipment, spending hours in the workshop and even missing meals to finish jobs.

In the evenings the sailing school *moniteurs* and their pupils sang French sailing and drinking songs. It was suggested that I should organise the diving instructors to provide some entertainment too. We set up something which the French called 'Reg et son Ensemble'. I borrowed a guitar and we sang various spirituals, shanties and less respectable rugger songs. The assembled hordes of French speaking sailors listened intently and applauded enthusiastically. Loran provided the squeak at the end of the chorus of the Roedean song.

When Phil Smith, the underwater photographer from Bournemouth Branch arrived, he was happy to project his strong professional-sounding baritone. He sounded like an opera singer standing in the moonlight above the port, but the words, which I doubt that the majority understood, were:

If forty whores with purple drawers
Were lying on the sand,
Do you suppose the Walrus said,
That I could get a stand.
I doubt it said the carpenter,
But wouldn't it be grand,
While all the time…

The beginners included a Swedish judge, Lars Schultz, and it seemed that most of the sailing staff wanted lessons too. We found ancient stone anchors at the Cathedrale and came across sea hares (*Aplysia*) that squirted beautiful light mauve ink when picked up. Ian Fraser's young son, Martin came as promised, together with his partner's son, Tony Gould. The two boys quickly took to diving and Martin later became a commercial diver in the North Sea, following in his father's footsteps. A new group of Tunisians from the lighthouse department of the Ministry of Public Works came on a course.

Yet another *moniteur* arrived from Belgium. He was called Joseph Dehopre. Lorenzo, who had first introduced me to Tunisia, sailed in on a friend's luxury motor yacht and we dived from it on an uncharted secca off the coast of Zembretta, finding many large groupers and bottom sharks. Mirella, his wife, who was on board was a very striking and characterful woman, whose father, Count Rocco had been a leading member of society in Kenya. Mirella, a brilliant photographer, had photographed the native African tribes and produced a stunning book called *Vanishing Africa*. I was somehow not surprised when, on her very first dive, we were followed for the second time by our old friend Boris, the seal. Seals have a 'harem system' – one male enjoying the attentions of up to seven or eight females. Sooner or later, a younger male arrives and a battle begins for possession. Often the older seal is driven off and may then become a rogue seal. Perhaps Boris had been driven from his home in the Galites.

Ron and Linden Blake, BSAC First Class Divers, who had previously holidayed with Club Med enjoyed their first visit to Zembra. On the 7th of September, I took them and another diver Neil Peterson in at the Grotte des Pigeons. We decided to look at a cave that had previously been found by Mike and Vernon after first diving deeper. Towards the end of the dive, we saw the cave entrance just above us at a depth of 31 metres. It was quite large and there was plenty of light inside, and so I took Ron and Linden in, while Neil stayed at the entrance. They had torches but did not need to use them. After a few moments, I turned to check the way out and saw, to my alarm, that the sand floor that we had been swimming over was in fact silt and was being stirred up by our fins into a fog that obscured the light.

I indicated that we should get out at once and took Linden's arm while Ron acknowledged my signals and started swimming out on my other side. Unbeknown to me, he saw a slipper lobster on the roof of the cave and left us to take it. When he turned round, he saw Linden's fin disappearing but then a huge cloud of silt billowed up and he could see nothing through his mask at all. He tried to find the way out, but it was impossible. He decided to stay where he was, near the roof of the cave and hoped that the sand would clear. He held on to his lobster.

Meantime Linden and I emerged from the cave through clouds of silt and mud. We waited for Ron. After a few seconds, if was clear that he was not following us and I made several attempts to get back in. As the visibility was now nil, I knew that if I went in too far, there would probably be two of us lost, thrashing around, trying to find the entrance again. Posting Linden at the cave entrance, I rushed for the surface to get a spare line from the boat some distance away.

Meanwhile, Ron was breathing slowly and still holding on to his lobster. After several minutes, the air in his single cylinder was becoming hard to breathe as the pressure dropped. He pulled his reserve lever, which gave him a few more minutes at that depth, but still held on to his lobster.

I used all my energy and as soon as I was within range, shouted to the boat that we had an emergency, and to get a line and a spare set of cylinders for me. They handed me a length of rope and another set. I knew that Ron's life was ebbing away in the blackness below and that every second counted. Whether he lived or died depended on me now. I didn't wait to take my nearly used set off, but clutched the new one to my chest together with the line, and spiralled downwards.

Back in the cave, Ron was calmly tapping on his cylinder and being answered by Linden outside, although there was nothing she could do to help him. His air became 'tight' again and he knew that he was now in a desperate position. He finally let go of the lobster. He was wearing one of the first adjustable buoyancy life jackets which had a small air cylinder for inflation, but which could be used to breathe from, in an emergency.

It was not easy changing mouthpieces and letting enough air into the bag for a few breaths. Ron decided to breathe each breath twice, although he knew that this would result in a build-up of carbon dioxide gas from his exhaled air. This gas began to make him weary and he could not think clearly. He slowly moved his mask on to his forehead to allow him to breathe out more easily. He felt a warm sensation, and everything became red and cosy. There was a roaring in his ears and he felt himself slumping over. His last thought was 'God, I could do with a good cup of coffee'.

I made my way through the clouds of silt welling from the cave where eventually

I found Linden, still guarding the entrance, but by now extremely short of air. She helped me tie one end of the line around a rock nearby, and then had to leave.

I started to make my way into the cave. There was nothing to be seen through my mask but impenetrable silt and blackness. The line ran out through my left hand and my right was waving up and down in front of me, searching for Ron. The new cylinder, that I was now breathing from, was floating away, only attached by the tubes and mouthpiece that I was biting into. Suddenly my right hand collided with something firm but soft and I felt an ankle in the blackness.

I began to back out along the line towing Ron, who I could not yet see. My high breathing rate did not help. I had a moment when I had the terrifying feeling that I was going the wrong way along the line and would come to the rope's end in the darkness. At last light began to appear and I saw, to my horror, that Ron's mask was off and he had no sign of life in his eyes. He still had the Fenzy mouthpiece in place though. He was, in fact, semi-conscious.

I tried to inflate his jacket but it was, of course, empty. I dropped both our weightbelts, and swam him upwards, checking that he was exhaling as we neared the surface. The boat was moored out of sight around the corner in the Grotte des Pigeons. I leant over Ron and blew into his mouth. To my delight, he began to groan and gasp for air. There was a horrible rattling in his throat, but to me it was the most beautiful sound I had ever heard …

I removed and dropped our cylinders and began to push him along the surface. He was blind and barely conscious. As he began to breathe, a narrow tunnel of vision appeared. It widened and he saw the sea and sun again. Back on the diving ladder, he finally regained full consciousness. I asked him if he thought he could go down again to decompress. He nodded. We hovered under the boat at 30, 20 and then 10 feet, hoping that no symptoms of decompression sickness would appear. Back in the boat again, we set course for home.

I was still worried about the length of time we had spent below, and we took two cylinders from the compressor house and moved offshore again. Ron was sick from the water he had swallowed, and was also suffering from diarrhoea, but had no more serious symptoms. We decompressed again. By this time, I had a slight ache in my left knee. We returned to the boat and a doctor insisted on giving me an injection against shock. After half an hour or so, the pain had got slightly worse in my knee. Ron's only symptom was a 'catch' in his breathing and some air in his stomach.

After seven hours my pain was lessening. Ron was fine. It had been the worst few hours of my life and the closest I had been to losing a diver. It had taught me several lessons that I would not forget.

I was diving again the next day, and Ron and Linden the day after. We were all thankful to be alive. Ron said that he had been sure that we would get him out. They later joked that they had been trying for a family for some years without success, but after Zembra, they had no problem in producing one. We have been friends ever since.

The season continued, but by now it was mid-September and most of the other instructors had left. Dominique, our bubbly commercial pilot, was back, as was Stan who helped me as a dive guide. Bill and Edna Weale from Shell came in from Tunis and Edna, an ebullient Gibraltarian and translator, had us in fits of laughter with her escapades. While learning, she managed to do a backward roll entry from a Caravelle dinghy with her fins securely trapped under a stowed oar. She made 'I am not happy' signals while hanging upside down in the water at a depth of two feet.

In early October I was back diving on Giglio with John Bowman. Costantino, I discovered, was now married to Nunziatina, the butcher's elegant sister. He and his cousin Pepe were still driving about on their ancient vespas with carts fixed behind. They were now investing in hydrofoils to run a service for the families of those held on the prison island of Gorgona to the north.

News of our ordeal in the cave had spread, and when I arrived back in London, the editor of *Triton* magazine was on the line asking for an article. I was not enthusiastic, but he said that if I didn't do it, it might be reported 'in a different way'. I decided that the article should be jointly written by Ron and myself, explaining what had been happening to each of us during the incident. It appeared, and my friend Tony Tillbrook, who had the concession for Fenzys, told me that he sold more life jackets as a result than he had with all the advertising he had done. We let them reprint a version for the *World Underwater Book* and then someone wrote the story up for *Reader's Digest* and it appeared in all their foreign editions.

A few weeks later, I told someone about our other cave with the Martinis. He said that I should contact the Martini company and tell them, in case they wanted to use the idea for their advertising campaigns. They were charm itself.

'I don't think we'll use it, but does your club hold a reunion?'

'Er, Yes, er, I think so'

'Well we'll invite you and your students to hold it on the Martini Terrace'.

On 16th December, several hundred 'members' of the Neptune Watersports Club were overlooking London from the 16th floor of New Zealand House and happily sipping drinks provided by Martini Rossi Ltd. Life seemed good.

CHAPTER SEVEN

A Valorous Hound & a
Girl with Hollow Legs

ALTHOUGH I DIDN'T KNOW IT AT THE TIME, 1967 would be my last season on Zembra. The CNIT had not been as successful as expected, and the Tunisian Bank had decided to do a deal with a large French tourist outfit called Voir et Connaître. They would take over the supervision of all sports on the island.

Back in London, I was trying out different kinds of diving. In March, I did my first helmet dive on a London branch visit to Siebe Gorman's under the supervision of a character called 'Rolly' Racketts, and then dived in Horsey Lake using oxygen sets, led by Lt Don McLauchlin RN.

In March too, I helped examine another lot of potential national instructors, including Vernon, who passed. He distinguished himself by dropping his glasses into Lake Windermere while watching a diver and having to drive back to London in his optical diving mask. He overcame all difficulties and became one of my closest friends.

I was back in Zembra by mid-May and it was already hot in the spring sunshine. On the foreshore, the 'farmer' had tethered a beautiful, but painfully skinny, Arab horse. It was tied to a post by its leg. The rough cord had caused sores to form and it was surrounded by flies and crawling with insects. I felt sorry for it. Although my sole experience of riding consisted of a childhood trip on a led donkey at Clovelly, I asked if I could try. I walked it down to the sea and they cheerfully hoisted me on to its back. There was no saddle and the bridle was a piece of string. I imagined that the horse looked grateful. 'I'll take it for a paddle', I thought.

The horse walked happily into the cool sea, but after a minute or so, I was almost swept off its back as it started to swim. I clung on in alarm. Luckily it decided to return after a short sortie in the direction of the mainland. I persuaded the farmer to find another means of tethering it.

I was delighted to find Oscar, our grouper at Anchor Bay, still in residence with what looked like a wife and child plus a lodger in the shape of an octopus, and, of course, our faithful Sacapuces. Dolphins now seemed to pass our village every day at mid-day.

I was soon teaching French and Tunisian beginners again. Together with John Davis we taught a number of the American Embassy staff and the Chief of the

Peace Corps, Fran Macey and his family. Ron and Linden, Bill and Edna and Angus all arrived back.

On the 6th July, Yves Baix, the editor of the French diving magazine *Plongée*, plus some of his staff, started diving with us. Yves wrote an article that described us as 'the only diving school run by a dog'. His theory was that when Sacapuces jumped over to chase rabbits, we anchored and dived – a nice idea, if not strictly accurate.

Sacapuces's exploits were amazing. One day I had a boat full of English divers and was guiding it through large rolling waves along the coast bound for the Bay of Caves that would be sheltered. Sacapuces saw what she thought was a rabbit and leaped fearlessly into the waves. Her small head could be seen bravely paddling over the crests. I pretended not to notice and also ignored the diver's entreaties to stop. There was no obvious place where she could land – only steep cliffs falling straight into the sea with waves beating up them. We turned the corner, moored up in the bay. Sure enough, after our dive, Sacapuces swam up and waited to be lifted up the dive ladder.

The only thing she could not cope with was the rat poison that the farmer spread around. Occasionally, tempted to eat it, she became very ill. I despaired at one point as she overheated, shook and was obviously blind. The farmer callously suggested throwing her into the sea. As a last resort, I carried her into the shallows to cool her down. She swam around pathetically, colliding with moored boats. It must have worked, as she survived.

I was now settled in the 'deputy chief's' bungalow below our mini-palace. I used to walk out in the early morning with Sacapuces to search for wild turkey eggs in the bushes that Vernon could use for breakfast. On one beautiful calm morning, I was looking out over a flat Mediterranean when I noticed a disturbance on the surface. A pair of field glasses revealed a swordfish jumping vertically out of the water with the sun sparkling on its sides. The moment has stayed with me ever since.

Bill Smith was back instructing and was soon joined by Joseph, Georges and a new French *moniteur national*, Jean Graux. I am sure that Bill was the only person to give up a highly lucrative career in civil aviation to become an itinerant diving instructor. He had a Welsh background and a lot of Celtic mysticism in his soul. He later went on to instruct with Club Med and then in his own schools in even more exotic parts of the world   When the CNIT asked if we would run the langoustiers ourselves to save on expenses, Bill was one of the few instructors who agreed to do so. We learnt a lot about boat handling.

Early in August, Taieb Slim arrived. He was a distinguished and important Tunisian, about 60 years old. He was the brother of the Secretary of State, Mongi Slim who was President Bourghiba's right-hand man. Taieb had also been Tunisian ambassador to the Court of St James and to the United Nations. He had come to the island to sail, but then asked me if I could just take him down once to see what it was like. He warned me that he could hardly swim.

We chose a calm day at Anchor Bay where we regularly took our beginners. I anchored and took him down hand-over-hand to the bottom at 20 feet or so. He watched with wide eyes as I broke open a sea urchin, put it gently in his hand, and the small wrasse clustered around him to feed. When I brought him up, he declared that this had been the most exciting moment of his whole eventful life. He was ecstatic and invited us to be his guests at his villa at Sidi Bou Said near Tunis. This was an important contact and resulted in my being able to declare Zembretta a fish sanctuary. Mohammed El Ghoul, the fisheries minister, made it a part of Tunisian law in no time at all, and unfortunate fishermen were suffering dire penalties for trawling there.

One day on Zembretta, after diving, we wandered over the island and passed a square hole in the rocks near the summit which we had noticed before, and which was filled with the bodies of sea birds. This time there was a huge and beautiful live bird walking about over the bodies of its predecessors. There was obviously not enough room for it to spread its wings to rise out of the hole. We jumped down the six feet or so and grabbed it, returning it to the skies. When we looked round, beneath the overhang inside, we saw ancient mosaic tiles around the walls. Perhaps it was a Roman or Carthaginian cistern or well. This turned out to be the *Cimitière des Oiseaux* that we had heard about from Hasan.

Brian May and Elise came in from London. They were now married and soon to be proud owners of a schooner called *Sylvia*. Elise had completed her pool training with London branch and I gave her her first open water lesson at the Cathédrale on the 9th August. We became extremely busy, all the instructors taking down parties of up to seven divers at a time.

On the 15th I took a young French blonde, Michelle Lambert, who had been diving with us since late July, to the Cathédrale. We were happily exploring under a large rock overhang at 130 feet when she made the signal that she needed more air and could not operate her reserve. This was, of course, in the days before 'octopus rigs' were thought of. Almost at once, she desperately signalled that she had no air at all. I gave her my mouthpiece and prepared to share air. She soon made it clear that she was not prepared to give any air back to me! I held my breath and we began to swim out from under the overhang. She clung on to my mouthpiece like grim death. I swam up with her, letting my air out in a slow stream of bubbles as we rose. When we arrived at 20 feet, she let me have two quick breaths. We hit the surface in a fairly heavy sea and she became hysterical, clinging on to me. There was no hold at the cliff face, so I got her cylinders off and swam her back to the boat round the corner. I was exhausted and was amazed at how strong a slim, slight girl could be *in extremis*. I had a pain in my left knee for some hours, but neither of us suffered any long-term damage and she was diving again in a few days.

Late in August, a rather bizarre group from London called The Atlantis Dive Club of Wandsworth High Street appeared. They said they had considerable experience, but their log books were homemade using crayons. They did contain some pronouncements from their 'Club Medical Officer', one of which was that to prevent bends, you should inject yourself with nicotinic acid. I persuaded them not to do this. We guided them carefully. After their return to the High Street, they sent me an formal letter, thanking me 'for my cooperation during their underwater researches on Zembra.'

The Canadian Ambassador, Alfred Pick came to learn with his family, and they also enjoyed fish feeding. I received a deputation from the more status conscious *moniteurs*, warning me that they were not prepared to dive with Edna any more.

'Why ever not?', I asked. 'Because she pulls our hair underwater'. It seemed the excitable Edna found this the quickest way to attract attention if she wanted to show them something. I assured them that I would dive with her. After all, the chance of her finding my follicles was fairly slight ...

One morning, the island was struck by an incredibly violent storm from Africa. Caravelle dinghies pulled up on the beach were lifted into the air and smashed down again. Tables from the Grand Bâtiments sailed out into the sea. People clung on to pillars to prevent being blown after them. After half an hour, it was over. The sea was calm again and we all helped to pick up the pieces. I was worried about Bill who, before the storm, had taken the *langoustier* out to Anchor Bay with a group. I motored round to look for him.

As he would have to leave the boat unattended while diving, he had luckily made sure it was secure with several anchors and lines to shore. His dive had gone well. As they returned from depth though, they found clouds of brown material spreading down through the water and were puzzled. They used up their air and surfaced to find everything calm as they had left it. The brown material had been earth washed in by the brief storm. They could hardly believe the damage back at the village.

In September Wendy Lloyd-Kirk, a lively young member of London branch arrived with a friend Jean Cracknell. Jean, who I christened 'Crackers', was even livelier. She was booked for a sailing course, but we soon persuaded her to change this to diving instead. Her performance of the Tahitian *tamouré* in the evenings mesmerised us all and I swore she must have had a Polynesian grandmother to move like that ... . Boris inevitably made another appearance. This time the two 'mermaids' persuaded him to come even closer. I estimated his length at nine feet, with whitish flanks, speckled with dark spots and a huge tattered tail. We chased him around for about 15 minutes and, when we left, he then followed our boat. Bill and I went in again and he got close enough to peer head-to-head into his face. The girls snorkelled above, unafraid. Afterwards I wondered what I would have done if Boris had become aggressive or amorous.

At the Cathédrale, there were vertical cliffs and at one point, a short horizontal tunnel at 70 feet. As I had been practising my snorkelling, I could not resist waiting until Bill's group of beginners were approaching along the cliff at 40 feet. I snorkelled down, passed them signalling 'OK', and disappeared into the tunnel below. They were suitably impressed. We toyed with the idea of getting one of the girls to dress up in a mermaid's tail and to be combing her hair on the rocks inside the 'Martini cave'. I wondered if this might produce more expressive results than London branch's usual, monosyllabic comments on the performance of their equipment at the end of each dive.

Sacapuces's most famous exploit came during one of our night dives. Her behaviour was no different at night and she would disappear into the darkness with the cries of worried holiday-makers echoing after her. Some ten minutes later we would arrive, moor the boat and dive. Half an hour later someone would notice that she was trying to climb the diving ladder. This time she swam back with a rabbit in her mouth. If any dog deserved an aqualung, this was the one.

As we were constantly putting our beginners through a series of training tests, we devised some more light-hearted competitive ones for the instructor team. The students could bet on the results. One test was an underwater striptease in which we took off cylinders, valves, weight belts, fins, mask and tubes at 30 feet and then free ascented back to the surface, before returning breath-holding, to put it all on again. A couple of us went further and sent our wet suit jackets and swimming drawers floating up as well.

Another hairier test was on our night dives. We anchored amid urchin-covered rocks at 30 feet. When the time came to leave, the instructor, without any equipment at all, not even a mask, had to pull his way down the anchor line in the blackness, dislodge the anchor and resurface. We were, of course, eating oysters underwater and discussed whether to bite a leg off a live octopus too, but decided it was too barbaric for a test.

Loran, now my wife, was diving with us again at the end of September and our tiny daughter was surviving happily amid the primitive environs of Zembra. Jean-Paul Carrier, the boss of Voir et Connaître had visited. He was friendly, but said nothing of his plans for the following season. We called him 'big wheel', and I was to hear from him again in the future.

We left Zembra for the last time at the beginning of October and I felt sad as I saw Sacapuces sadly watching our departure from the shore. I wondered how long she would survive without us.

A few days after arriving back, it was time for the next NUIA exam. We were examining the BSAC London coach, Alex Double (who would become a future partner), Keith Nicholson (DO of London branch), and my right-hand man, Bill, just back from Zembra. They all passed with flying colours.

At the end of October Bill, Stan and I had the opportunity to make a TV commercial for a washing powder. We spent all night in Waltham Forest Baths with underwater scooters, dressed in black or white wet suits, acting as 'dirt fighters'. It was hilarious, if tiring. In the morning, Bill and I went to watch the rushes. The ancient producer, a rose in his button hole, pronounced them 'Very posh, very posh indeed'. Perhaps, mercifully, the ad was never shown.

I dived with London branch on the wrecks of HMS *Hood* and the *Himalaya* in Portland Harbour with Bill and Keith. Bill had now been accepted as a *moniteur* with Club Med and would be in Cadaques in Spain the following summer.

In June 1968, we were invited to do a survey of the diving potential off Bunbeg in Donegal, where Anthony Marreco, the treasurer of Amnesty International had bought some old houses which he was considering turning into a watersports hotel called The Fisherman. The countryside was dramatic with rugged mountains and a coastline of sandy beaches, rocky outcrops and islands. He put us up in gypsy caravans on his land. A number of ex-Giglio divers took part including Bill Butland, Jill Stokoe, Geoff and Jill Harwood plus Loran with Nicola, who was already a year old. We found the sea life interesting with many lobsters and crawfish.

The Sports Council were now encouraging the BSAC to appoint a full-time Director to oversee its potential expansion and to liaise with government and military agencies and formulate new policies. It sounded exciting and a new kind of challenge. I was approached by the Club Vice-President, Colin MacLeod and Harry Gould, now Chairman, who felt I should apply. In the Autumn, an impressive selection board was set up with representative from the Club, the Sports Council and Ministry, who would be paying most of the salary. I felt anything but sure of the result, as I knew that several distinguished Royal Navy officers who had been involved with the Club were also candidates. To my delight, I was appointed. I would start in January 1969.

It was suggested that I should now sit for the First Class Diver exam, the only one I hadn't passed. The theory papers posed no problem, but in those days, the practical consisted of a one-day project overseen by an existing first class diver. I decided to organise both London and Croydon branches on a survey of sea urchins on the Lulworth Banks. My examiner was Peter Cornish, the enthusiastic DO of Hampstead branch. All went according to plan on the day and I asked Peter if he was satisfied. He was. I then suggested that I hand over to Keith Nicholson, who had put a lot of work into calculating the position of a wreck called the *Alex Van*

Opstel. I invited Peter to come with us on the Sunday to dive on the site.

Keith was something of a perfectionist, especially with his own projects. He and Jeannie or 'Crackers' were now fairly inseparable. I had suggested that she joined London branch on her return from Zembra, although I hadn't suggested that she dated the DO We spent all day bobbing about in a number of inflatables some five miles out, while Keith fiddled with his sextant. Finally at 4 p.m., he announced 'This is it, it's underneath us now'. At that moment the Croydon boat came up and cheerfully reported that they couldn't stay any longer. Keith threw a wobbly, seized the tiller and drove us landwards again. Half way back, we noticed that one of our inflatables, containing Peter, was still over the wreck. The Croydon branch boat overtook us. 'Why are they still out there?', we asked. 'Waiting for your orders', came the reply. We hadn't enough fuel to get out there again.When they returned, Peter reported that I had failed my exam, as I should never have let this situation arise.

Later the national diving officer, Derek Cockbill, who was not too happy with this decision, asked if I would be prepared to take the 'practical' again. I swallowed my pride, and said 'Yes'. Innumerable buoyant lifts in Stoney Cove in freezing conditions followed, supervised by the most dogged of Midland coaches. I passed.

I had agreed to go on a Club Med holiday with Keith and 'Crackers' to the island of Caprera between Corsica and Sardinia. Loran was unable to join us but they had invited a friend of theirs called Margaret Kuyper from Rhodesia.

Keith had decided to drive his powerful Ford all the way, although we could all drive. The Alps to him were a detail. He made his route plan via Switzerland and North Italy and we booked a ferry from Marseilles. 'Crackers' was detailed to map read. I relaxed in the back with Margaret. We roared through France. 'Crackers' only made one mistake in her map reading, which entailed our going for a mile in the wrong direction.

Keith was furious and I was unwillingly moved into the front seat and presented with the map. His Ford had never experienced anything like climbing the Alps and screaming down the other side. As we came into northern Italy, his brakes collapsed and we came to a clanging halt at the edge of an Italian lake. There was a small restaurant. 'Take the girls for something to eat', ordered Keith, 'I'll get this fixed at the local garage'. We sat on the terrace on a warm evening with cool wine and pasta. The moon shone over the lake. Every so often, Keith would rush by swearing about the lack of decent mechanics. We waved sympathetically, but our eyes were glazing over. We eventually missed the ferry from Marseilles, but caught one the next day.

Club Med included all watersports free in their holiday costs, but had a nasty habit of upping the medical requirements if they had too many applying to dive. Their medical check was called the 'Ruffier test' and involved doing 36 knee bends,

alternating with blood pressure checks. Miss Kuyper, who besides having a magnificent figure, was extremely fit, passed effortlessly. So did 'Crackers'. My results were
a bit marginal. I heard them discussing them from the other side of the curtain.
Luckily I'd reported my 2,000 dives under 'previous experience'. They decided that
they had to accept me. Keith failed.

However much noise he made, didn't alter their decision. We decided we would
wait for him to pass. Meantime, after practising hundreds of knee bends, he decided, 'We're going to get fit'. He drove us out into the *maquis*. Half an hour or so later
he parked the car by the sea, and led us on a circular hike. We were slowly garrotted
by the gorse-like *maquis* bushes. Bare legs began to bleed. Finally, in desperation,
we decided to swim back to the car although this would take a lot longer.

Margaret swam fast and was soon ahead of us and out of sight. The three of us
staggered ashore at the car but there was no sign of her. By this time it was getting
towards dusk. We guessed that she must have taken the decision to swim all the
way back to the village. The distance on the map was huge. We drove back and after
checking that she had not arrived, warned the *Chef du Village* that one of our party
was missing. It got dark. Just as they were about to alert the rescue helicopter, she
swam in having covered a number of miles in the dark.

Keith passed the 'Ruffier test,' and we enjoyed the diving, collecting oysters
and finding Roman anchors. One of the *moniteurs* was an easy-going Englishman
called Mike Coltman who was destined to become the chief of all Club Med diving.
He was then working at Caprera under the current overall chief, Michel Lendrin.
Lendrin (nicknamed 'Banane') was mad about collecting red coral and led us down
to 50 metres. I watched dive times closely and brought the group back before we
ran into decompression time. On one dive he spent 30 minutes at 50 metres and
decompressed for an hour. I interviewed him for *Sub Aqua Magazine* discovering
that he had been in charge of the five Club Med diving schools for four years, had
done less diving than I had, and that he was called 'Banane' because he had nearly
died from eating them when he was three.

We only saw Maggie Kuyper on dives as she was being pursued by a number of
French instructors. When 'Crackers' performed her *tamouré* on the beach one night,
we had to rescue her from an ardent *moniteur* who swept her off into the shallows.

We arrived back in time for me to organise the Sixth National Instructor exam.
This time we had a lively bunch of candidates including the examiner on my First
Class, Peter Cornish, Mike Coltman from Club Med and John Bevan, a young
physiologist from Southsea branch.

On the last weekend, I supervised the 10-metre snorkel dive off Babbacombe
beach. The water was cold. I sat on the bottom breathing with my aqualung and
watching purple faces appear and disappear above me. They were supposed to sign

their names on my slate. Some managed it. Most signatures were unreadable. Then John Bevan came down. He had spearfishing experience. He signed calmly, and printed his name underneath. Then his address. He thought a moment. Then came his girl friend's name. Then … I signalled for him to go up.

On the second weekend at Stoney Cove, we had decided to spring something new on the candidates. I offered to act again. I quietly paddled out in an inflatable to the other side of the cove. The other examiners were discussing results with the candidates. At a signal, I fell noisily overboard, shouting for help. The candidates' equipment was elsewhere, but the examiners were looking at them expectantly. They plunged in and swam over-arm all the way across to me. Strong arms seized me and threw me into the inflatable. I acted drowned. 'Cut his wet suit off', I heard a voice order. I came back to life. 'The first one who touches my suit fails'. Another voice shouted, 'He's hysterical, hit him'. A large fist waved. I didn't try that game again.

As Director of BSAC, I was given a tiny office on the floor occupied by the South East Sports Council at 160 Great Portland Street in London. The next thing was for me to appoint a secretary. This would take a little time, so meantime I made do with a temp who wore a mini-skirt and see-through blouse. She was quite efficient, but after a week or so, asked if I knew whether Interpol could extradite her to Cyprus where she and her boy friend were wanted for armed robbery. I checked for her, and kept a tight hold of my small petty cash box until it was time to interview candidates.

Harriette Rancom was to be my longest serving secretary. She had a sweet and long suffering nature that hid a wild and adventurous streak. She also had a splendid sense of humour and 'hollow legs' when it came to alcohol consumption. I am not sure which of her qualities was the most valuable. I discovered later that her previous boss had been an insufferably meticulous man, constantly rejecting her efforts for the slightest of reasons. One day, she got the biggest and broadest roll of sticky tape she could find, stuck one end on his back as he sat at his desk, and walked around him until he was completely trussed up. She then walked out.

We got on very well, although we both had to squeeze into one small office, most of which was occupied by my oversize desk. Those were the days when we would dictate into hand-held tapes, and secretaries would then play them back through earphones while they typed.

Lord Wakefield, a tall, commanding figure, was then the President of the Club. He had captained England at rugby and was a pioneer flier. He came to see me one day when he was passing, and I sat him in front of my desk while Harriette was in 'another world', listening to my dictation, and typing. We talked about the future of the Club.

At one point on her tape, I had obviously changed my mind again. In frustration she shouted 'Shit!', threw down her earphones, pulled open a drawer in her desk, took out a bottle of gin, had a quick swig, put it back, replaced her earphones and carried on typing without another word. Lord Wakefield was impressed 'Who is that amazin' girl?' he asked.

Working as Director of the Club was, of course, a serious business. I was directly responsible to the Chairman who at that time was a very civilized architect called Alex Flinder. I felt that it was important that I visit each of our ten newly appointed part-time regional coaches to find out what problems they had, and to put them in contact with the regional representatives of the Sports Council who could help them in many ways. I also wanted to dive with them when possible. Alex initially believed that I shouldn't leave my desk, but be like 'a sponge, absorbing all the news and problems that came through from branches.' I got my way and found that making direct contacts throughout the country was vital.

In the North East, they were a dour lot, suspicious of Londoners like me. A sort of initiation ceremony was to drink eight pints of Newcastle Brown ale with them. I had no problem with this and was then accepted.

During my Scottish visit, I met Thurso branch and dived with their chairman and diving officer, Bill Stewart and George Gibson off their village on the northern tip of Scotland. They had just rescued the entire crew of a Belgian trawler that had foundered on the rocks off the harbour in a 70 mile-per-hour gale at midnight on a January night. This had involved not only getting a line from shore to ship, but getting the crew down it and recovering one who had let go and been carried out to sea. I persuaded them, against their will, to come down to tell their story to the Diving Officers' Conference. They became the first winners of the BSAC Alan Broadhurst Medal for bravery in saving life.

I was still somewhat nervous of public speaking, but was soon to be in at the deep end. One of the largest dinners of the year followed the DO's Conference. My first, just after my appointment, would not entail a speech from me. The menus had already been printed: 'Surgeon Rear-Admiral Stanley Miles, CB MD MSc DTM&H QHP' would propose the health of the Club with a response from the National Diving Officer, Leo Zanelli. Stanley, who I knew as a member of the advisory board of NUIA, was a scintillating and thoroughly obscene speaker, greatly loved by divers everywhere. I relaxed and looked forward to hearing his latest tales.

Between the fish and the meat courses, a note was passed down to me from the Chairman. 'Reg', it read, 'Leo doesn't feel up to it. Can you respond to Stanley Miles?' This was a challenge and a half. I looked towards Leo who was further up the top table. He looked normal enough to me, but I could hardly refuse.

I racked my brains and remembered something that Stanley had once told me. He recited his diving version of 'Eskimo Nell' and sat down amid gales of laughter and wild applause. I rose, thanking Stanley, and referred to his orders and awards. 'What does QHP stand for?' I asked. No one knew. 'Queens Honorary Physician', I told them. 'What's that for?' 'Well, when the Queen gets the bends, Stanley treats her'. I was on my way.

CHAPTER EIGHT

To the Mysterious East &
a Sunken Submarine

L ONDON WEEKEND TELEVISION had decided to make a series of programmes on Scuba diving. They were produced and directed by Ed Goldwyn, a dedicated film-maker, who learnt to dive as part of his preparations and later became a good friend.

Dick Harris and I were chosen as the instructors, and we demonstrated different teaching techniques in the deep pool at Crystal Palace using Gilly Lythgoe and Fred Lock from London branch and Mike Maloney from Holborn. We also raced each other in a 'ditch and retrieve' race from the bottom. Each programme, besides our teaching sequence, showed a different aspect of diving, such as photography and archaeology. The programme on cave diving featured Ron Blake talking about our incident in the cave at Zembra.

In April '69 I went down to Plymouth to take part in the first SNAP Course (School of Nautical Archaeology Plymouth) run by Alan Bax, who with Jim Gill, was considering leasing Fort Bovisand nearby and opening it as a dive training centre. I walked around the Fort with him amid piles of rubble. It would be a huge job. One of the other students on the course was Martin Deane who would become Britain's first professional underwater archaeologist.

In May I got an invitation to join a party to dive from a new launch belonging to Tony Titterington in Jersey. We drift dived in a strong current at the Minquiers Reef and came upon a wreck, believed to be the *Silvania* which had been sunk in 1936. We could only cling on to it for a few seconds before being swept on by the tide.

Derek Cockbill, the previous NDO, now Vice-Chairman, had pioneered a scheme to provide the club with a national boat that could accommodate divers and move around the coast, running branch holidays and expeditions. As a trial run, he hired *The Provident*, one of the last Brixham trawlers, which belonged to the well-established Island Cruising Club at Salcombe. He could not get enough bookings for it until he opened it to branches as well. Keith hired it for a week in June '69 for a London branch holiday.

We would have to follow the Cruising Club's rules, as far as the ship was concerned, and help with the sailing. 'Provi' was a beautiful old boat with huge sails and a wheel that stood proud on the aft deck.

We arrived and Keith briefed the skipper. 'We want to be at Guernsey for the first dives, then on to Jersey and Alderney'. He pointed to sites on the chart. The skipper, nodded wisely, but said nothing. We were shown to our bunks. Mine was a top one, above Fred Lock, and I was provided with a small piece of cellophane to cover the blanket in case water came through the deck above. We were assigned watches. During the night watches, we would steer the ship, polish the bell and wash down the decks under the supervision of the Skipper or Mate.

We sailed out into a wildly rolling sea and several members turned green and disappeared from view fairly permanently. It was exhilarating steering her across the channel and shining torches on the sails as tankers came roaring over the horizon. I crawled into my bunk in the early hours, but was awoken by water dropping on to my face and blankets as they washed the deck above.

We arrived at Roscoff in Brittany after a stormy 24-hour passage and didn't leave again until it was time to return. Keith was not pleased, but could do nothing to change the situation in view of the weather. We dived in the kelp forest and collected scallops that were fried in butter as a delicious hors d'oeuvres. I was not too popular when I went ashore with the skipper, mate and cook to enjoy drinks and a meal at a restaurant they knew.

In August, Cy Corder, a public relations man, and member of the branch, invited me to accompany him to Norway where a newly-built coastal hotel wanted a report on the diving potential. The hotel was built on the side of a beautiful little fiord called Godoysund (God's island sound) just south of Bergen.

Scientists from the Bergen Marine Biological Station dived with us amid the most gigantic jellyfish I had ever seen and we were passed in the distance by whales and porpoises. I walked into the fiord one day from the shore. My first step brought the water level to my knees. The second and I was up to my neck. The third and I was in 3,000 feet of water. We took care to adjust our buoyancy before leaving the surface.

One of the students who dived with us told us about the Vevatn (Holy) Lake nearby where the Vikings of 500 BC were said to have made sacrifices and which had never been dived. We were soon on our way up to it. Huge rocks towered above us and an inscription recorded where a British geologist had been killed by falling rock in 1908.

The estimated depth was 51 metres. We stepped off the side in excitement and started to sink. At 50 feet, the water temperature suddenly dropped to 10°C. We had no gloves. At 75 feet it got dark. We had no torches. We decided to call it a day. Rising from the cold layer, I felt as though my hands were being immersed in increasingly hot water.

Returned to England, I dived with our Eastern Region coach, Mick Glover, an

RAF technician, in Lattersey Hill Clay Pit near Peterborough. We stalked a number of small pike until I looked over my shoulder and saw a huge pike apparently stalking me.

Cy had another invitation up his sleeve. Murison Small, the travel people, ran an 80-foot cruise boat through the Peloponnese islands in southern Greece and had invited a group of us to join them when they arrived on the island of Hydra. Roger Hale and Leo Zanelli also agreed to come.

We took all our own diving gear, but when we arrived on Hydra, we heard that the boat was blocked by weather in Athens. Leo and Cy went snorkelling in the harbour as our compressor, which had arrived a day late, was still being prepared. Leo happily collected a couple of discarded plates off the bottom. He returned to a tavern to sample the ouzo.

A régime known as 'the Colonels' were then in charge in Greece and it was something of a police state. While Leo enjoyed his drink, we were visited by an inspector with cold blue eyes, who had been told that we had been recovering 'antiquities' from the seabed. We rushed to show him the plates that Leo had left in his sink and he saw the name of the local hotel engraved on them. We were given a clean bill of health again.

The next day, cylinders fully charged, we decided to have a look at nearby Miramare Bay. It was three miles east of our port, and too far to carry our twin-sets and gear, so Cy hired some mules and donkeys. We strapped the cylinders onto their backs, eyed suspiciously by the owner, and set off.

It wasn't long before we came across the traditional problem with mules. They decided that they had gone far enough. We used all the usual methods of encouragement without success. Then someone had a brainwave. The pillar valves were hovering over the rumps of the unwilling animals. We let them have a quick burst of compressed air. Their ears went back and they moved – so fast we had to restrain them and they kept going from then on.

We dived happily down to 150 feet finding many sponges, and I made the mistake of picking up bristle worms, that I had never seen before, and was promptly stung by them.

We spent the evenings at Lulu's' the local hot spot, and met a young Greek called Pantalis who was, among other things, the local skin diver. During my absence, the others challenged the friendly but boastful Pantalis to a deep snorkel contest against me. He joined us the next day after we had dived from the small island of Petasi.

I unwillingly agreed to the challenge and we were lined up together on the surface with the others watching. We both took a deep breath. At 40 feet, Pantelis turned back up and arrived on the surface, stuck his head under again in time to see me arrive at 80 feet. Although he lost, he proved a good loser and the ouzo flowed in celebration after he had told the locals the story.

It was now the conference season back in UK and I was speaking regularly. On New Year's Eve I addressed my biggest audience, 3,000 students in Central Hall, Westminster. I was also writing articles for *Triton* to encourage branches to apply for government grants for equipment and to help them gain pool space and the use of open water sites. My title was changed to Director General which I thought was a bit over the top. One Council member objected that I could not be a DG because I had no other directors to 'general'. They remedied this by changing the title of the national coach to Director of Coaching.

By March 1970 I could report that the Club's growth rate had risen from 12% to 22% per annum, and we were forming new branches all over the world. I had visited Loughton independent sub-aqua club and, with the help of their Chairman, Bob Bulgin, persuaded them to become a branch. Bob became a good friend. At the Diving Officers' Conference I gave a paper with ideas for the next ten years' development. I forecast that branches would need a qualified instructor and that National Instructors would become coaches and run commercial diving schools. My ideas were considered so radical that my paper was initially censored by the NDO before it was published. The club was regularly consulted by the government, Sports Council, CCPR and the, newly formed, Society for Underwater Technology who invited me to talk at their first conference on the work of the BSAC.

At our 1970 AGM, the Minister for Sport, Dennis Howell, promised further financial support. We were encouraging Dave Bellamy to organise pollution investigation projects which involved hundreds of BSAC members around the country. Keith Nicholson became part-time National Coach.

I found another useful attribute – a strong stomach – was valuable when we visited the Northern Federation's Annual 'Windive' event. After the formal dinner, they sat the visiting guests, the club officers and myself, down to have a 'black pudding race' which I won by a short head from Derek Cockbill.

Harriette continued to entertain me at HQ. One day she arrived, announcing that she had booked up to do a parachute jump.

'An excellent idea for a young girl like you', I said.

'I booked you in too'.

I gasped, remembering my fear of heights.

'I don't know whether I want to do parachute jumping', I ventured.

'Are you scared?' she asked.

'No, but'.

'You're scared', she decided.

'I'm going to tell everyone that Reg Vallintine is scared of parachute jumping'.

'Hang on', I countered, 'It's equivalent to jumping off a ten foot wall, and I'm likely to break something at my age'.

'Five foot wall', she corrected me.

'Ten feet'.

I went next door where the General Secretary of the Amateur Rowing Association happened to be an ex-parachutist. 'Five feet', he confirmed, 'and you shouldn't break anything if you're moderately fit'. I capitulated and we measured up the bookcase on our back wall. It was just about five feet high. I climbed on top of it to try.

'Jump', she shouted, as the door opened and Lord Wakefield entered on one of his unannounced visits. I landed with a crash at his feet.

'Don't do it, dear boy', he advised kindly, 'Nothing's that serious'. Luckily for me the parachute jump was cancelled due to weather.

In May, I was on the way to Eddystone again with the branch. On the way, excitement broke loose on board as a huge fin broke the surface. Then two black points on either side of it, as the nose and tail of a 20-foot shark appeared. Our boat crept closer and we could see the shape of a basking shark just below the surface. As we left, I told the others, 'They're harmless, we should have got over the side and had a proper look'.

The next day, diving on the wreck of the *Newholme* off Start Point, two sets of fins broke the surface.

'Remember what you said yesterday?' chorused my fellow members.

Grabbing my fins and mask, I jumped over, shouting 'Follow me!'

I could see the shark's fins above the surface ahead of me as I swam out towards them. All was mysterious dark green beneath and ahead. I looked round to check the boat position. No one seemed to be following. It looked as though they were taking bets on what might happen next. Suddenly a shark with mouth wide open was charging towards me. I felt distinctly uncomfortable, although I told myself that their diet was planktonic.

I moved out of the way and the largest body I had ever seen drifted passed me. There were scattered markings on its back and lampreys clung to it flanks and streamed from its tail. Ian Graham finally joined me and we swam from one shark to the other. The second shark stopped in front of me, as though thinking. It shallow dived just below me and I brushed its back with my fins as it glided past.

It occurred to me that, with their eyes way out on the sides of their massive heads, they couldn't see ahead and if I got entangled in the open mouth what would they do? I imagined they might shut their mouth and dive. Was there a signal for 'I am in the mouth of a basking shark, OK, but cannot clear my ears'. The situation did not arise.

The Club was now organising marine biology courses for divers and I booked

myself on one of the first held at the Dale Fort Field Centre on an isolated prom-
ontory in Pembrokeshire. The young engineer who had built the fort in 1856 had
written 'I pity the officers and men who will have to live here, for this is a desolate
place'. He went on to know triumph and tragedy as Gordon of Khartoum.

The Fort was now a bit more cheerful with George Skuse, the regional coach
organising, under the course director, Dr Robin Crump, an engaging biologist who
had recently returned from working in New Zealand and on the Great Barrier Reef.
Each morning we had a lecture, followed by a dive to collect specimens We then
identified and observed them at length in the tanks in the laboratory.

I dived with an eccentric lady called Zoë Gardner, who had arrived by motor-
bike from Zambia with her air cylinders strapped on to the side. We explored and
picnicked on Skomer island and had a wonderfully unscientific scallop feast on the
last evening cooked by the 'Prof'

Soon after, I passed the first of many visits to Lundy Island in the Bristol Channel, where Don Shiers had set up a small dive holiday operation. Lundy was then
privately owned, and had an interesting history, and the ruins of a pirate castle. It
boasted a pub with no closing time. We stayed in an old lighthouse above the cliffs,
and daily diving was run by Alex Double, who I had examined for NUIA. We enjoyed taking crawfish and watching grey seals.

Brian May was now the proud owner of *Sylvia*, the 70-foot ketch that he had
bought from 'Mad' Mike Hoare, the mercenary leader. He was touring the Med as
he had always dreamed of doing, while Elise was back in Spain, bringing up their
two small daughters. He persuaded me to book a cruise and in August 70, Loran
and I got together a group of friends including Bill and Edna, ex-Zembra and Ed
Goldwyn, the TV producer and his wife 'Chum' who was a local GP.

Unfortunately Brian was getting so laid back that he was almost horizontal. He
had had a party of hippies on board before we arrived and the boat was a mess with
junk piled in every corner. His 'hippie-type' meals left a lot to be desired by hungry
divers and we persuaded him to give us the money he had set aside to buy food and
the ladies would organise the cooking under the leadership of Edna. We ate much
better.

He had picked us up in Nice and we planned to sail via Corsica to the islands
that I knew and loved. By the afternoon of the first day, we were out of sight of land
and motoring gently along over a calm sea. Most of the party were dozing in the
sun and I was idly looking over at the sea when I suddenly became aware that there
was something huge just below the surface. I only had time to shout once before
a huge body, as long as *Sylvia*, rolled over and a huge tail extended in the air as a
sperm whale sounded.

Sperm whales are not too common in the Med. They have a 'harem' system, like the seals, and it is recorded that in the waters off the South of France, it is always old males that are seen with a harem of six or seven young females. They can travel for thousands of miles through the oceans of the world and so my theory is that the crafty old males with their females, enter the Med through the Straits of Gibraltar, and spend their declining years off the Côte d'Azur while the young males who should be taking over, are roaming the Atlantic, wondering where they went.

We dived off the north-west Corsican coast before sailing on, passed the rocks of the Scoglio d'Africa to dive again off the West cost of Montecristo in a very blue evening light. A few hours later we were back in Giglio. The magic of Giglio was felt by Brian as well and we didn't leave again until it was time to return except for brief forays to Giannutri where we dived the Punta Secca and in the Grottoni to collect red coral.

Back in London, it was time for me to visit the Institute of Baths Managers' conference in Douglas, Isle of Man. This was an attempt to reassure them that diving would not ruin their pools or cause hundreds of pounds worth of damage to their tiles. I was warned that they might be hostile, but they proved a very sympathetic audience and my talk was even applauded.

I took the opportunity to dive with Isle of Man branch and also with Norman and Joanna Jones of the Port Erin Marine Biological Station, admiring their luxurious plumose anemones and 'dead-men's fingers'(*Alcyoniums*).

In March 1971, the Club had a new President, Lord Ritchie-Calder, who was a distinguished writer on science and the future. He asked me to brief him on the value of underwater archaeology and wrecks as 'time capsules' and afterwards, invited me into the House of Lords to hear his speech on the subject. Afterwards we went for a drink with a number of his cronies including Lord 'Bob' Boothby.

The Club's growth rate was still 20% per annum and we now had 335 branches I was also trying to bring other organisations to come closer to, if not within, the BSAC. I visited the officers of the Scottish Sub-Aqua Club, but found them determined to preserve their independence. I was also working on bringing Don's Aquatic Club into the fold and also the NUIA. I was soon to be successful with both.

Harriette returned from a holiday in Gibraltar with a girl friend and some news. On impulse, the two girls had taken a side trip on to Tangier. Dressed in mini-skirts one evening, they had crossed the road into a night club. A sports car screeched to a halt. Two men followed them in. One was very attracted to Harriette, and turned out to be a Swedish Baron. He later invited her to tour Europe as soon as she could get away again, visiting the castles of his friends. As her holiday entitlement was finished, she asked if she could have unpaid leave to go. I was not enthusiastic, but could see that she intended to go whatever I said, so agreed.

A few days later, I answered the office telephone while Harriette was getting our sandwiches.

'Zis is the Baron Dobranie speaking from Stockholm, I vish to speak to Miss Harriette Rancom.'

'Sorry', I replied, 'She's out at the moment'.

'Well', said the voice, 'Go and fetch her'.

I did not comply. She left for the tour a week later and came back full of stories of fairy-tale castles. Some time later, I asked about the Baron. 'Barons are not good enough for me now' said Harriette ', I'm looking for a King'.

In mid-summer I was invited by the Lebanese Tourist Bureau to visit their country and produce a report on how they could develop their diving tourist industry. I flew into Beirut and was met by a driver with a huge American limousine.

'My mission', he said gravely, 'is to satisfy your every desire'.

'Every desire?', I queried timorously.

'Yes'.

'Well, firstly I need to arrange some diving'.

'You want to dive?' he sounded surprised, 'OK'

I was taken to meet two of the very few divers in the country at that time. Raymond Abdelnour and Zareh Amadouny, who belonged to the exclusive Clam Club. Raimond was quiet, calm and knowledgeable. He proved to be one of the most reliable of divers. Zareh was a slighter figure, with a constant smile. He was a qualified instructor, expert underwater photographer, and a veteran of many visits to the Red Sea.

The hospitality of the Lebanese was second to none, and I enjoyed visits to the world-famous casino, where shows included such exotic sights as girls hanging from the roof in cages and simulated fires and floods. There were also live dolphins as actors. I met Pepe Abed, the ex-Lebanese ambassador to Mexico, who had an extraordinary collection of ancient objects and during the day was guided to the best dive sites by my two new friends.

We dived off the ancient harbours of Byblos and Tyre, finding groupers, flying gurnards, parrot fish and the remains of ancient pots. Raimond told me about a submarine they had dived on further out and which they thought they could find again if the weather settled. Luckily it did.

Meantime they began to tell me the story of its sinking on a calm morning in June 1941. France had fallen to the Nazis and the French Navy now under the collaborative Vichy government, was at the disposal of Germany. The French submarine *Souffleur* (Blower) had spent several weeks patrolling off the coast with two 'sister' subs. The *Souffleur's* mission was to prevent hard-pressed troops, particularly the British, from getting reinforcements or supplies by sea.

Her commander eased up his periscope. There was no sign of enemy ships, and after exchanging sonar signals, the other two submarines departed eastwards. Through his periscope, the *Souffleur*'s captain could make out the sprawling city of Beirut in the far distance. He swung round and the low-lying coast came into view. There was no sign of life.

Souffleur had been submerged for a long time and there was a need to recharge her batteries – both electrical and human. 'Blow 2, 3 and 6', he ordered. 'Stand by to surface'. The long, dark shape broke the surface. She was two-hundred-and-fifty feet long and was soon rolling gently on the calm surface under a hot sun. The French sailors clambered gratefully out of the conning tower, savouring the sun and fresh air. Although far from shore, two of them decided to swim. They knew the Mediterranean well and, after testing for currents, swam strongly away from the submarine. They never guessed that at that moment the eyes of the experienced Commander 'Bim' Rimington of His Majesty's submarine *Partheon* were checking out the *Souffleur*. The hunter was hunted!

Conditions were ideal for the attack. Rimington kept his periscope up all the time and fired four torpedoes. With a great explosion the first struck *Souffleur* right beneath her conning tower. All was chaos, shouts, cries and roaring water. And then there was silence, as a wave subsided and *Souffleur* took her last plunge.

The two French sailors, treading water, watched in horror and then began fearfully to swim for the distant coast. When they staggered ashore, they knew that they were the only survivors. Forty-five officers and men had disappeared forever.

The sub was slowly forgotten until twenty years later, when Zareh and Raimond heard the story and became interested in finding her again. What they lacked in numbers, they made up for in persistence and ability. They started by quizzing the local sponge divers and fishermen, having to overcome their suspicions that they were trying to steal their living. The stories they heard were contradictory, and resulted in many months of fruitless searching.

Finally the remaining evidence suggested that *Souffleur* had gone down well out to sea off the village of Khalde, south of Beirut. After more searches, they were finally successful and found her dark shape outlined against the white sand bottom.

It was now 30 years, all but a few days, since she went down. We chartered a tiny open fishing boat with just enough space for the three of us to kit-up on board. The sun was so hot that the sand burnt our feet as we brought the equipment down to it. A brown, wizened boatman swung our cylinders and weight belts easily aboard and we were away over a sea that looked like blue silk.

Zareh was unusually serious. He had forgotten to bring his photos of Beirut and the coast taken over the wreck site, which served as his 'marks'. He peered through field glasses at Beirut far astern through a heat haze. I began to feel that the chances of finding the wreck way out here 'in the blue' were becoming less. Abeam of us, VC10s and Boeings reared into the air from the new airport and turned out to sea over our heads.

The boatman produced a battered bottle of arak, radiated bonhomie, and took no further part in proceedings. Raimond took over the tiller and followed Zareh's instructions. We headed further out towards the horizon – a search for a needle in a haystack – I thought. A sign from Zareh, and Raimond cut the engine and we lay, rolling gently over a deep, clear, bottomless blue.

It was sheer ecstasy to fall backwards into the coolness of the sea after the sweating preparations on board. I put my mask on as I sank, bubbling the water out as I watched the others close towards me under the boat. We set our watch bezels and Zareh led the way down. Blueness in all directions, as I 'fell' effortlessly, feet first, with my fingers pressed into my mask. I watched the needle of my depth gauge move gently round 20, 30, 40, 60, 80 feet and, suddenly a sand bottom appeared far below.

Zareh took an instant decision and pointed the direction along the featureless sand. We followed, not very hopefully, spread out widely on each side of him. On this huge plain of sand, you could lose fifty submarines. Two minutes later a dark mass was looming up and we shouted into our tubes. I dropped down, took out my mouthpiece, and blew mock kisses in the direction of Zareh. He bowed formally, covered in self-satisfaction. I sank further and wrote on my slate 'Standing on the deck of a submarine at 105 feet at 05'.

It looked enormous as we swam along the hull and picked out the depth-keeping planes below. Raimond explained their function with hand movements. Then a small turret came into view and, suddenly, the high conning tower with its machine gun pointing upwards. Zareh flashed with his Nikonos as we hung on the gun. I came upon a steering light firmly fixed to the superstructure.

I joined up with Raimond and we entered the gaping hole where *Souffleur* broke in two. Struts and bars, rubber gaskets and a vent with a moray watching us. 'Are there still bodies in the sealed section?', I wondered. Raimond emerged with two slipper lobsters. We joined up with Zareh and swam towards the stern.

I wrote 'Bottom time 16 minutes, depth 130 feet' and made a questioning 'thumbs up' signal to Zareh. He nodded and we rose with the submarine spreading out below us in the clear visibility. The sinister conning tower looked like a great stern face under a helmet.

Slowly it disappeared, and we were 'in the blue' again, alone with our streams of bubbles. – 70 – 50 – 30 – 20 and we 'flattened out'. We hung happily together decompressing and comparing decompression meters, depth gauges and watches as we waited. The mood was jubilant.

After five minutes we crept upwards again and broke surface. We picked out our boat in the distance, and it altered course towards us. Its white hull cut the water beside us and we passed up cylinders and weight belts. We didn't feel like leaving the water and lay on our backs on the surface, joking about sharks. It was one of those great moments.

Before leaving the Lebanon, the tourist office arranged an outing to the ancient Roman city of Baalbek. I was accompanied by the Balmain models who also had an assignment in the country. Not surprisingly, I got on well with them. All went well until I was put onto a camel. The camel keeper struck the animal smartly on the rear end and it rolled into violent action. I'd never been carried so fast in my life and had no idea what camels did when they stopped running. Eventually the keeper re-appeared grinning and helped me down. The camel then tried to bite me. The first of a number of unfortunate encounters I was to have with this animal.

The last months of 1971 saw a return to Dale where I explored with a young Irish marine biologist, Liz Sides who I had previously dived with at London branch, and to Lundy with Alex Double. Both times we swam with grey seals. On Lundy, Alex arranged a night dive at the Knoll Pins that was so peaceful that I nearly went to sleep underwater.

Examining on the NUIA event in October, we went to 200 feet in the chamber that had been used by John Bevan and Peter Sharphouse in an experimental 1500 foot dive two years before. I supervised the arithmetic tests to check the effects of narcosis.

Loran and I were now living in a small cottage in Mortlake. We overlooked the tomb of the explorer Sir Richard Burton which was in the churchyard across our tiny cul-de-sac.

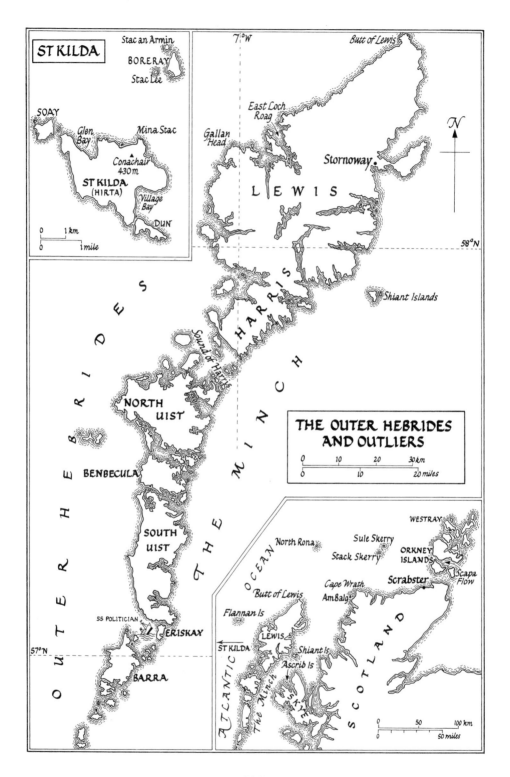

ST KILDA

Stac an Armin
BORERAY
Stac Lee

SOAY
Glen Bay   Mina Stac
Conachair
430m
ST KILDA
(HIRTA)
Village Bay
DUN

0   1 km
0   1 mile

7°W   Butt of Lewis

East Loch Roag
Gallan Head
Stornoway

L E W I S

58°N

Shiant Islands

N

O U T E R   H E B R I D E S

H A R R I S

Sound of Harris

NORTH UIST

T H E   M I N C H

BENBECULA

SOUTH UIST

THE OUTER HEBRIDES
AND OUTLIERS

0   10   20   30 km
0   10   20 miles

WESTRAY

ATLANTIC OCEAN   North Rona   Sule Skerry
Stack Skerry   ORKNEY ISLANDS
Scapa Flow
Cape Wrath
Am Balg   Scrabster
Butt of Lewis
Flannan Is
LEWIS
ST KILDA
Shiant Is
Ascrib Is
The Minch
SKYE

S C O T L A N D

SS POLITICIAN
ERISKAY

57°N

BARRA

0   50   100 km
0   50 miles

120

CHAPTER NINE

The Land of Demons &
the Seven Hunters

A T THE CLUB'S MARCH 1972 AGM, I reported that we now had 500 branches on six continents. Derek became Chairman, and my old friend Vernon took on the Treasurership. It was to be a very fruitful period and Derek, Vernon and I met up regularly at our tiny cottage to plot policy and future action. Derek foresightedly encouraged me to dive as often as possible, knowing how suspicious the members could be of those who did not.

Keith resigned as national coach to take up an appointment as chief diver at Trust House Forte's new tourist village at Santa Margherita di Pula in Sardinia. 'Crackers', of course, would go with him. She had now become the first female BSAC instructor.

Since Alex Flinder's time as Chairman, I had been the Club's chief trouble shooter. Messages were received from Scarborough branch in Yorkshire reporting that they were unhappy with the Club and were planning to break away. It was a large branch and I went up to pour oil on troubled waters.

The Chairman, Jim Lassey, was very reassuring, but they had called a meeting to discuss grievances. I listened carefully, and afterwards, explained our thinking, sympathised with some of the points they made, and promised improvements. It seemed to take the wind out of the sails of those proposing a break. They voted to stay in.

The most aggressive campaigner came to see me afterwards. 'You've got away with it this time', he said, in impotent fury, 'but, I'll take you diving, and scare the pants off you.' 'Yes, please', I replied. 'Anytime'. Active diving was certainly a requisite for this job. I dived through the summer with London branch and examined candidates on the Club's new advanced instructor course, which had been inaugurated by Derek.

In May '72, Jock White was successful in his third attempt to dive the isolated Wolf Rock lighthouse off Land's End. I dived there with him and an old friend, Ken Hay. We were on the look-out for one of a number of sunken U-boats, but only found crawfish and pieces of brass.

I had long been planning a series of expeditions to explore the farthest islands of the Outer Hebrides. As far as I knew, they had never been dived before. I was especially fascinated by St Kilda which lay 110 miles west of the Scottish mainland and 45 miles from the nearest Outer Hebridean island. It was on the edge of the continental shelf and had the highest cliffs in Britain at over 1300 feet. I devoured books written about the tiny island group.

The first book had been written by Martin Martin in 1753. He was rowed out the 45 miles from Lewis in an open long boat, the rowers guessing their course by following migrating gannets who nested there in huge numbers. The passage took his crew 24 hours during which they were out of sight of land for sixteen. They found local inhabitants who suffered from excessively zealous ministers of religion and scraped a living by harvesting eggs from the gannets and other sea birds. The gannet is our largest sea bird, has a six-foot wing-span and a habit of suddenly folding its wings and plummeting straight down through the surface to catch fish. Local folklore told that sometimes captured rival clansmen were floated out to sea with hands tied, corks under their armpits and a fish tied on top of their head to await the first gannet to split their skulls. The sight of these dramatic isles on the horizon was not easily forgotten. R.A. Smith wrote in 1879: 'Had it been a land of demons, it could not have appeared more dreadful, and had we not heard of it before, we should have said that, if inhabited, it must be by monsters.'

The original inhabitants had been finally taken off in 1930, so now the only occupants were soldiers of the tiny St Kilda garrison, which was a tracking station for the missiles that were tested from the mainland. There was certainly no ferry and the only anchorage, in Village Bay, was unusable when the wind was from the east.

During my previous tour of Scotland, I had met and dived with the young diving office of Dundee branch, Pat Barron who, I discovered by chance, was a second cousin. We decided to run the expedition between us with me responsible for the diving. To get to St Kilda, we reckoned we would need a seagoing fishing boat (MFV), a very competent skipper, strong stomachs and a lot of luck.

We thought about who to take with us. After crossing the Atlantic by sail, Clement Freud had once proposed that ideal companions would be 'Two soft, non-women's lib women, preferably, placid, hardworking, short-sighted nymphomaniacs, who could do the washing up and embroider towels with my crest.' In fact we took eight active divers from eight different BSAC branches. On 10th June '72 we all converged on Ardfern, a small anchorage and yacht basin in Argyll.

Jock White from Harlow, brought two weeks' provisions and a decant rig and my friend Ken Hay from Bournemouth brought a compressor. Dr Joan Lamb, our only girl was from Hampstead, Graeme Hall from Salford, Chris Sullivan from the new Loughton branch and an amazing giant of a man, Seamus O'Reilly, the DO of Belfast, who arrived direct by fishing smack carrying his inflatable.

We settled aboard the 45-foot Motor Fishing Vessel *Old 797* that we had chartered and met the colourful skipper, Boyd Keane, whose exploits were becoming known throughout the isles. We had heard that he could navigate through the most distant and dangerous waters and that his seamanship was second to none. His weaknesses were as yet unknown.

Old 797 had four berths in the forward cabin, another amidships and a double in the saloon. Joan took over the galley and began to produce a series of memorable meals. The wheelhouse served as dining saloon and chart room.

Next morning we set course for Tobermory and dived the site of the supposed disappearance of the famous galleon. The eyes of scallops twinkled on the bottom, but no doubloons. On northwards next day, to the island of Canna where we found 40-foot underwater visibility and crabs, squat lobsters and dead-men's fingers that seemed to beckon us further north. That night we reached Loch Maddy in the Outer Hebrides, our 'target area' where we aimed to wait until the weather was good enough to cross the remaining 45 miles of open Atlantic.

We had read of the difficulties of reaching St Kilda. Recently a wind speed of 130mph had been recorded at sea level there. What the speed was on the summit of Conachair, the island's peak, 1400 feet above the sea, can only be imagined, but a strong radar aerial that had been fixed using reinforced angle-iron was bent through ninety degrees and the anemometer fixed to it had been blown away.

Miraculously we awoke to a fine dawn and Boyd decided to attempt the crossing. Picking our way through the tortuous channels of the Sound of Harris, we came out into the open sea. Our spirits rose as we made good progress over the long swells. Five hours later, St Kilda appeared on the skyline – islands with sheer cliffs and vertical rocks sticking out of the sea, which were known as 'stacs'. As we drew closer to the northward islet of Boreray, Stac Lee and Stac-an-Armin gleamed white in the sun.

We thought that the whiteness must be a covering of bird droppings until we were very close, and then the 'covering' suddenly rose into the air blotting out the sun. Boreray and the two stacs form the world's largest gannetry with nearly 45,000 nesting pairs. They also form Britain's largest fulmar colony.

Thousands of sea birds swirled above, and squadrons of ungainly puffins or 'sea parrots' began long, laborious efforts to take off and escape. The little round birds are slowly losing the power of flight like penguins. Around Stac Lee dozens of heads appeared above the surface, huge curious eyes blinking and bristling whiskers twitching, as a colony of seals ogled their first divers.

We decided that Stac Lee, which stood like a pillar over 500 feet high, was the best place to start. Seamus and I led the way, rolling backwards into a moderate sea with 25 feet of underwater visibility.

A large female grey seal rolled curiously into sight and followed us down the vertical cliff face. She was joined by another, and the two swam warily closer as we coasted over vast fields of 'dead-men's fingers.' Corals, sponges and sea mats decorated the rock faces, but there was not a fish in sight. The gannets and seals had seen to that.

In the days that followed, we explored the main island of Hirta and the other islets around. Off the north coast another rock, Mina Stac, rose to 212 feet above the sea. Legend had it that it had originally been joined to the nearby cliff by a natural archway. One day a Spanish ship from the Armada was driven in and struck its foremast against it, dislodging tons of rock, which fell and disappeared with the galleon into the channel. Underwater, the site was impressive with great boulders, valleys and rock clefts. Seals played hide-and-seek with us but there was no sign of the galleon.

Coming ashore at Village Bay, we met Captain Simon Hopkins, commander of the small St Kilda army post, and Donall Stuart of the Nature Conservancy. Donall showed us the remains of the houses in Village Bay evacuated by the last inhabitants when they left in 1930.

We climbed to the summit of Conachair, passed wild orchids, mountain flowers, and nests on the open hillside. Black-backed gulls swooped menacingly. The cliffs here dropped 1400 feet straight into the sea and we could look across the three and a half miles to Boreray and the Stacs.

St Kilda provided opportunities to explore caves and vertical submarine cliffs. There were sunken gardens of corals and anemones and kelp forests with isopods on their fronds. I always kept an eye over my shoulder, knowing that the blueness we saw stretched unbroken down to the abyss and as far as America. I wondered whether whales or sharks might suddenly materialise out of the distance.

The weather began to change and Boyd advised leaving. The wind rose as we battled our way back eastwards, hour after hour, towards the low line of the Outer Hebrides. In spite of the weather, Joan continued to produce wonderful meals from the galley including joints of beef with all the trimmings, as *Old 797* rolled on her beam ends. I was to benefit from her culinary ingenuity again in another few years time. Seamus lashed anything that moved to the wheelhouse, and at 8.30 in the evening we limped back alongside the pier in Loch Maddy.

The sheltered Sound was rich in scallops and therefore a paradise for starfish which fed on them. We found no less than six kinds from huge spiny stars to tiny purple sunstars. There were starfish resting, starfish digesting, starfish walking and starfish testing out their muscles on unfortunate scallops. One hung acrobatically by one foot from a rock overhang and seemed to be sampling the plankton.

We sailed north-east into the little Minch, fabled home of the 'storm kelpies' or sinister 'wee blue men', whose influence on the weather is feared in these parts. We arrived at the Shiant islands. Their name in Gaelic means 'enchanted islands' and the vegetation includes flowering plants and palm trees. The Shiants used to be owned by Compton McKenzie of *Whisky Galore* fame and were later bought by Nigel Nicholson and then passed on to his son, Adam.

We chose to dive on the isolated and seal-haunted Galtachean rocks to the West of the group. Huge boulders covered the slope below the kelp forest and we were surrounded by huge shoals of pollack. The rocks were covered in sponges, anemones, hydroids, tunicates and beautiful nudibranch sea slugs. Lobsters and crawfish roamed the bottom.

We spent the night at anchor in the only bay on the east coast and Jock and Joan dived into a convention of squat lobsters and their relatives. The next morning, white breakers were forming outside and we fought our way south against a Force 8 gale. The 'storm kelpies' had been at work. *Old 797* rolled and lurched and we clung on as sheets of spray flew overhead.

By tea time we were forced to run for shelter on the west coast of the uninhabited island of South Rona. Then on southwards through the Sound of Sleat to visit Tex Geddes, author of *Hebridean Sharker* and an old friend of Ken's. Tex had been Gavin Maxwell's chief harpooner when they had operated a basking shark industry, and still lived on Soay with his wife and a friend who helped him with his new lobster farm.

We set a final course south-east through the Sound of Mull to Ardfern. Boyd gave us all a report that stated that 'we had steamed 472 nautical miles, consumed 400 gallons of fresh water, 4 gallons of vino and got the skipper stoned 2.75 times.'

The image of St Kilda and the Stacs stayed with me for many months and I planned to return. At the end of August I was back on Lundy and saw my favourite ocean sunfish again as we explored the wreck of a paddle steamer off Rat island. We dived into a magnificent garden of soft corals off Virgin Spring in the north, and sighted a basking shark.

Derek Cockbill, the new Chairman, persuaded me to come down to Devon to dive with him. We took turns to dive off a small inflatable he had borrowed to 'find lunch'. I successfully recovered a lobster. Back at his home he tried me out on a diet of Southern Comfort, chased with Carlsberg Specials. I survived that too.

In September we got an invitation from the American National Association of Underwater Instructors (NAUI) to speak to their annual conference about the achievements of BSAC. It was to be held in Miami Beach. I flew out with Mike 'Bus', now National Training Officer, and Vernon, and it was decided that we would take advantage of our being three BSAC Examining Instructors, to run some courses and exams for West Indian branches.

I was given the opening session of the conference and was listened to by over 500 American instructors who were amazed to hear of the Club's growth, activities and publications. Mike later detailed the instructor programme and introduced 'emblemism', a new badge disease, to the Americans. We got to make three new friends, Dr Glen Egstrom, the President of NAUI, Art Ulrich, their full-time administrator and a captivating professor of diving psychology, Dr Art Bachrach.

Art Ulrich invited us to join him on a private flight to dive from the Underwater Explorers Club in the Bahamas and we flew in to a mixed reception from the newly independent local immigration police. The Explorers Club and the Caribbean were revelations. We dived around their underwater habitat 'Hydrolab', discovering warm tropical water, coral heads and hundreds of fish. I discovered my first piece of fire coral when I sat on it by mistake. We watched through the windows of the Hydrolab while a lady aquanaut did a striptease.

From Miami, we flew on to the Cayman Islands to give the first of our Club Instructor Course/exams. The Club's main representative in the States, Fred. D. Leete III, travelled with us and became the USA's first qualified Club Instructor. My old friend, Liz Sides also passed together with a number of the Cayman Islands branch members. She was now working on brittle stars at the University of the West Indies and acting as Secretary of Jamaica branch. At Gerry Wilcox's hotel we were given cylinders and told to 'help ourselves' to the 'drop-off' just off the beach. Out of the mysterious deep blueness beyond, a large silver barracuda appeared and circled twice around Vernon, making us fearful about the future of Club funds.

On to Jamaica and the next course which, thanks to the efforts of Liz, was held at the University, where nine of her branch members became instructors. We then moved up to the north of the island and Montego Bay where the smaller branch also wanted a course. We ran it from the Chalet Caribe where a diving school was run by members. One of the examinees was a young nun called Sister Stella Rose who had got special permission from her Mother Superior to take the course. Tragically she died a few weeks after we left, on a misguided world record depth attempt organised by her branch diving officer.

We were back in London in time for the DO's Conference where I gave a paper 'Which Way Up?' to stimulate thinking on the best methods of emergency ascent and to make a plea for the re-introduction of 'assisted ascent', a term I coined, for sharing one mouthpiece in emergency. The Navy, the Club's advisors at that time, capitulated and assisted ascent was back in the training programme again.

I used to meet up with Bernard Eaton, editor of *Triton* every week for a drink and discussion on BSAC policy and initiatives. In November he launched a new bimonthly diving newspaper under the title *Diver* and asked me to provide a regular column. To my horror, he insisted on calling it 'Vallintine'.

Sadly our marriage was crumbling fast and Loran and I were now officially separated. She had two air package tickets for a Christmas visit to Moscow that she was not using, and passed them to me. Harriette agreed to go at short notice although she had been put under house arrest in Moscow some years before when her plane landed there in emergency. Beryl Brooshooft's daughter, Nikka, was now working in Moscow although temporarily absent, and Beryl asked me to take a few Christmas presents for her and friends.

No sooner were we on our Russian Aeroflot plane than announcements began, stressing that it was against the law to take presents to Russian citizens, and the need to declare the names of any we knew. I began to realise the significance of our instructions to contact the Russian after midnight by a public phone.

We had been told by the tour operators to take Christmas puddings for the hotel to prepare on Christmas Day. They burnt them into our plates and we ate them like biscuits. Moscow was freezing, but impressively beautiful in the December sun which lit up the golden domes above the Kremlin. We were taken there and admired the Tsarist treasures still held within the walls. It was an honour to be buried in the walls of the Kremlin, and I was amused to read some memorial stones reading 'Fergus McTavish, Glasgow, 1921' or some such. It was the Soviet Union's 50th Anniversary Year and everywhere I looked there were effigies of Lenin that looked rather like me. I was even embraced by a drunken Russian in a lift – not to be recommended. We went to see Lenin and Stalin lying in state and I was pleased to see that Lenin in the flesh had reddish hair and a less distinguished nose than mine.

The Russians who I had met on my visits to the World Federation meetings in Paris collected us for a visit to the Moscow Club of the Sea. They were mainly engaged in fin-swimming along the surface, but showed us Spiro equipment and, when pressed, some Russian regulators too. We visited Ivan the Terrible's Palace and were entertained by gypsy dancers, who mingled with us, to the horror of our Intourist guides.

Our hotel was a huge modern tower with innumerable floors and lifts that scarcely moved. On every floor there was a large female guardian with all the door keys. At last it was time to deliver the dreaded presents. I phoned the number from the pay phone in the lobby. 'What number is your bedroom? Stay there 'til I arrive', said a voice. Harriette gave me moral support. There was a quiet knock, and a young Russian in a huge top coat swept in. He sat down on the bed, perspiring heavily. He began to tell us how awful it was in Russia, and how he could not work as a film director any more.

It was like a dream. I even began to look around for hidden microphones. He stuffed the presents into his great-coat pockets and then, as I feared, said 'You must help me … I cannot take them all. Wait five minutes and go down to the hotel entrance. Turn right, second left and there is a dark corner on the left. Bring them down, I'll see you there.' He disappeared. I took the remaining carrier bags. Avoiding the guardian, I pressed impatiently on the lift button. I felt a step behind me and a hand came down on my shoulder. 'Ah, you are ze man viz de bag'. My heart sank. I looked round to find one of our fellow tourists had made an obscure joke. I was out of the hotel like a rocket. A figure detached itself from the dark corner. 'OK, thanks, I will remember'.

The 1973 AGM was held in Edinburgh with pipers piping us into a splendid civic reception in the castle. It was perhaps the most glorious meeting we had ever organised, and *Triton* magazine chartered a special train from London for delegates. It was Derek's first AGM as Chairman and in the 12 months since he had taken office, we had reappraised and streamlined the administration and reorganised all the Club departments. Vernon was a new vital force, running the Club finances and we were planning to run a World Congress 'Oceans 2000' in October. Peter Cornish was now salvaging aircraft and torpedoes using lifting bags and oil drums. I presented him with the 'Diver of the Year' trophy and suggested his motto should be 'Have oil drums, will travel'.

I had interviewed and appointed a new Administration Manager, Ivor Emberey and he had taken over the branch administration from our agent Hume Wallace. We also benefited from a new, far-sighted National Diving Officer, Bob Darby. Over 2,000 members had joined in the three months since January and the Sports Council grant had increased.

The May bank holiday was approaching fast when my phone rang in the office. A lady made it clear that she was the secretary of someone pretty important. He wanted a private diving instructor to fly out by private plane to St Tropez for the holiday where he had a villa and motor launch. I phoned all the coaches and instructors I knew. No one was available at such short notice. I suddenly thought: 'Why don't you go? You're qualified?' Not ethical I decided, then changed my mind.

The VIP concerned was called Godfrey Bradman who was a mysterious young chartered accountant and tax expert, director of 27 companies and with his own 'fringe' bank. He sat in his office wearing white gloves, and I found it difficult to imagine him on the average diving boat.

His friend, Brian Stein, flew me out in a tiny 2-seater plane with his leggy model girlfriend draped around us from the tiny bucket seat behind. We flew over London on a clear day, admiring the river and streets below. Some hours later, over the middle of France, I sensed something was wrong. Brian was quite calm. 'Just going to pop down to fix a minor technical fault', he shouted over the noise of the engine.'There's a French Air Force field very close.

As we came in, I looked over the nose and saw the ambulances and fire engines

33. Whisky Galore: Sound of Eriskay, February 1966.

34. With bottles of *Politician* whisky after diving. L to R: Bill Smith, Horace Capaldi, Reg, Iain Davidson.

35. In the Grotte des Pigeons, Zembra. Stan Hayward (*centre*) and Hasan el Bey (*right*).

36. Ready to dive, Zembra 1967. L to R: Bill, 'Crackers', (Jean Cracknell) and Reg.

37. With the 'Atlantis Dive Club'. Loran and Stan (*sitting foreground*), Reg, Jean Graux, and Bill (*back right*).

38. The 'red *langoustier*' was our main dive boat in 1967.

39. Reg, 'Banane' (Michael Lendrin), and Mike Coltman at Club Med, Caprera 1968.

41. PA to D-G, Harriette Rancom.

40. The new 'Director-General', 1969.

42. Mule power, Hydra, Greece 1969. L to R: Reg, Roger and Cy Corder.

43. Ed Goldwyn directing TV series at Crystal Palace, 1969. *At poolside*: Reg, Ed, Dick Harris; *holding on to sill*: Slim McDonnell, Mike Maloney, Gill Lythgoe.

44. *Sylvia* moored in Giglio Porto in September 1970.

45. Liz Sides & Mike Busuttili at Negril, Jamaica during exams.

46. Conning tower of the *Souffleur*, 125 ft down off Beirut, 1971.

47. *Moniteur*, amphora and Maggie Kuyper, Caprera.

48. First visit to Village Bay, St Kilda, June 1972. L to R: Captain Simon Hopkins, Reg, Graeme Hall, Seamus O'Reilly, Pat Barron, Joan Lamb, *Old 797*, and 'Jock' White.

49. The deserted village at St Kilda.

50. With lobsters and Boyd Keane at the Flannans, June 1973.

51. The Flannan Light and sheep's skull.

52. BSAC office staff. February 1974. L to R: Fred Lock, Jerry Hazzard, Ivor Emberey, Harriette, juniors and Reg.

53. The Duke of Edinburgh's visit to the office. L to R: Reg, David Nations, HRH.

54. *X-5* expedition, North Cape, Arctic Norway 1974. John Harris and Reg displaying their finds –a German coffee pot and the bootee from a British submariner's suit.

55. The bow section of the X-craft being raised.

56. A group of expedition divers, Kaafjord, Norway. ʟ to ʀ: Joan Lamb, Wayne Bennett, Reg, John Harris, Linsay Cole, Geoff Coxon, and Jens Assued.

57. Nigel Kelland with side-scan sonar in the fishing boat cabin.

58. Reg erecting transit markers at Kaafjord.

59. Desert accommodation, Ras Muhamed, 1976. L to R: Rubi Eviatar, Janie, Margaret Witts and Reg.

60. Room for four divers and one snake.

61. Local inhabitant: Napoleon Wrasse at Ras Muhamed.

62. Pensive Janie in new wet suit
before first dive, Fort Bovisand,
September 1974.

63. Four years later as an experienced diver,
on *Colonna IV* in the Red Sea.

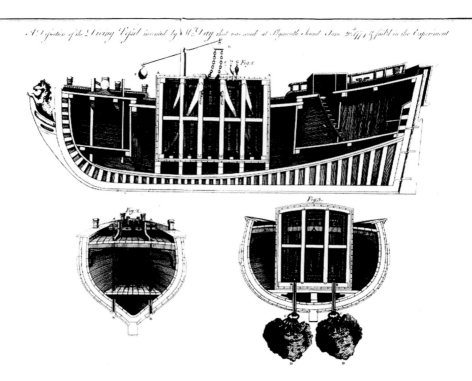

64. Dr Falck's plan of Mr Day's 'diving vessel', 1771.

65. The search for Mr Day, April 1979. L to R: Phillippe Dumortier, Tony Smith, Reg and Peter Edmead.

66. Sanganeb Light, Sudan, October 1979.

67. Lunch with the keepers of Sanganeb. L to R: Fiona Bennett, Mo, Alex Double, and three keepers

68. Accommodation for two, Sanganeb. 'It never rains'.

69. Surtsey, the newest island, Westmans, Iceland, July 1981.

70. Sunset and Sudurey from campsite, Heimaey, Westmans.

lined up along the sides of our runway. One of our engines had apparently lost all power. We landed safely and Brian asked me to take his girlfriend for a coffee while he got the engine repaired. We walked into a huge hanger where a thousand or so French airmen were having their break. A huge gasp went up at the sight of the model in a mini-skirt. We were deluged with coffee and cakes before being on our way again.

I had never landed at St Tropez before, but it was a tricky operation and needed previous experience. We dropped down suddenly between the mountains while girlfriend held her head in agony. Instead of the usual set radio procedure on approach, most of the conversation seemed to be about getting G&Ts ready, and seeing mutual friends.

Godfrey was already in residence in his villa, entertaining young banker friends. We went out to dive using his Riva speed boat that had very little room for the equipment. He was initially apprehensive and refused to touch anything underwater, but we made progress over the next few days.

I returned at the end of May and then it was already time for me to organise a return to the Hebrides. This time I decided to explore the mysterious Flannan Islands (or Seven Hunters), twenty miles off to the west of Lewis.

There are over 5,000 islands around the tortuous coast of Britain. You may think that this must include large rocks, but I prefer the old Hebridean definition of an island, 'any piece of land, surrounded by water, with enough grass to support one sheep'.

Why are the Flannans mysterious? In 1899 the first lighthouse had been built on Eilean Mor, the largest of the uninhabited Flannans, and twelve months later, keepers James Ducat, Thomas Marshall and Donald MacArthur were in residence there. On the night of December 15th 1900, the steamer *Archer* passed the islands and reported that the lighthouse was not operating.

The Northern Lighthouse Board's ship *Hesperus* was sent out to investigate and when their crew landed on the silent island, they found no trace of the keepers. To add to the mystery, in the living room of the lighthouse, a meal was laid for three and one chair was knocked over. Eventually a theory was put forward. It seemed that the log book of the chief keeper, Ducat, was found with entries up to December 13th and a slate taking the rough record to 9 o'clock on the morning of the 15th. This record told of gales and heavy seas, and of damage to the west landing. The west landing is a steep inlet called Skiopageo which ends in a cave. During storms, the sea is funnelled into the inlet until the escaping air explodes throwing tons of water over the gulley.

Testifying to the severity of the storm, the searchers found that a crane set in concrete 100 feet above high water level in the inlet had been torn from its foundations, that a concrete box built 140 feet above had been demolished, and turf 200 feet above had been torn away. Ducat's and Marshall's oilskins and sea boots were missing, and as the keepers only used these when visiting the landings, it was deduced that they had been visiting the west landing to survey the damage.

It was suggested that the third keeper, MacArthur, glancing out to sea, saw a huge freak wave making for the west side. In his rush to warn the others, he knocked over the chair before running down towards the landing. He probably had to go right down, they thought, before he could make the others hear, and all three died as the great wave came in and Skiopgeo's cave exploded with its death wall of water.

This was convincing, though closer analysis showed up some anomalies in the recorded accounts. If, as supposed, the meal had been breakfast, why did it consist of 'cold meat, pickles and a dish of potatoes'. According to another account 'utensils used in the preparation and consumption of breakfast were all clean.' I hardly expected that our two-week expedition would turn up any new theory, but there I was wrong.

Jock White came with us again, and we were joined by Gordon Wilson, Derek Woulds and Tricia Sinclair from Hampstead. They brought their home-made Domino inflatable *Baggy Wrinkle*. Dave Molyneux from Putney and Russell Hay (my friend Ken's son) completed the party. We joined Boyd Keane again at Ardfern and found that he had taken on a dark-eyed local girl called Clare as cook. Boyd asked me to dive over the side before we left to check the rudder. It seemed to be firmly in position. He did not explain why.

We travelled north through the Sound of Mull until a tiny, low islet with an automatic light appeared ahead. This was Green Island, scene of the wreck of the cargo ship *Rondo* which had managed to collide with the islet head-on in January 1935 and completely demolished the original lighthouse. The *Rondo* was a magnificent wreck. Balanced vertically on a ledge on to which it had slipped, the stern was 20 feet below the surface and the bow at over 200. She was a beautiful sight, covered with plumose anemones, tunicates, feather stars and tube worms. She looked mysterious in the late evening light as we swam down collecting a crawfish on the way.

After the dive, we spent the night at Tobermory, and made the acquaintance of the local pub, run by Bert Hall, where licensing hours could be conveniently forgotten. We also made the acquaintance of Boyd's latest girl friend, who followed our progress over hill and dale in her Mini-Minor, and pitched a tent where Boyd sometimes spent the night.

The next day, the first of the gales that were to haunt us, started and we fought our way passed Rhum in a Force 8, eventually seeking shelter at the hamlet of Isle Ornsay on Skye. Boyd warned us not to speak unless 'in the garlic' (Gaelic) as the local laird was a fervent Scottish nationalist. He duly arrived with an English accent and a swagger cane and exchanged a few words with Boyd 'in the garlic' while we stood silently by.

We left this unwelcoming place the next morning on the rising tide, bound for Kyle of Lochalsh. We sheltered in Kyle amid a gaggle of local fishing boats. A young fisherman/diver came on board and talked about the industry and local characters including the colourful 'Captain Midnight'. He complained about the thousands of scallops that were being taken each day from Loch Roag by the new professional scallop divers. Many of them had apparently suffered from bends, but others used the Decompression Meter successfully to prevent them. Boyd, primed with whisky, just managed to miss the fishing boats as we left. His weaknesses were becoming clearer.

On to Portree in the north of Skye where again we met the well-connected 'laird' who, it transpired, was a Knight of the Realm and founder of a bank. He was patronising the fishermen in the local pub that he also owned. A local fisherman plied us with delicious fresh shrimps. The weather took a day or so to improve and then we were off northwards again to our favourite islands, the Shiants.

I manned the inflatable for the first dive off House Island and while the divers were down, watched hundreds of razorbills and puffins skimming overhead. There were also cormorants, fulmars and many other sea birds. A wonderful sight. I later dived with Jock and we found four different species of nudibranchs amid the luxurious beds of Dead-Men's Fingers, plumose anemones and encrusting sponges. Soon it was time to move on and we arrived at Stornoway the same evening.

Horace appeared like magic to greet us and immediately organised an impromptu ceilidh, featuring the local singer. According to Horace, I suffered from 'butter legs' in the early hours,

We left Stornoway, heading north round the wild Butt of Lewis, the northernmost tip of the Hebrides. As the seas crashed against the cliffs, fulmars hovered above and gannets gave displays of aerobatics. Tiny puffins, not to be outdone, demonstrated expert 'duck dives' and we turned into the fiord-like East Loch Roag. The wind had not dropped and we decided to dive in the loch while waiting for a chance to make the Flannans. We were visited by clam divers and later saw their launch. They were very much 20th-century buccaneers of the seabed, happily ensconced in local crofts with bottles of whisky and local lassies and with seagoing boats and the latest Scandinavian dry suits. They harvested thousands of scallops each day.

The wind finally dropped enough for Boyd to chance the long run out into the open Atlantic, and two hours later we sighted the tall, dark shapes of the Seven Hunters through a confused sea and heavy waves. In the afternoon we arrived under the east landing on Eilean Mor with the lighthouse towering above us. As we prepared to dive, a family of grey seals poked their heads up. We tried to charm them with singing in the traditional way, but without success. It was exciting to be the first divers to swim down the dark rock slope, passed jiggling crawfish 'feelers'. The kelp stretched down to 100 feet, deeper than we had ever seen it before. I searched the bottom for any trace of missing keepers.

After the dive, we took a quick run ashore to look at the lighthouse, now fitted with an automatic light that needed no tending. A steep climb up the old rail track used for refuelling the light, brought us on to the spongy turf that covered the top of the island.

I scrambled over and down to the west landing, the supposed site of the disappearance. Anywhere wilder it would be difficult to imagine. Great waves broke into the narrow inlet and clouds of spray drenched me as I peered into the cave. There were hand rails on the stone steps high above the water, but they had been wrenched from their mountings by enormous forces. I felt the ghosts of the keepers all about.

As I climbed up again to the top of the island, I passed the skulls of sheep and was pecked at by puffins from their burrows on either side of the path. The lighthouse was serenely white in the early evening light. The wind was freshening again from 6 to 8, and we headed back for Loch Roag. Now used to the rolling, we were eating dinner when suddenly Boyd put his head down the companionway and asked to speak to me on deck. I went up. He looked as white as a sheet. 'What's the trouble Boyd?' 'The f---ing rudder's dropped off!', he said.

I looked in towards the shore five miles away where waves were beating up the black cliffs of Gallan Head. We were wallowing helplessly with the wind increasing and night falling. 'What are we going to do Boyd?' 'Don't know. We could cut the wheel house away to try to make a jury rudder.' That seemed a bit extreme. As so often in an emergency, all the divers quietly donned their diving life jackets. Luckily we also had two quick thinkers on board. Gordon and Jock decided to launch the inflatable and try to steer *Old 797* with it.

We all struggled with the launch of *Baggy Wrinkle* in difficult conditions and then got the outboard on to the transom. Gordon was joined by Jock and they disappeared into the waves with the strongest line we could find. Boyd put his engines slow ahead. It proved impossible to manoeuvre the inflatable against a taut line until we tried a longer version. *Old 797* at last began to make slow progress. Meantime, Boyd had made several emergency calls on the radio, but got no acknowledgement. An hour later Stornoway coastguard announced that the Stornoway lifeboat had been launched but was not expected to get to us until 2 or 3 a.m. as it was 50 miles away heading round the Butt of Lewis. Boyd could not get through to recall it.

Long, nerve-racking hours followed. Several times the rope parted and as darkness fell, we used torch signals to indicate direction to the distant inflatable. We estimated we were now making 3-4 knots successfully guided by Gordon and Jock, who was becoming seriously chilled without his wet suit.

At last we approached the coast and the trickiest part, which was to get through into the loch. If the rope failed now, we would be on the rocks. We stood in the spray, holding all the emergency boat gear including the axe and life raft. After three hours we were through into the calmer waters of the loch and a local fishing boat towed us in to berth at Great Bernera at 2.15 a.m. We learned that the Stornoway lifeboat had mercifully returned before traversing the Butt of Lewis.

We were now unable to move any further until repaired, but carried on diving from *Baggy Wrinkle*. The next evening we were visited by the local harbour master, Donald MacLeod, a gentle, white-haired, quietly-spoken islander who rowed across to see how we were. He had been a keeper on the Flannans and on one occasion both the other keepers had been taken ill and he had operated the light alone while looking after them for weeks until the relief ship could get out. Asked what he thought about the disappearance of the keepers back in 1900, he said that many subsequent keepers had discussed it and many did not agree with the official theory.

The lighthouse keepers' working day began at 10.30 a.m. in the winter, he said, and they always had breakfast first. He also told us that the oilskins and boots of all the keepers had eventually been found in the lighthouse, and that the meal was half-eaten and there were half-filled cups of tea on the table. In weather such as they had had, it was inconceivable that they would have ventured to the west landing.

What had happened then?

'Well,' he said, 'they say that one of he keepers was an alcoholic, on the Flannans to try to "dry himself out". Did you notice that the edge of the cliff on one side is only seven paces from the lighthouse? The feeling is, that the only thing that would have taken them outside in such weather was if one of their number had tried to do away with himself over that cliff. The others might have tried to stop him and all could have been carried over struggling into the sea.'

The lamp flickered in our wheelhouse and I looked across the darkened loch in the direction of the Seven Hunters. What had really happened? No one, I guess, will ever know.

We continued diving around the loch. I got the news that a message was waiting for me at the harbourmasters office. The message read: 'To Reg Vallintine, Old 797 via Oban radio. I confirm that I wish you to join me in south of France for coming weekend. Reservation on plane to Nice on Friday evening for you. Please confirm availability and acceptance soonest. Godfrey Bradman.'

How could I resist? The next day was one of outstanding contrasts. At 6 a.m. I quietly left the boat and paddled myself ashore under a beautiful dawn. A girl called Liz was waiting on the tiny quay and drove me to Stornoway airport, narrowly missing stray sheep on the way. I caught the morning plane to Glasgow. Then one to London. I joined up with Godfrey and his girlfriend, Rosemary Adams. We caught the evening plane to Nice and drove on to St Tropez. I sat sipping G&Ts, looking out over a calm Mediterranean, the farthest Hebrides already becoming a memory.

CHAPTER TEN

The Mystery of X-5

ROSEMARY WAS A PHOTOGRAPHER, and a pretty serious one too. She had her expensive camera with her, and an even more expensive underwater case that she had hired for the occasion. I suggested that, for her first lesson, she left the camera behind.'No way! My camera goes everywhere with me'. 'But, you'll have to learn to take your mask off and other exercises.' Just tell me what to do, and I'll do it.' She did, and was astonishingly competent for a beginner. Even the fish looked astonished, and an octopus she discovered must have been the most photographed ever.

We dived off the Isle du Levant, the famous nudist site, and French fishermen laid their nets around us as we dived. I had a day off, and wandered around the cliffs and swam in a deserted cove. The water was crystal clear, but there was a gobbet of oil every foot or so and a plastic bottle every 20 yards.

There was no sign of pollution back on Lundy in August. The island was now administered by the Landmark Trust, having been bought for the Nation by phi-lanthropist, 'Union' Jack Hayward. I took young Bart Smith, the son of the Trust founder, diving.

Some days later, a basking shark came into the Landing Cove where we were based and Bart and I snorkelled with it. We explored the wreck of HMS *Montague*, a First Class battleship wrecked on Lundy in 1906 and now owned by Don Shiers.

Vernon and I had been invited to sample the diving from the Trust House Forte holiday village in Sardinia, where Keith and 'Crackers' were now working as diving supremos. When we arrived, we found that 'Keithie' was *hors de combat*, having dropped equipment on his foot, and the diving was being run by 'Crackers'. They had a converted ferry boat called the *Cirio* on which they packed a mass of holiday makers and divers every day. We had a lot of fun underwater and I perfected my shark-biting technique, practising on the most interesting parts of 'Crackers' and her German girl friend, Pifke.

Vernon perfected a different technique. When we arrived back close to the sur-face near to the boat, he would turn face down, crouch, remove his swimming trunks and with whirling movements of his hands, manage to surface his backside up and down above sea level. There was a rush of tourists to the side of the boat. Several thought it might be a dolphin, others a shark. When it became clear what it was, we received an obligatory lecture on the importance of not being frivolous, from 'Crackers'.

Peter Dick was also instructing there, and we discovered a floating missile, 'the property of the French government'. It had obviously been in the sea for months as it was covered in acorn barnacles and surrounded by pilot fish. The police arrived to remove it.

The moment we got back, we were working on the final arrangements for the Oceans 2000 World Congress organised by the Club. It was held over six days at the Grosvenor House Hotel in Park Lane. All the great names of the underwater world were speaking, Hans Hass, Jacques Cousteau, Hannes Keller, Arthur C. Clarke, David Bellamy, Philippe Tailliez, Commander Scott Carpenter, Margaret Rule and Art Bachrach. At the CMAS meetings during the event, I was elected on to the international executive bureau. The event was extremely successful and culminated in a banquet in the Great Room of the Grosvenor House for nearly 1,000 delegates and visitors, with a cabaret by the Band of the Coldstream Guards.

Harriette and I celebrated the successful conclusion at our 'local', The Mason's Arms run by a friend, Mike Bunyon. We met a tall Texan, in Western boots, just returned from an oil rig, who introduced us to 'Southern Comfort Sweet and Sours', which even had an effect on Harriette. At the DO's Conference in December, a number of evil coaches took secret bets that they would be able to drink her 'under the table'. An hour or so later, she was still upright (more or less), but several of them were horizontal under the furniture.

I had met the Diving Officer of Salford branch, and was invited to their branch dinner. When I arrived at the station, I was met by a young blonde with sparkling eyes. 'My job, this weekend', she announced with a smile, 'is to keep you happy.' Where had I heard that before? I resisted the temptation to make a number of suggestions, and she made it clear that her mission must include my attendance at the branch dinner. She was Jan Chapman, wife of Dave, a leading member of the branch.

By the beginning of 1974, I had managed to bring our National Instructors organisation into BSAC, and the original organisation went into voluntary hibernation. A few weeks later Don Shiers finally agreed to bring the Aquatic Club and all its branches in too. This swelled the Club's membership numbers again. On the 1st January, I was able to appoint Jerry Hazzard as full-time Director of Coaching. He became the third of my departmental heads. Besides Ivor Emberey, I now had taken on Jill Sarsby from London branch as Publications Manager.

We moved offices with the Sports Council to IBA House at 70 Brompton Road, opposite Harrods, where they gave us 1500 square feet of office and storage space rent free. The Director of the Sports Council, Sir Walter Winterbottom had commented on our recent grant of £30,000 for the national boat, saying 'I am constantly amazed at the foresight and initiative of the club'. I had a very good liaison with Fred Briscoe their liaison officer who made many useful suggestions for further applications for aid. Our growth rate was still 15% per annum and we now had 20,000 members.

A few weeks later, our ex-President, the Duke of Edinburgh, was chairing the AGM of the CCPR at Brompton Road and it was agreed that he would be brought in to see us on his way out. I briefed the office staff as to modes of address and made a plan which involved a quick tour from my office to Harriette and Jill's, and then to the general office where Ivor supervised a number of girls.

The Duke was brought in by David Nations, Chairman of the Water Recreation Division, and we chatted about worldwide diving, our overseas branches and wrecks. He was interested to hear that Peter Cornish was now planning an expedition to North Cape in Norway to look for a missing RN X-craft midget submarine from the war. I prepared to take him into the other offices, but he was whisked away by his entourage before I could do so. A few moments later there was a tap on my door. It was Harriette. 'Would you like a cup of tea, your Royal Highness?' she asked. 'Sorry, he's gone'. She curtsied and went out backwards. She continued this method of approach and withdrawal for some days until I threatened to throw something.

One floor up in IBA House lay the offices of the British Water-Ski Federation. They were run by a wild Australian called Sandi Primo. She was slim, dark and a barefoot skier and judge. My friends said that she must be less of a judge of men since we began to spend so much time together.

The Club AGM was held at Butlin's Honeymoon hotel at Brighton and I took her along as my guest. She finished up standing on a table after the dinner, conducting AGM delegates in renderings of 'Waltzing Matilda' and 'Tie yer Kangaroo down, Sport'. The Vice-Presidents were not amused, but the members loved it. She had a heart as big as Australia.

The Butlin's hotel had been Derek's idea to save delegates' money, but had left something to be desired, especially in the food department. Due to my friendship with Mike Bunyon in the Mason's Arms, I was able to speak to Bobby Butlin who was a regular there. The next morning, I had three of his managers in my office apologising, and a large refund cheque followed.

Harriette finally decided to follow her destiny in the shape of a young aeronautical engineer called Pete whom she had known since childhood. He was currently working in a dive shop but soon became a gliding instructor. Harriette became administrator of the airfield. On her last day with us, I was out at a meeting. When I got back there was a note on my desk in her handwriting. It read:

'Bye, Bye Reggie,
What a 4 years it's been – wonderful.
Very sad to go.
Shall keep in touch.
Please ring me anytime…
See you soon, Super Mush,
Love, H.child'

Probably the best testimonial I ever received.

By May it was time for the third of our Hebridean expeditions. This time I was involved with my new friends from Salford branch. We took a different boat, a 62-foot motor yacht called *Pentland Wave*. It had a sizeable crew. A local, Alex, as skipper, a lively engineer called Willy and two young New Zealanders as cook and steward. The Salford divers were Jan and Dave Chapman, Peter Schofield, Sylvia and Frank Shenton, Tim Hatch, Roy Hyde, Mike Leech and Dave Percival.

My aim was to reach the lonely rock isle of Sule Skerry, source of the seal legends, 40 miles north of Cape Wrath. There was an old ballad, 'The Grey Selchie of Sule Skerry', selchie being the ancient name for a seal. They were said to have come ashore in ancient times and married local women. The song included the words:

I am a man upon the land,
I am a selchie in the sea,
And when I'm far frae every strand,
My dwellin' is in Sule Skerry.

I had dived from Scrabster on the northern tip of Scotland where the *Pentland Wave* was based, and we were met there by Bill Stewart, chairman of the local branch, who brought charts and pointed out wreck locations far into the night.

The next morning, we were on our way, and had a warm-up dive in Loch Erriboll on the way to our target area. It was evening, and we were surrounded by Aurelia 'jellies' as we dropped down on to a dark bed of scallops and oysters. A ripple broke the surface on our port quarter, soft brown eyes sparkled in the evening light, a moustache bristled, and the first of the selchies checked us out.

Next morning we woke to a freshening wind, but nosed out to sea and then decided to head due north for Sule Skerry. The hours went by, and a slight roll developed as we left land far behind. The Salford compressor grumbled away, filling bottles on the aft deck. Excitement mounted as the morning wore on and more and more seabirds appeared – fulmars, a sprinkling of puffins and isolated gulls and gannets, sitting on the sea.

Soon the 130-foot high pillar of Stack Skerry, the neighbouring isle was on the horizon. As we arrived, the skies cleared and the sun streamed down on the thousands of gannets and guillemots whose home is on this twin-humped pile of hornblende gneiss rock. A dozen seals lolled in the surf around the guano covered cliffs. At the last count, this rock had apparently held 2,800 pairs of nesting gannets on the upper reaches, with the guillemots lower down. The skipper was not happy to stay and so we left for nearby Sule Skerry.

It was low-lying with a prominent lighthouse. The seals had bred extensively there until the building of the light in 1895. Early in the twentieth century they were hunted extensively, as were the birds, by raiders from Port Ness on Lewis.

As we approached, more seals appeared swimming up to us with curiosity. The scene was inviting and underwater, great rock gullies opened through the kelp and led down to a fairy-tale world of crystal clear water. The rock walls were covered in anemones, Dead-Men's Fingers, hydroids, crabs and lobsters. The lobsters had evidently not seen divers before. The seals eyed us through the kelp.

There was no anchorage and so after diving, we rolled off eastwards towards the northern tip of the Orkneys where our anxious skipper hoped to moor up. The sun sank slowly and in the evening light a piebald dolphin led us to Westray, the most northerly of the Orkneys, where there was already a small BSAC branch established.

The next morning it was overcast and windy, but we dived at Noup Head, a magnificent cliff 260 feet high that pointed out towards Iceland. As we got close, we saw that there were many ledges which held row upon row of sea birds, standing upright, with hardly an inch between them. Underwater was an impressive sight, with great boulders and huge fields of alcyoniums and anemones. Rounding a rock at 100 feet, I disturbed two large ling that were lying in a sand gulley. When we surfaced, we were surrounded by guillemots sitting sedately on the sea around us.

We spent the night on Stronsay further south. The next day we explored Burgh Head where Dave caught a magnificent lobster, and we watched razorbills, guillemots, cormorants and gulls whirl by overhead. By the early evening, we were in Kirkwall, capital of the Orkneys, a quiet little town with cobbled streets where pedestrians had priority over traffic and the influence of the Norsemen could still be felt. Our small MFV was dwarfed by a cargo ship, a symbol of the new affluence brought by the recent discovery of oil offshore.

On we travelled south-eastwards to the tiny isle of Colinsay and the wreck of a trawler that had grounded two yeas before and was still visible from the shore. We ran in under the cliffs where curious guillemots surrounded our boat. We dived down the rock face passed shoals of pollack. When we rose up again to 45 feet at the end of the dive, Tim and I suddenly froze. We were surrounded by fast-moving black bodies, milling around us only a few feet away. Closer and closer the guillemots came, beating their wings and rolling their eyes, with streams of bubbles pouring from their beaks, until I was sure that they would hit us. Their speed and mastery of the alien element amazed us as they plummeted and whirled around. It seemed like a dream. As suddenly as they had arrived, they were gone and we were alone in the greenness, hardly believing what we had seen.

On southwards, into what the Sailing Directions calls 'the most dangerous stretch of water in the British Isles' – the dreaded Pentland Firth, where tides frequently run at over 10 knots. There is a race there called 'The Merry Men of May,' where the water just off the shore is travelling at lightning speed in one direction while just a few yards further out it is travelling just as fast in the other. Between them is a mass of confused waves that give the race its name.

We watched apprehensively as *Pentland Wave* swung drunkenly past whirlpools and overfalls. Sometimes it felt as though a great hand had gripped our hull and moved it suddenly sideways. Still visible on the rocks was the remains of the cargo ship *Irene* whose call, the ill-fated Longhope Lifeboat had answered when she herself struck a freak wave and capsized with the loss of all the crew.

Before leaving the Orkneys, we turned north again into Scapa Flow where Cox and Danks had bought and raised much of the first World War German navy. We located a U-boat and found an impressive wreck with fish swimming through its twisted girders and scallops lurking beneath. Unfortunately, our anchor then became stuck at 125 feet and I volunteered to clear it. The visibility was now nearly nil and I was confused to find the anchor chain going through a small hole in the deck that could not possibly have let the anchor through. Finally, I found a narrow gap in the metal sheeting of the deck along which the chain must have dragged. I worked to free it from the hole and then went down to the anchor in the darkness to manhandle it up and over the side of the wreck. It was exhausting work, but eventually came free.

A last dive with Jan, south of the famous Old Man of Hoy rock and we were homeward bound to Thurso at the end of a week of wonderful weather and the magic views of selchies and guillemots underwater and a million magnificent birds.

Early next morning we arrived back, and I jumped into my Opel Manta and drove 380 miles without stopping to see my new girl friend at her family home near Shrewsbury. I had met Janie at an election party in London. After the usual introduction, she had asked me if Reg was short for something else. Rather unwillingly I disclosed, the not surprising information, that it was an abbreviation of Reginald. She laughed and later explained apologetically that in her childhood home they had had a rabbit called Reginald and she had never met anyone with the name since.

She was small, blonde and extremely lively (Jane, not the rabbit) and had been a nurse, midwife and the owner of a nursing agency. It wasn't long before I enticed her back to my little cottage in Mortlake. She called me 'Reginald Rabbit'.

Peter Cornish had written to me asking for my help to get a Winston Churchill Memorial Scholarship to finance his leadership of the expedition to try to solve the mystery of the missing midget submarine, X-5 in the Norwegian arctic. I was happy to help with this and also with another grant from the World Expeditionary Association and became so interested in the story of the disappearance, that I asked to join the expedition as a member.

Before leaving, we met Admiral Godfrey Place VC, the only X-craft commander who had taken part in the operation and was still alive, who came to my office to brief us. He was extremely modest and referred to the difficulties they had had in controlling their buoyancy, partly due to the amount of fresh water coming into the fiord, an unexpected complication.

X-5 had disappeared back in 1943. It was on a sunny morning and the smooth surface of Kaafjord, 400 miles north of the Arctic Circle glinted. From the trees above the fiord, a group of Norwegians could hear the early morning noises coming from the giant ship that lay motionless below them. She was a beautiful sight, the biggest, sleekest battleship in the world; 56,000 tons of impregnability and power and the pride of the German Navy.

The time was 7 a.m., the date September 22nd 1943 and the ship, the *Tirpitz*. Captain Hans Meyer, tall and thin with blue eyes and bushy eyebrows, was just finishing breakfast. He had commanded the *Tirpitz* and its crew of 2,300 since February and was confident of the power and efficiency of his ship. She was not a match, of course, for the British Home Fleet with their greater numbers, air support and efficient radar. It was for this reason that Hitler and his Naval Commander-in-chief, Admiral Raeder, had decided to keep them immobile in this fiord, tying up the British fleet who feared his occasional forays out into the North Atlantic menacing our vital convoys to Russia.

Winston Churchill could not tolerate the existence of a battleship more powerful than any of His Majesty's ships. He had given the order to 'sink the *Tirpitz*' in January 1942, adding that 'the whole strategy of the war turns at this point on this ship.' He discussed the methods of destroying 'the beast', as he called her, with the First Sea Lord. Bomber Command and carrier borne aircraft were both used, but the unique armour, steel fifteen inches thick on her sides and eight inches over the deck, together with an efficient smoke screen, had prevented serious damage. The next line of attack would be human torpedoes or midget submarines.

Captain Meyer had little cause for anxiety that morning. He had four batteries of anti-aircraft guns on the surrounding hills, a considerable armament on his own ship, a new smoke-laying apparatus that could hide this ship in three minutes and minefields off the coast and nets surrounding him. Suddenly the door opened and his second-in-command's head appeared. 'Sorry to disturb you, sir, but a look-out has sighted an object inside the nets. A small submarine, he says.'

For nearly three years, before the air attacks started, Royal Navy scientists had been working on a device that could pass through all the German defences to place bombs under the *Tirpitz* and escape. It would be a miniature submarine, small enough to cross minefields that started only 15 feet below the surface, but strong enough to dive to 300 feet and versatile enough to avoid detection, cut through nets and travel submerged for 36 hours, with a range of 300 miles. In March 1942 the prototype was launched and soon after the first six operational 'X-craft' arrived from Vickers, numbered X-5 to X-10.

They were 48 feet long, weighed 39 tons and the maximum diameter was only five and a half feet. In every place except directly under the periscope, a man had to crouch, sit, squat or crawl. They were run by batteries underwater and on the surface by a 40-hp London bus engine. There was a small 'wet and dry' chamber that could be flooded to allow a diver to leave the sub. The crew consisted of a Captain, helmsman, engineer and diver. Along the whole length of each side were detachable charges, each containing two tons of Amatex high explosive with a clockwork time fuse.

A call had gone out for volunteers. The first was a quiet 26-year-old Scot, Donald Cameron, a Royal Navy Reserve Lieutenant who was soon joined by three more crew. They took over X-6.

The next recruit was Sub-Lieut. Godfrey Place, the only RN career officer among the volunteers. He was 'short, dapper and dark and already a veteran of submarines'. He was also known to be 'incredibly cool under pressure', having won the DSC on a previous operation. He took over X-7 and its crew.

X-5 was commanded by a very different figure, a young red-haired Australian, 'Tiger' Henty-Creer, an ex-film director from the RN Reserve.

It was decided that the X-craft, manned by passage crews, would be towed across the North Sea by full size submarines. Off the coast of Norway their operational crews would take over and motor the craft under their own power through the 50 miles of mined and closely guarded fiords to the *Tirpitz*.

X-6 and X-7 had perilous crossings with many breakdowns, and Godfrey Place used his foot to push off a German mine that was tangled in his towline. On the evening of September 20th, they cast off from their parent subs and set off through the minefields. The plan was to attack, escape and meet up again with their parent submarines three days later.

They got through the first minefields by night and took shelter at the Bratholm

Islands, only a few miles away from *Tirpitz*. In the early hours, they all set course to cover the final most dangerous part of the attack, through the nets to the battleship (*see front endpaper map*).

Misting periscopes and unreliable compasses forced them to surface several times, but Godfrey Place in *X-7* slipped through the gap in the anti-submarine boom at the entrance to Kaafjord on the surface in the early dawn. He dived and was caught by anti-submarine nets. He had a long struggle and finally surfaced with compass and trim pump out of action, to see *Tirpitz* only 30 yards away in bright sunshine.

Meantime Donald Cameron in *X-6* was also travelling blind with a fogged periscope. The boom at the entrance to the fiord was closed when he arrived an hour later at 04.45. As he watched, it opened to let a coaster through, and he took a chance and followed through on the surface. The *Tirpitz* was now two miles ahead of him and Cameron continued on compass and managed to force his way through the surrounding nets, only to crash into an uncharted rock. Caught in nets again, *X-6* broke loose and shot to the surface out of control just 60 feet off the port bow of *Tirpitz*.

The warship's crew were finally taking notice and machine gun bullets rattled off the hull and then the boom of depth charges could be heard. Cameron gave his last orders and the tiny, incapacitated X-craft scraped against the hull of the *Tirpitz*, too close for secondary armament to be brought to bear. He released his mines and they slid to the bottom with their automatic clock set for one hour.

Cameron then had to move fast. 'Open the pumps, destroy equipment and get out on the deck with your hands up.' As the water rose inside the crew stepped out on to the tiny deck and into a waiting German picket boat. The Germans put a line on *X-6*, but to their horror it began to sink beside them.

Fifteen minutes before, Godfrey Place had also got into position and released his charges and then tried to get away. Almost immediately he was stuck in a net. Minutes later they slid over the top of it, and machine gun bullets bounced off their hull. Back at the bottom, depth charges started bursting around them and their compass and diving gauges were out of action. Place tried to escape on the surface, but it was hopeless. Each time he came up, *X-7* was hit and he realised he would have to abandon ship.

He knew that as soon as he re surfaced, he would become a target, and decided that he would be the first to take the risk of leaving the craft. He waved his white sweater out of the hatch and leaped after it, shouting, 'Here goes the last of the Places'. He was met by a hail of bullets and shells. Miraculously he was not hit and managed to swim to a nearby gunnery target. When he turned round, *X-7* had disappeared! She bottomed at 120 feet, her vents opened.

Bob Aitken, the diver in the crew, instructed the others on how to put on their Davis escape gear that included a small oxygen cylinder which would give them a limited time to breathe. They then had to wait for the water to rise and equalise the pressure so that they could escape. The icy sea rose very slowly in the submarine, covering first ankles and then knees. When it was up to their thighs, an electric current blew, and filled the interior with smoke and fumes and plunged them into darkness.

They had to start breathing from their sets, conserving the oxygen as long as possible. Bob Aitken tried to open the hatch, but the pressure was still too great outside. His oxygen bag was nearly empty and he felt for the other two to help. Whitley, the third crew member was close beside him, but his bag was flat, and Aitken realised he was already dead. He could not reach the further member and with his last few breaths, struggled alone with the hatch in the darkness. He passed out. The next thing he remembered was a stream of bubbles around him as he shot to the surface. He was picked up by the Germans and delivered, shaken and haggard, but breathing, to the *Tirpitz*.

The survivors clustered together, saying nothing. Eventually Captain Meyer sent down coffee and schnapps for them. The charges were still quietly ticking away on the sea bed beneath them. Suddenly their knees buckled as the exploding Amatex blew the mighty battleship five feet upwards. Steam gushed from broken pipes, oil quickly covered the fiord, and injured German sailors were brought up from below. The *Tirpitz* heeled to port, still afloat, but crippled. Suddenly there was a stir on board and X-5 broke surface to port. The 35mm and 105mm guns opened up and X-5's stern rose and she disappeared in an eddy of foam.

For Godfrey Place, Donald Cameron and the survivors of X-6 and X-7 the war was over. They were transferred to a German Navy prison camp. When the war finished in 1945, Cameron and Place returned to receive the Victoria Cross from King George VI for 'pressing home their attack with courage, endurance and utter contempt for danger.' No trace was found of X-5 or Henty-Creer or his crew.

The years went by and the mystery of the whereabouts of X-5 was slowly forgotten, except by the families of its crew. Henty-Creer's mother and two sisters researched the operation and became convinced that X-5 must have pressed home her attack and laid her charges before surfacing.

They argued that when the 56,000 ton battleship had lifted out of the water, some Norwegian observers had reported that her propellers had come out too. Cameron had laid his charges under the bow, Place amidships and Henty-Creer had planned to lay his under the stern. He had not received a posthumous VC, and they felt he deserved this recognition. Such an award might hang on what we found on our expedition.

After his previous successful lifts, Peter Cornish had become interested in the *X-5* story and the possibility of finding the remains of the sub. He was encouraged by Henty's sister, Pamela and her husband Colonel Gerrard Mellor. He did some trial dives in Kaafjord, but found nothing at the spot where the Germans had reported that *X-5* had sunk.

He began to organise a 16-man expedition and the provision of side-scan sonar, Decca 'sea-fix', and the latest proton magnetometer. He got sponsorship from Fine Fare, diving companies, Comex (UK) and the Imperial War Museum. All the diving equipment, search instruments and tents had to be transported by ship to Alta, 400 miles into the Arctic circle in the extreme morth of Norway.

A number of the divers came from Hampstead branch and were members of Peter's 'octopush' underwater hockey team. Jock White and Joan Lamb who had been with me in the Hebrides were also there, and some members of RAF branches and a young member of the US Air Force who had volunteered as expedition cook.

As the expedition left London airport we were warned about the virulent Arctic mosquitoes and issued with tablets to deter them. After a brief stop in Oslo, where at a briefing session, I was 'put in charge of relations with Mrs Mellor', we took off again into a pink sunset. 'This sun will not set tonight', announced the Captain as we flew north into the 24 hours of daylight of the Arctic summer. We arrived at Alta after changing planes at two in the morning and then drove to Kaafjord to begin assembling the tents. It took till 5 a.m.

Kaafjord was a beautiful sight, with plunging green mountainsides, topped with snow and mirrored in the calm clear waters of the fiord. Arctic terns swooped around us as we worked and light rain showers blotted out the sun. I grabbed some sleep at 8 a.m.

We were joined by Nigel Kelland, an expert on side-scan sonar, and Lindsay Cole, ex-Australian Navy whose previous experience with X-craft would prove valuable.

Along the shore, close by the camp, twisted metal girders still rose out of the grass – the mooring posts of *Tirpitz*. Her old berth had been next to our tents. Relics of the giant ship, forks and pottery decorated with swastikas were still about, as were the remains of German smoke canisters .

I did my first dive that evening with John Harris, the Hampstead DO on the wreck of the tug *Badenfeld* which had been serving the battleship. It looked unreal in the half light. The water temperature was seven degrees centigrade, only a few degrees colder than British seas, although it felt icy.

The next morning the cook was already in denial. We survived two pieces of 'cinnamon' toast and no coffee or tea for breakfast. As there were no washing or toilet facilities we began to dig locations for them. I began to think that the information

I had received about the Arctic summer had been unduly optimistic. The cold rain persisted and after foraging around, we found a battered metal stove left by the Germans.

Underwater we were already beginning to collect plaice and flounders to supplement our frugal diet. I volunteered to help Nigel Kelland with the preliminary survey work. On my second dive with our erstwhile cook we became aware of the halicline, or fresh water layer. The river flowing into the fiord produced strange 'oily' effects that were disorienting. At other times the fresh water mix produced a visual effect as if we were surrounded by fine fishing nets. It was extremely weird.

The expedition had hired a local skipper with a small fishing boat and its tiny cabin and deck were soon stacked with our Decca and side-scan gear. Two Decca 'slave stations' were set up on the shore and Nigel explained his plans to traverse up the fiord along set lines. We searched for wood and constructed transit line markers which we painted red and green. The skipper lined up on them, but we later found that he was colour blind!

The large containers had arrived before us at the camp site, but didn't seem to contain food. We dined off fresh flounders from the fiord but the supply was running out. The weather continued wet and miserable. We were issued with a crate of whisky each from a sponsor, not perhaps the most suitable drink at this time. It resulted in some young members spending the 24 hours of light drinking on the hillside where we feared that if they fell asleep, they might die of exposure.

A few days later the weather did finally improve and we glimpsed occasional sun. When it appeared, so did the arctic mosquitos. They were like no others I had known, and quite capable of biting through a woollen sweater.

On the morning of 26th June I dived with Nigel on the site of the disappearance of *X-5*. We found wreckage – 'rods' and girders and remains of a hull. Peter checked later and decided that it was too large to be an X-craft.

The next day I dived with Jock on the site where the *Tirpitz* had been anchored. It was no longer there, as the Germans had moved the crippled battleship south to Trondhem after the attack. We found a featureless silt plain with occasional starfish and more smoke canisters.

After lunch, Pam and Gerrard Mellor arrived with her sister Deirdre, and Jack Owen from the *Daily Telegraph* put in a brief appearance. I worked with Nigel and Peter on the survey and fixed new points along the fiord at 30-yard intervals with Peter, Tony Speight, Tim Ayres and Bjorn, our local translator. The survey runs began and very soon anomalies were being marked on Nigel's master chart and buoys flung over. The side-scan sketched out details of wrecks on the bottom. We dived to investigate each anomaly.

Breakfast now consisted of cereal, and bread and jam with a lunch of soup and bread and cheese. Dinner was fish with a few potatoes and tinned tomatoes. I began to have a lot of sympathy with Oliver Twist and found myself secreting bits of cheese and bread in a plastic bag in case the supply ran out. I was now in charge of the shore party and equipped with a 'walkie-talkie' radio, assistants, two targets, tent pegs and hammers. We set up the targets against the pegs and Nigel supervised the skipper in lining up.

By the 29th, the survey was in full swing and Nigel and his team could place each anomaly within a few feet and give us information on its size, shape and depth. The divers checked them each day, but there was still no sign of X-5.

That night at midnight the sky lightened and the clouds cleared away. By 1 a.m. the sun began to shine on the mountain tops. We decided to dive and I ran out in our inflatable with Nigel over a flat calm sea. We dived at the centre of the *Tirpitz* position where an anomaly had showed up. It turned out to be anti-torpedo nets. The sea was so clear that we could see our boat 130 feet above us.

The next morning I was on compressor duty, a deafening operation, as the silencer was not working. In the afternoon I laid more lines while avoiding dive-bombing mosquitoes. I was invited for drinks with Pam and Gerrard who had now pitched a small tent some distance away and we talked about the original operation. They told me that, apart from the circumstantial evidence of the ship's stern being seen, they felt that it would be unlikely that 'Henty' would have approached the target for the first time when he was seen, as he would have known that the other charges were due to go off then. More likely, they thought, that he was trying to get away after laying his charges. Even more interestingly, a Norwegian sea-captain had sworn on an affidavit that he had seen a periscope returning up the fiord the day after the attack. Other observers had reported seeing a man 'standing on a log' (which an X-craft resembled) and moving into Sternsund Cove, 10 miles north of Kaafjord which was a proposed possible repair site, which the intelligence officer who had briefed the crews said Henty had been particularly interested in.

John Owen and Mike Nicholson (ITV *News at Ten*) appeared together with Dr Chris Rhodes, a well-known diver and Deputy Director of the Imperial War Museum. Daily reports on our progress were now being printed in the *Telegraph* and interviews with the Mellors and Peter were shown on *News at Ten*.

On the morning of July 4th, high winds and torrential rain hit the camp and penetrated most of the tents, delaying diving and depressing morale. Some of the local Norwegian divers from the 'Draugen' club had now joined us and Jens Aassved arranged a free visit to a sauna and indoor pool in Alta that was much appreciated.

The weather slowly improved again and we carried on diving. The wind was freezing as we continued fixing pegs for the transit lines. The cook had decided that he no longer wanted to cook, and Joan Lamb filled the breech. Due to the shortage of food, we tried harpooning the wolf fish (*Anarhichas lupus*) on the bottom. They were ugly and very aggressive with nasty curving teeth. On the plate, we found them full of bones.

After diving on the 7th, more Norwegians from the diving club arrived and we held a party. Some time later at 1 a.m., Lindsay suggested that the two of us went waterskiing as the sun came up over the water. It was flat calm with early sun and shadows streaking the cliffs. He towed me for a mile skiing up the fiord, an experience I will never forget. My coordination was probably not improved by the drink inside, but I kept dry most of the time, before changing places with him and driving the inflatable back again. We rejoined the party, and discovered that two of the Norwegians had brought some 'moonshine' with them. This was homemade spirit allegedly 95% alcohol. John Harris and Brian King found themselves suffering from 'butter legs'.

The next day we saw our first real sun of the summer and everyone changed into swimming trunks. Time was running out but there was still no trace of *X-5* among the hundred or so anomalies studding the master chart. Peter wanted experienced deep divers to check the deeper sites and on July 9th I checked the deepest of them at 165 feet with Peter and John Harris. Peter said he had a feeling that something would be found that day. He was right, but we didn't find it. He had asked for some of the anomalies to be re-checked and Lindsay reported that he had seen what appeared to be the nose cone of a submarine. The position was in the middle of the fiord roughly between the points where *X-7* and *X-5* had last been seen. Excitement mounted.

If it was an X-craft, which one was it? *X-6* had been scuttled under the *Tirpitz* and destroyed in the explosion. At least half of *X-7* had been recovered by the Germans, and a Norwegian had reported that it included the bow. Other members examined the site but because of our deep dive, we could not return for several hours.

We dived it at 10 p.m. While Peter examined the bow, John and I explored further afield and suddenly came upon a long, narrow wrecked hull that I estimated was 20 feet long. It was remarkably similar to the wreckage I had previously found but which had been dismissed as 'too large for an X-craft'. We laid a line to it from the nose cone.

On our return to the surface, Peter announced that he had positively identified the nose cone as belonging to an X-craft and the following day also identified our further discovery as part of the same vessel. There were no signs of the submarine's charges, and the extensive damage it had sustained seemed to have been caused by shells or depth charges. We surmised that if its charges of Amatex had still been in position, they would have been set off by the explosions and the whole submarine would have disintegrated. The implication was that if this was *X-5*, the probability was that she had already laid charges under *Tirpitz*. I dived the wreckage again with John on the 10th July in 70 feet visibility. After the dive Peter asked me to phone the *Daily Telegraph*, ITN, the *Daily Mirror*, *The People* and the *Birmingham Post* all of whom had been covering our story.

We continued to dive on the wreckage and on the 11th, Jens and I found a diver's rubber boot and lead sheeting from batteries. The batteries were in the forward section of the X-craft, which was further proof that we had found a bow section.

After much discussion, it was decided to raise the smaller bow section to the surface for more accurate photography. A huge lifting bag was manoeuvred into position. It was slowly filled using spare air cylinders. The minutes ticked by and a frothy patch began to form on the surface. Suddenly the huge red buoy exploded through, closely followed by the working divers. The nose cone lay, gently rocking beneath. After photography, it was returned to the seabed for later lifting, if permission was forthcoming. Peter sent a cable announcing that he believed that we had found the remains of *X-5*.

There was a widespread air of achievement, but I was having doubts about the reports of what had been sent to Germany. Other reports now mentioned that it had included the prop of the craft and I became increasingly convinced that we had found *X-7*. I discussed these doubts with Peter and sadly, much later they proved to be justified.

So the expedition ended. Peter was asked by the Imperial War Museum to recover all the remains which he did during a subsequent expedition a year or so later. Sadly the chance of a posthumous VC for 'Tiger' Henty-Creer was still as far away as ever. The Kaafjord Expedition had, however, proved the capabilities of well-trained club divers to undertake major projects. Peter's drive and leadership had ensured this.

When Jane met me at London Airport, her first words were 'You look as though you've been in Belsen'. She proceeded to fatten me up.

CHAPTER ELEVEN

From the Ascrib Islands to Annaba

M**Y DIVORCE WAS NOW OFFICIAL**, and I had asked Janie to marry me. She said 'Yes'. Our main problem then was finding suitable dates between our many commitments. We finally chose Friday 13th of September 1974, invited 13 people to the reception and moved into a new home, numbered 13, a mere stone's throw from the cottage I had previously rented in Mortlake.

Vernon was our best man and managed to sign the register in the wrong place – so I almost married him by mistake. My brother John, Harriette and Pete, Harry Gould and Stan were all at the small reception.

We left next day for Fort Bovisand, where I was examining on a weekend instructor's event. Alan Bax and Jim Gill were now running the fort as a successful diving centre and Alan put us up as his guests in his flat at the top of the fort. Janie now had a smart tailor-made wet suit and asked me if I would take her on a shallow trial dive in the harbour.

Mike 'Bus' who was running the event gave me 'passionate leave' on the Sunday afternoon and I was briefing her on the foreshore when he appeared with the candidates and other examiners. 'Ah,' he said, 'What have we here? An instructor briefing a pupil. Let's listen to what he has to say.' 'Get in now', I whispered to Janie, and we disappeared from view. The dive was uneventful and enjoyed by my new pupil. When we came out, she said 'I was surprised at how noisy "the silent world" was'. I then told her that Jim's underwater explosives course was operating in the next bay.

Only a few weeks later, I was on my way to America with Mike and Vernon where we had been invited to take part in the IQ6 conference in California. First we flew to New York to arrange instructor exams for our new branch in Peconic Bay on Long Island. Greenport, where they were based was an old whaling village with white wood houses and an old cannon in the centre. The branch was enormously hospitable and we enjoyed diving with toad fishes before leaving for Gloucester, Mass. where we stayed with a diving magazine editor and dived again with lobsters, flounders, angler fish, sand dollars and hermit crabs.

We flew on to 'The Village of Mackinaw City' on the Great Lakes and went down with Indianapolis branch on some of the largest fresh water wrecks in the world, the *Cedarville* and the *Minneapolis*.

On to California, where, during the conference in San Diego, our NAUI friends arranged for us to dive in the giant kelp forest. It was my first dive in the Pacific. We were given a small launch crewed by a muscled NAUI instructor as skipper and a beautiful blonde NAUI instructor as mate.

The giant kelp is the fastest growing plant in the world reaching up to 150 feet high. It grows nearly 18 inches each day. They say that if you watch it very closely, you can actually see it growing before your eyes. The seaweed surface was not particularly inviting, but once through it was like being in a submerged pine forest. We swam down the giant 'trunks', through bands of sunlight, on to what looked like a 'forest floor', populated by tiny striped 'garibaldis', abalone mussels and nudibranchs. We collected the abalone for a later 'clam bake' on board. At the end of the dive, we swam in across the stern which had been lowered to just below water level, lying on it like beached whales. The skipper then sprang forward, unclipped our cylinders and replaced them with new ones. Meanwhile the beautiful blonde gently opened each of our mouths and put a slice of ice-cold water-melon between our dry lips. We gratefully munched before being pushed off backwards to continue the dive. 'Bus' was heard to mutter: 'Too much of this could be bloody fantastic.'

During the following months, between conferences, meetings and banquets, Janie continued her training with London branch and we dived together at Challaborough in Devon in May 75. On my return I introduced a series of programmes on Radio 4 under the title of *Secrets of the Deep* and completed the sections on diving and its history in the *Oxford Companion to Sports and Games*. The Club still had a 14% growth rate which was unequalled by any other sport.

The new BSAC chairman, Kendall McDonald, and I, were invited by Alex McKee to see the progress on the *Mary Rose* and went down on the 23rd of June. The *Mary Rose*, had been built in 1509, and sunk in 12 metres of water in 1545 in full view of Henry VIII during an excursion by the French into the Solent. Although the pioneering Deane brothers had rescued cannons from her in the early nineteenth century, Mac McKee had had to search again in 1965 to re-find the wreck. When he finally did find it, under the silt bottom, it became clear that most of the starboard side had been perfectly preserved by the silt.

When we arrived, the support vessel, a small catamaran called *Roger Grenville*, that had been presented by a local businessman, was already out over the wreck. We went out to her and were welcomed by Mac. Margaret Rule was also on board, checking divers' reports, and munching cheese sandwiches. The weather had been good and Mac reported the underwater visibility as 12 feet. We dived on to a line of wood posts, part of the port side of the ship. There were also larger blocks, part of the transom, being uncovered by his divers using suction pumps. A few weeks later the Club's president, Prince Charles, did his first dive on the site.

We had arranged for the last of my series of expeditions to the Hebridean out-liers in July. The final goal lay forty-four miles north-east of the Butt of Lewis, the most isolated, uninhabited and inaccessible of all the outer islands, North Rona, also sometimes known as the Isle of Seals. It had a macabre history. The original inhabitants had died out many years before, but in the 1880s, two men from Ness in Lewis had exiled themselves there following a religious quarrel. Eleven months later, they were found dead, from natural causes and exposure and exhaustion.

It had been visited again in 1940, during the Second World War by RAF air-men recovering a crashed Whitley bomber. The small party camped in the long-deserted village of dark, stone houses, built three feet into the ground as protection against the continually roaring winds. They explored a number of old cave-like ruins. In the windowless depths of one, they made out a dark form. The light of a torch picked out the body of a German naval officer in full uniform including cap, sitting upright against a wall. How had he got there? Had he been landed to report on British convoy movements? Had his U-boat not returned to pick him up, leav-ing him to die of starvation? The RAF buried him beneath the floor.

Twelve years later, two visiting ornithologists followed a sea bird into one of the old homes. Peering with a torch through the darkness, they found a skull lying on the floor. Examining it, they came to the conclusion that it was of no great age. The teeth were in good condition. Why was it lying there? Whose skull was it? Next morning they buried it under the turf before leaving. Six years later re-visiting, they decided they should disinter it and perhaps search for the rest of the skeleton. They could find no trace of it.

We would be the first to dive there and had again chosen *Pentland Wave* to make the voyage. Janie and I drove 800 miles to Scrabster to join her and the other ex-pedition members from Salford branch. The leaders this time were Jan and Dave Chapman and the others included Peter Schofield, Tim Hatch, Paul Croome, Ian Nicol and Paul Hardy. At the last minute, my old friend Stan Hayward joined us, though he had had little experience of diving in British waters. We planned a warm-up dive in Loch Erribol, 50 miles west of Cape Wrath, and sailed in the early afternoon, expecting a smooth trip along the coast. Wind and tide built up and we were soon pitching and rolling and lashing down our air cylinders.

After a while, some of us began to change colour and the black-backed gulls sur-rounding us, screamed enthusiastically as the remains of lunch left from the rails. Janie and the two Pauls were the only ones unaffected. We finally turned into the calm of the loch and the more hardy dived in the twilight, collecting scallops. The next day, watched by seals, Jane, Stan and I did our first dive amid hermit crabs, scallops, sea pens and whelks. Stan found a large roseate lump sucker guarding her eggs and *Luidia* and *Henricia* starfish, doubtless attracted by the scallops.

The forecast was good and we left for Rona soon after 6 a.m. North Rona had been described as 'the loneliest of the isles of Britain once inhabited, with an area of 300 acres, about a quarter being occupied in the breeding season by grey seals, forming the largest population of the species in the world.' We climbed the long Atlantic swells on a course NW by W, passing puffins sitting on the sea and fulmars, gulls and whirling guillemots above. We watched the gannets, with their six-foot wing spans, beating up wind, immaculate in black and white with yellow and black heads. At midday, we could see Rona on the horizon, looking like a huge bull seal, remote and menacing.

The hours passed, and our excitement grew as we approached this last, most impressive and most remote isle. We decided to dive the high cliffs and caves on the west side. They are formed of Lewisian gneiss, the oldest known rock in the world. Fascinated guillemots and gulls watched us as we went in.

It was a pleasure to relax and crash through the surface in a cloud of bubbles. Janie and I sank down until a dark bottom came into view at 60 feet. I remembered that killer whales were often here, attracted by the pupping seals, but we saw only yellow alcyoniums, sponges and tiny daisy anemones. Lobsters and crabs scuttled amid the rocks and, in the kelp were tiny delicate nudibranchs and flatworms.

Anchoring later off the east of the isle, Janie and I climbed 300 feet up the steep grassy slope to the top of the island. Baby black-backed gulls cowered in holes in the turf as we passed, and their parents began to dive-bomb us. At first, we tried to ignore them, but their screeching rushes got closer to our heads, and we were relieved to get over the crest and see the remains of the sinister village below us.

The original inhabitants, some 30 islanders, had lived here, and the earliest account of them dates from the middle of the sixteenth century. It mentions them as 'a simple people, scant of ony religione who catch whales and others grate fisches.' The families eked out a living through the centuries, growing barley, pasturing sheep, and collecting seabird feathers. Towards the end of the seventeenth century, a plague of rats had devoured the islanders' corn and hungry seamen landed and stole the island's only bull. As a result, the entire population perished. The island was re-populated, but the numbers dwindled, until by 1814 only one family remained. They were evacuated in 1844.

We stumbled down the steep turf slope, into the long deserted village of low stone huts cut into the hillside. In one old house we found a millwheel and in an inner room in darkness, a solitary fulmar squirted oil at us from its beak. We saw a ruined chapel, supposedly built by St Ronan early in the 8th century. In a disused graveyard was a solitary modern gravestone, recording the two Ness men who had died here in 1884.

As we came back down the slope, chased by the angry gulls, we counted seventy sheep grazing. We boarded our inflatable and drove back to *Pentland Wave*, watched by razorbills, puffins, fulmars and seals.

Diving in these waters was like visiting another planet. We went down a cliff face of wildly swinging and rippling kelp into a deep gulley and a dream world of anemones, cup corals and multi-coloured vegetation. A baby octopus jet-propelled itself away and then wound its legs around a kelp plant, changing colour to resemble it. At 100 feet, a huge rock formed an underwater island, covered in a mass of anemones. We slowly swam back up the slope, watching the huge swells bursting down towards us from the surface as the waves hit the sheer rock wall. A small white form was rolling in the surf, a young seal, playing effortlessly and gracefully in the waves. We edged closer, unwilling to leave.

It was a difficult night, rolling at the inadequate anchorage, and, after breakfast, we were forced to make for Sule Sgeir, ten miles to the west. We circled the islet, but the wind was freshening to Force 5 and we reluctantly set course for Stornoway, and an afternoon dive in a bay on the Eye peninsula where the water teemed with dogfish, pollack, sea hares and millions of brittle stars.

We berthed in Stornoway, and looked-up Horace and Annetta, who immediately arranged a mini-ceilidh with James, the local singer and a school teacher who, shaking my hand, said: 'I remember you; a diver of great note, and a guitarist of some promise.' I was suitably flattered. Much later we arrived back on board with bottles of whisky and cointreau, which we drank in the late evening light as a 'tame' seal surfaced alongside and watched us across the smooth dark water.

The next day, we ran southwards to the Shiants and dived off Mary's Island where we found cushion stars and an enormous spiny starfish nearly three feet across. Acting as boat cover off Home Island, I was mesmerised by the thousands of guillemots, cormorants and fulmars swirling above me. We visited the small house that was in good repair, with a sign reading 'Shiant Isles' on the door. From the saddle of the hills, we looked down on to dark rocks filled with seabird colonies, and gulls hanging a hundred feet below us with a smooth sea crawling beyond.

At midnight, *Pentland Wave*'s sister ship, *Pentland Firth*, arrived in the bay with a party of divers aboard. Their skipper asked us if we had any water or food he could have. Our crew asked why he couldn't go up to Stornoway only two hours away. 'They won't let us', he complained, 'We have to go night and day'. Much later, I discovered that their party was organised by Gordon Ridley, a new 'super-human' driving force who was to take me as far as Iceland in future years.

After diving the Galtachean rocks, we made for Uig on Skye for the night, and then set sail over a silky calm sea for the Ascrib Isles. Close in, our echo sounder still read 50 fathoms. We anchored and I dived with Jan down to 100 feet past lion's mane jellyfishes. An unexpected current surprised us, and we fought our way back, through rocks covered with plumous anemones, alcyoniums and siphonophores. Back on board, we ate crab sandwiches, soup and cakes and relaxed under a hot shower as *Pentland Wave* crossed Loch Snizort, bound for Loch Maddy and then, hopefully, St Kilda again.

Next morning, a pilot in a small green fishing boat took us through the Sound of Harris passed porpoises and sitting auks. The gannets led us on to St Kilda and we again dived at Stac Lee where seals followed us underwater like friendly dogs. After a night at anchor in Village Bay, we took a party from the National Trust for Scotland to Soay islet to make a puffin count. We waited for them in our inflatable watching the thousands of puffins strutting over the islet like little overweight dancers, occasionally rubbing each other's beaks affectionately. They took long runs on the sea to take off, like overloaded airliners. I watched two of them flying by in different directions and they both turned their heads to look at the strange humans on their island and collided in a mass of feathers in mid-air. I imagined the gannets, soaring above, laughing derisively at their discomforture.

Returning to Village Bay, we found that a submarine, HMS *Rorqual*, had surfaced beside us. We were invited on board for a tour and hospitality. The Captain was surprised to learn that there was an Army outpost in the bay. The inter-service liaison seemed to be somewhat lacking.

In the following days, we dived Glen Bay on the north coast of Hirta where the remains of ancient Viking habitations dotted the hillside, providing shelter for sheep, and off Soay in 'another world' of gulleys, anemones and cup corals. The evenings we spent with the Officer Commanding St Kilda, drinking his beer and watching an oyster catcher on his lawn stabbing with its beak for grubs.

Soon the weather was breaking. We headed out past the Flannans to Gallan Head, where we had lost our rudder with Boyd, and into East Loch Roag. The next day the sea was amazingly calm again and we made for the Butt of Lewis and our best dive. From the surface, below the lighthouse, we could see the bottom 50 feet below with huge rocks covered in sponges, anemones and corals. We swam down and through crystal clear gulleys over innumerable crabs and passed huge shoals of pollack to where occasional dogfish weaved through the short kelp holdfasts. Deeper down, thousands of sand eels hung like a huge cloud in the water and lobsters walked stiffly over the bottom. A perfect dive.

We set course for Cape Wrath while dolphins played around us. The sea was now flat calm and we dived there with more seals. We moored in Kinlochbervie for the night and drank at the small hotel nearby. I spoke briefly to John Ridgeway at his outward bound school regretting that we would be unable to meet up with him as planned.

Our last day, and we dived at the isle of Am Balg, where nearly 100 seals were

hauled out on the rocks. Janie, Ian and I dropped through the surface to be surrounded by the ducking and rolling white bodies of the females. They were curious
and came up wide-eyed to take in every detail of our laboured progress. We swam
into a shallow rock bay and found that we had cornered a very young seal inside. It
was torn between curiosity and fear, and after a while put its head in a cleft, ostrich-
like, hoping we would go away. Janie swam closer and the baby seal actually came
up to her, gently nuzzled her face mask and stroked her with a flipper. Then it was
off like a rocket between her legs and out to sea again. Another wonderful dive during which time seemed to stand still. At last we set course for Thurso over a velvet
sea, again surrounded by dolphins rolling on to their sides to watch us above.

My ambition to dive the most isolated islets of the Hebrides had now been ful-
filled. St Kilda, the Flannans, Sule Skerry and North Rona had all been explored for
the first time. I carried away memories of 'the people of the sea', soft-eyed seals, and
friendly dolphins, beneath graceful gannets, whirling razorbills and comic puffins.
A world of magic diving animals, far away among the strange islands of the farthest
Hebrides.

A month later, Janie and I were back underwater, swimming with a young basking shark off Lundy and enjoying her first dive to 100 feet.

The CMAS World Congress was held in Stockholm in September, and Peter Cornish and I gave a combined presentation on the X-5 expedition. We explored one of
the last midget subs, still operated by the Swedish Navy and learnt a lot about the
limited amount of space that the crew had inside. In October, I was in Montreal for
the IQ Conference where we had the frustrating experience of waiting while every
word was translated into French although all the audience understood English.
I stayed with Ben Davis, the 'grand old man' of Canadian diving in his beautiful
home in the woods outside Toronto. The red and yellow of the autumn trees made
a lasting impression and the Canadian hospitality was second to none.

I had received an invitation to visit Jordan and to write a report for King Hussein on the possibility of the development of the sport there. Janie was also invited,
and we flew out first class on Royal Jordanian Airlines. On arrival we were hosted
by BSAC instructor, Conor Craig, who was attached to the University of Jordan.
Conor was somewhat eccentric and enjoyed chasing cats and driving us into the
desert and up a number of wadis in his four-wheel-drive jeep. Jordan only had a
short Red Sea coast, but we enjoyed diving with him amongst the tropical fish, clear
visibility and warm seas. We were also provided with an Army lorry, complete with
driver and armed guards. They seemed to take more interest in Janie changing than
in protecting us from unknown perils around.

As part of the report, we dived with the existing centres run by expatriate Dutch-
men and Germans along the coast. On a dive near the Saudi border we were sud-

denly approached by curious yellow-fin tuna, each about four feet long, and later dived with the King's brother-in-law, Taymour Daghistani on a bed of garden eels. On the 1st of December, I took Janie for her first night dive. At first apprehensive of sharks, she soon relaxed and enjoyed herself.

At the end of our time in Jordan, we were due to have an audience with the King, but he was unexpectedly delayed and we were waved off by Taymour and left for the airport surrounded by armed soldiers in an armoured car. It drove us direct to the airliner which had been kept waiting on the tarmac for us.

Not long after we got back, I got a phone call from 'big wheel' in Paris. Jean Paul Carrier announced that he was negotiating to take over a hotel at La Calle (or El Kala) on the Algerian/Tunisian border and asked if I would run a dive school for him there. I told him that I was no longer available, and he then asked if I would go out and do a report on its suitability for diving. December was a difficult month, but I managed to snatch a long weekend and tickets arrived from Paris with a short note from Jean Paul, mentioning that he hoped to meet the Algerian Minister of Tourism with me before my return. Algeria was not then a tourist destination, having been locked in fighting with the French for a number of years.

I took off into a clear blue sky on Sunday 7th December '75. On arrival at Orly, I was told that there was no such flight as the one that I had been booked on to Algiers. However, there was another Air Algerie flight at a similar time, so I was re-booked.

Air Algerie's idea of in-flight catering consisted of a number of sweet and sickly cakes, but I ate them, not having had anything since an early breakfast. Algiers airport was dark and forbidding. It was packed with screaming Arabs and queues of people. I had a desperate time collecting my baggage from the only carousel where the crowd clustered six deep fighting to get to the front. My shins were slowly garrotted against the turntable by pressure from behind, but I eventually got my case and carried it, battered and shaken to a customs official who was enthusiastically going through every item of baggage. 'Diving equipment?' I could see his eyes registering disbelief. I produced Jean Paul's letter that mentioned the Director of Tourism. There was no response. He picked out each object of equipment, asking what it was for. Finally he held up a neoprene bootee. 'And this?' 'To keep my left foot warm.'   Although true, this reply seemed to upset him. 'I won't pass any of it. You will have to see the Chief Inspector himself.'

A grim-looking door opens into a windowless room with a number of sinister figures in plain clothes. I can imagine blood-stains on the walls. I produce my letter and brightest smile. 'Just a little diving equipment for an important report for the good of Algerian tourism.' Blank looks. This was obviously outside their comprehension and experience.

As a last resort, I try out my few words of Tunisian Arabic. 'Barakaloufic' – 'may all that's good shine upon you'. There is a pause, followed by ecstatic laughter. 'Parle Arabe!' they gasp between bouts. I am escorted out through the waiting crowds.

The girl at 'Information' directs me to Sonatour, Jean Paul's agents. A smooth-looking Arab mans the desk. 'Who? Where? He looks at the letter and some light dawns. 'But, you have missed the connecting aircraft to Annaba.' 'The next? Eight tomorrow morning, but you will have to see the director first and that means an afternoon flight.' I realise that I am due to return the morning after.

After more negotiations and a half-hour wait, a more senior representative appears. He is all 'sweetness and light'. 'Welcome to Algeria'. By this time, I am wishing it was Siberia. 'You are fools and idiots', he shouts at the reps. 'Mr Vallintine's ticket is in the drawer there.' Ah, possibly, but no one can find the key. Eventually the air ticket emerges so my early plane is back on.

I am taken to the biggest hotel in Algiers, a sumptuous establishment, obviously built by the French. My bedroom has no less than three chandeliers, Louis XIV furniture, floor to ceiling mirrors, delicate writing desks and a variety of bells, knobs and switches to play with. I visit the *concierge* and try for an hour to convince him that La Calle and its new hotel exist. Later I go down, walking past scenes of French maritime history into the hotel restaurant. The only alcohol available is gin, martini or beer. I sleep in a huge double bed and am up at 6 a.m.

An excellent French breakfast and a driver arrives and I catch the flight to Annaba. We fly along the coast in bright sunshine and it is good to see the Mediterranean again. I feel I'm coming home. At the tiny airport of Annaba, I contact 'Information'. 'Yes, they were looking for you last night.' 'Who was looking? 'I don't know that.' I try to contact the hotel by phone without success. It is already 10.30 and I will have to dive today if I am to complete the report. I leap in a taxi, although warned that it is 40 kms to La Calle and it will cost more Algerian money than I possess. An hour later we finally arrive at the newly-built Moorish-style hotel on a shining white beach.

The reception clerk knows nothing, but, to my relief, the sub-manager does. 'Welcome to Algeria' he says, and, more importantly, agrees to pay off the taxi. 'Diving tanks?' 'No we don't have any.' 'Nobody told us.' 'We will try.' After further discussion, we have a stroke of luck. Sogetram, the French commercial diving company, is building a jetty nearby and employing a local diver.

It is 12 midday and the manager is encouraging. 'We will arrange things for 1 o'clock so that you get a dive this afternoon and use of our boat.' Sounds good, but I know it will be dark by five.

At one o'clock there is no sign of the manager or transport. I sling my dive bag over my shoulder and set off for the site of the jetty that is visible in the distance. I climb over sand dunes, through a river valley and up through huge concrete anti-erosion blocks. No manager, but I manage to speak to the diver. 'It is not possible to use the cylinders this afternoon, due to my work. Yesterday would have been fine, or this morning or tomorrow.' There is no moving him. Back at the hotel, I wonder whether I can risk changing my flights at short notice and also break the rules about not flying immediately after diving. I decide to do so.

The sub-manager agrees to take my tickets to Annaba at 6am and change them to the 1.30 flight. I relax and order a drink, 'Only gin, martini or beer.' I order all three and sample their 'out of season' menu of raw onions, tomatoes, olives and steak to a noisy accompaniment of thickly painted ladies singing endless songs of love on Algerian television. I sleep fitfully. No breakfast ready, so I shoulder my bag again and stagger out through the dunes. Unbelievably, the plan works, the diver is there with equipment and also the boat.

We chug out of harbour and they decide on a suitable site for me to examine the beauty of Algeria underwater. The diver announces that he will not after all be able to come with me as originally planned. He also tells me that 'the valve vibrates'. I nod cheerfully and jump off into the sea. The valve not only 'vibrates', but seizes up every few seconds. It sounds like a battery of clanging hooves. Eventually I get it to settle down and manage to get some evil tasting air through.

There is no sign of the bottom in the low visibility due to spoil tipping nearby. Eventually I find low rocks at 10 metres and start to see numbers of fishes including a four-foot grouper. At 15 metres there are caves and more groupers. Good news. The diving is as good as I remember it in Spain many years before. Back on the surface, I am relieved, delighted and feel my problems are over. Standing in the little port, I am approached by an Algerian naval officer. He is friendly, but says that we should really have got a permit to dive, in case I had an accident. I agree cheerfully, and leave.

Back at the hotel, I begin to pack. The phone rings. 'We have need of you in reception.' The *concierge* has a long face. 'You must go to the police station at once.' I am led to another sinister inner office. This time I am sure there are blood-stains on the walls. The chief of police announces that I have contravened Algerian law by diving without a permit. I smile, look as assured as possible, mention the Minister and even try my 'baracaloufic'. No result. I am passed to a junior official to give endless details of my ancestors including their middle names. Time is ticking by and I imagine my plane warming up. They let me out at 10am.

Back at the hotel again I quickly finish packing. The phone rings again. 'The Algerian navy wishes to speak to you at reception.' I contemplate disappearing over the back wall to find a taxi but decide I will probably be hunted down and shot. A long-haired Sub-lieutenant and a Commander, who looks like Charlie Chaplin in

159

a uniform two sizes too big. 'Do you know you have broken the law? Illegal diving and possession of maps of our country.' 'Why don't you come and see them?' I ask and take them to my room. I point out that the chart has 'From a British Admiralty survey 1933' printed on the bottom. They now suspect I have been engaged in espionage since then. I give them my letter and they take it away to the phone. I am finally released.

I jump into a taxi and arrive in Annaba to find that, miraculously, the deputy hotel director is there with my new ticket. I will only have fifteen minutes turn around time in Algiers though. My case can't go in the cabin. We arrive in Algiers and I run to the departure desk waving my ticket. I fill in yet another form and run on to customs. 'Just diving equipment.' 'Money? I've only got these dinars.' Although against the law to export them, they wave me through. I run on to the tarmac. The aircraft has its engines running just 20 yards away. They restrain me. 'No, you must go by bus.' I bite my nails and wait. It finally arrives and I am driven the 20 yards and run up the steps, subside into a seat. We take off.

How much did that one dive cost? I thought. Probably the biggest cost was taking about two years off my life. I pick up the Air Algerie magazine and read: 'There is an old Arab saying: He who goes too quickly does not come back.'

At that moment, I rather hoped so.

CHAPTER TWELVE

A Surfeit of Eels &
the Search for Red Maria

THE CLUB'S AGM IN 1976 was at Bournemouth. We had now formed branches in Italy, Holland, Borneo, Saudi-Arabia, Fiji, Libya, Abu-Dhabi, Nicaragua, Thailand and Japan. The Diving Officers' Conference attracted 622 delegates from 250 branches. Our formula for expansion seemed to be working well and there seemed to be no limit to the boundaries for the Club.

Janie and I began a two-year part-time course in marine biology for divers at City Poly. Their first excursion was to Bovisand where we dived in a fog, collecting and identifying specimens.

In May, a Swiss tour operator, specialising in travel for divers, invited me to look at their Red Sea operation. The Israelis had occupied the Red Sea coast down to the south of the Sinai. My new holiday manager, Maggie Witts was also invited, and I persuaded them to take Janie too.

We started at Eilat and met Hans Fricke, the distinguished Austrian biologist and author who had a caravan on the beach from which he studied a bed of garden eels offshore. He had a back problem, which Janie solved by jumping on him a couple of times. A landrover then whisked us further South to Dahab, or Di-Zahav, where we were accommodated at a bungalow hotel under palm trees and by the sea. Here we met Rubi Eviatar our 'safari guide', an ex-Israeli frogman and underwater photographer.

My secret ambition was to see Red Sea sharks, and so, whenever they were mentioned, I told Rubi that I did not believe that they had any. Jane was not too sure about sharks, but thought she should be all right, providing that they were not the 'evil-looking ones' (Hammerheads).

At Di-Zahav we swam down through shafts of sunlight illuminating the dark walls of 'the canyon', a vertical shaft through the reef with slowly turning shoals of fish. Three dives and 20 lagers later, we were on our way south again. 'Must get to those sharks', said Rubi. 'I'll believe it when I see them', said I.

Sharm-el-Sheikh was then a village with Howard Rosenstein running the only dive centre. He introduced us to giant bushes of gorgonia, a forest of soft corals and even black coral, but no sharks. Our goal was Ras Muhammed, the southern point where the bottom dropped out of the ocean, or at least, down to 3,000 feet. Rubi, now under pressure, warned us that we would have to get away from hotels and camp in the desert for three days, getting up at dawn to guarantee sharks. We enthusiastically agreed.

Rubi found a ruined hut in the desert with no roof or water, but just 10 minutes from Shark Reef. We soon discovered that there was another occupant, a snake, which was promptly dispatched by Rubi. We spread our sleeping bags on the sand outside the hut as we felt there might be less chance of rats or insects being at-tracted by our cooking. We bartered with the Bedouin for fish and cooked them over an open fire, or, at least, Janie and Maggie did. Hans Zimmerman the Swiss travel agent and I washed up, and Rubi gave advice. Our compressor chugged away outside.

Dawn broke and the camp stirred. Water was put on for a morning 'cuppa'. We took our jeep, with gear, and arrived at the beach as the sun was just creeping up over the still water. We picked our way across the reef and began to snorkel to con-serve our compressed air. The sea felt like warm silk and we eventually fitted our aqualung mouthpieces and dived down through shoals of batfish to the edge of the reef, as a turtle paddled away in the distance. Rubi signalled to us to sit quietly on the reef edge, looking out to sea over the abyss. I winked at Janie who was wide-eyed and pointing as the first shark climbed effortlessly towards us out of the blue distance. He was a beautiful sight with the sun glinting on the white tips of his fins. In the distance was another … and another. They seemed very aware of us but kept their distance.

The next morning we were back again, watching barracuda and jacks, when there was a movement at the limit of vision. A weaving evil-looking creature with a strange flat head tipped with malevolent eyes – a hammerhead. Janie's eyes were as big as saucers as a second and a third followed. They all banked and weaved to-gether before gliding out of sight. We were ecstatic.

I took my knife and banged on the rock, managing to attract the attention of the large amberjacks that swam closer to look; then suddenly the hammerheads were with us again. Rubi swam out towards them and they melted away in the blue.

Eventually we rose up and began the long return swim through the shallows. I noticed Maggie snorkelling above us in a white bikini. 'That should attract any marauding hammerheads', I thought unkindly. Our air got shorter as we swam up, against a strong current. I sensed that Janie was having problems keeping up with our super-fit frogman and watched her until she broke surface, and then arrived like magic, to take her weight belt off to make things easier. My stock went up 100% instantly and I lugged her belt back to the beach. A wonderful dive, the track of which would be followed by hundreds more divers in the years to come.

In the following days we continued to dive with Howard, sailing through endless shoals of barracuda down to crinoids and feather stars off Dahab and managing to stroke a sleeping parrot fish on a night dive.

Some days later I stood with Rubi looking across the Red Sea at four different countries, Egypt, Israel, Jordan and Saudi-Arabia that could all be seen from the same point. With a telescope you would have been able to pick out our dive sites in Jordan directly across the Gulf. Rubi said that they felt sympathy with King Hussein who they called 'little Husy'. I remembered just a few months before, standing with the King's brother-in-law, Taymour Daghistani, and looking back across at ships unloading at Eilat. 'We don't interfere with the Israelis', he said, 'Their oil is too important to them and our potash is too important to us'. Good diplomacy all round.

Our last days were spent paddling on top of the Dead Sea and through the colourful casbah of Jerusalem. The memory remained of weaving sharks and circling fish against the deep blue of a Red Sea, still largely unexplored by divers.

Later in 1976, Janie and I organised a trip to Malta with Bill and Edna Weale, Stan, and Maggie and Martin Marks. We dived in the 'blue grotto' and at Comino finding parrot fish and bristle worms that we had never seen in the Western Mediterranean. Near the blue grotto was a little museum of the sea. It was full of stuffed sharks. 'Where do you find them?' I asked. 'Filfla', was the reply.

Filfla lay on the horizon, a rocky islet looking like 'Bali Hai'. An old fisherman confirmed that many sharks were seen there and that it had been used for target practice by the RAF. It was difficult to get to, but I resolved to dive it at sometime in the future.

* * *

Our marine biology course at City Poly was continuing and in June, Janie and I left for a course of field work aboard the Club boat *British Diver* which had been chartered by Dr Paul Cragg, our teacher. The plan was to tour the Scillies, studying marine life and collecting specimens. We left Falmouth at 4 a.m. and arrived mid-morning, in time to dive off St Agnes with anemones, starfish and nudibranchs. We visited St Marys amid changeable weather and enjoyed a brief visit to the fairytale landscape of Tresco with its gardens, lakes and birdlife. There was a magnificent show of jewel anemones (*Corynactis*) off the West coast of St Martins, and we were surrounded by bottle-nosed dolphins. We dived on the site of the sinking of Sir Cloudesley Shovell's flagship, the *Association*, off the Outer Gilstone.

A month later, I was rolling backwards again into a gentle choppy sea some 100 miles further to the North East. I followed Mike, the dive leader, down from an improvised raft on the surface. A flat mud bottom broke into view at 15 metres. It was covered with holes. Mike swam above and pointed to one of them.

I swam down and, as planned, switched off my imagination and began to wriggle my hand down into the narrow hole. My knuckles were scraped by the gravel sides. The burrow went straight down and I thrust and squeezed until I was trapped up to my armpit. I could now just feel a terminal chamber and began to explore it …

It had been only a few months before that the first marine biology student had asked his supervisor what lived in these holes. His tutor didn't know the answer, so suggested he put his hand down to find out. He had felt a squirming body in the bottom and 'taking his courage in one hand', he grabbed it and pulled it out. They could scarcely believe their eyes.

Wriggling in his grasp was one of the most fantastic fish he had ever seen. It had an orange-red body, purple-edged fins and a long eel-like shape. What was it? Why had it never been seen before?

Research showed that they had found a Red Band fish or *Cepola rubescens*, a species normally found in the Med and rarely in British waters and then only trawled from depths deeper than 70 metres. This shallow bed off Lundy would provide the first opportunity to study a fish about which very little was known and which had never been seen by divers.

The first expedition to the island was mounted from the Marine Biological Station at Port Erin in the Isle of Man. They found that the fish had a 'lodger' in the shape of a burrowing crab (*Goneplax*) which lived in an adjoining burrow. A 24-hour TV watch was organised, and it was found that the fish were not hermaphrodites, as previously thought, but developed male and female characteristics early in life. They lived permanently in their burrows, emerging at fixed times to feed.

Janie and I had joined another of their mini-expeditions based on the Isle of Man research vessel *Cuma*. Dr Roger Pullin, one of the biologists, told us that he thought that they had now observed courting behaviour, 'approaching, biting, lying side-by-side, and quivering'.

We stayed in The Old Light, a disused lighthouse with Don and Jeannie Shiers and their family and enjoyed diving with them too. The island was full of birds – razorbills sitting on the water, guillemots, puffins and oyster catchers in flight above. Jane dived on the battleship HMS *Montague* with Don, who owned the wreck. We dived off the west coast collecting an orange and purple nudibranch (*Greilada elegans*) that was once thought to be rare. Greg Brown, a nudibranch expert, who was also on the island identified our specimens. We collected six different kinds for him, not to mention two flatworms.

At the north end of Lundy was a race called 'The Hens and Chickens'. Here at 'Virgin Spring' we encountered whirlpools and strong currents. It was exhilarating diving, although Jane had had an unhappy experience when she and another girl had both been forced downwards by the current. They inflated their life jackets, but continued on down until the current dispersed at the bottom of the cliff.

A few weeks later we were buying food and staying in a chalet at Lanzarote in the Canaries. The Atlantic was warm and clear amid black, volcanic rocks. We were welcomed by Bob Wright, an ex-RN instructor, who ran the Clubulanza dive centre.

Most of the diving was from the shore, but the 'drop-off' was only a short swim away with a variety of fish. We were again joined by Maggie and Martin Marks from England. The sea life seemed to be half Mediterranean and half cooler Atlantic species. We bought a huge tuna from one of the fishermen and the girls marinated it before cooking.

Lanzarote's best-known son was an artist called Cézar Manrique. Apart from designing and building a fabulous house on the island, he managed to influence the locals into banning the construction of high-rise buildings. He built a stylish art gallery overlooking the sea and a really astonishing night-club in a cave. We visited it, and arrived at a car park with just a huge unmarked rock in the middle. In the rock was a door. It opened on to narrow steps leading down underground. Lights dimly illuminated the walls. The cave began to open up. Suddenly a long lake came into view cunningly illuminated from below the surface, disguising the depth. In the lake was a type of blind white crab (*Munidopsis polimorpha*) found nowhere else. The others laughed as I stood fascinated in my new safari suit, up to my knees in the warm water watching them. We walked along the edge until we came to a restaurant and dance floor, all cunningly constructed by an imitation tropical lagoon.

We started boat diving with Bob's assistant, Miguel, finding garden eels, liche and caves of shrimps and then, finally, decided to explore Fire Mountain where active volcanoes were still erupting. Unfortunately this involved camels again. We set off in a long line. As I feared, the camel in front sprayed me, while the one behind tried to bite me. My own camel tried to unseat me. Friends were unsympathetic.

Fire Mountain was impressive, with bushes spontaneously igniting, and when water was poured into holes in the ground, it exploded out as steam. There were 300 volcanoes on the island and the last major eruption had been in the eighteenth century. The next evening we took Bob and Miguel for dinner and finished up drinking 'Cuba Libres' and watching buxom German girls chasing the Spanish waiters around the restaurants

A few weeks after our return it was time for me to attend the next CMAS World Congress. It was on the other side of the world in Brisbane, Australia. The hosts, the Australian Underwater Federation, had high hopes and made extravagant arrangements, booking a small liner for a 12-day cruise through the Great Barrier Reef. It had to be cancelled due to lack of bookings and the full-time administration of the federation got the blame while elected officers quietly passed the buck. Andrew Maluish, the organiser kept smiling as did the programme organiser Dr Peter Saenger and the liner was replaced by a week's holiday diving from Heron Island in the South of the reef.

Mike 'Bus', still National Training Officer, and the Club's chairman-elect Nick Fleming, came too. We gave presentations to the conference, mine on the X-5 story and also a 'Historie of diving'. The climax was an evening with shark experts Ron and Valerie Taylor.

Before departing for Heron Island, the Australians asked if we would like to visit Sea World in Brisbane and maybe dive there in one of the sea-life tanks. We agreed.

Mike had been his usual forthright self when discussing problems at the conference and some of the 'ozzies' were less than enthusiastic about his approach. The visit organiser quizzed him:

'You Poms are supposed to be good divers aren't you?'

'No', said 'Bus', 'we're the best'.

'Do you want to dive in the shark tank then?'

'We'll dive anywhere you do', he kindly replied on our behalf.

'Get ready, you'll be in, in ten minutes'.

Being a cautious lad, I slipped round to look through the windows of the shark tank, expecting the odd bottom shark and dog fish. It was full of the most gigantic sharks I had ever seen, with so many teeth they appeared to be escaping from their mouths. There was no going back now.

We did our last preparations standing in the water on the shallow shelf round the huge tank. Meanwhile purposeful shark fins swept passed us. I was happier when I got to the bottom at 15 feet and could see what was going on. There was a shark cage down there but we were not invited to use it. The sharks appeared unsettled in the presence of so many strangers and some exhibited nervous behaviour patterns. Fortunately we all came out in one piece.

The Australian seemed a little disappointed, and reported that one of the regular tank divers had received 40 stitches in the leg a few weeks before. The second wave of divers included Bernard Eaton who had done only three open water dives while training with 'Bus'. There were some 500lb groupers in the tank as well.

I watched through the window as Bernard backed away from a large specimen that came slowly towards him, head on. Each time he backed away, the grouper advanced until his back was against the wall and all he could see was its huge head. It was a stand-off. Luckily the grouper took things no further. We were pleased to have retained our Editor for future issues of *Triton* magazine.

We were then delivered by helicopter to Heron Island, 45 miles off the coast and forming part of the Great Barrier Reef. It was run by Walt and Jean Deas, international underwater photographers and film makers who were originally from Scotland.

'Heron' was a small and idyllic tropical island with white coral sand beaches and clear blue sea. I dived among the 'bommies' or huge coral heads with Bernard and Vicki Fontaine, a talented artist, who had accompanied us to Australia . The batfish were so demanding that we had to push them away – obviously the result of fish feeding. Huge morays were almost tame.

The few Australians on the island spent most of their time consuming cans of lager in the bar, ignoring the beautiful suntanned girls surrounding them. I watched, fascinated, as one girl sitting at the bar, used her bare foot to try to produce some reaction from a comatose male, without result.

We met a very different Australian female a few days later. Walt took us to visit the tiny Wreck Island which hovered as if in space on the horizon. 'There's one woman living there', he told us. 'who's crazy about turtles'. Julie Booth was about 40 and the mother of one of the Heron Island staff. She had built a rough lean-to in the trees and swam with the turtles every day. Bernard interviewed her while Vicki sketched and 'Bus' photographed. She had lived in these primitive surroundings for a number of years and told us of her long friendship with the turtles.

'Don't you get lonely or bored?' Bernard asked.

She turned and gazed at the sky line.

'See that other island on the horizon?' she asked.

We nodded.

'There's a guy lives alone there and he rows across once a week – and bores the pants off me.'

When we got back to Sydney, Sandy Primo, now married to an Australian, was on the phone. She moved her new husband and herself into our hotel and announced that she would show us the sights. We finished up eating succulent sea food and happily singing in a café in The Rocks where they had offered free drinks as long as we did so.

Australia had exceeded all my expectations.

* * *

The World Underwater Federation still seemed important to the club and I was now appointed as Secretary of their Technical Committee that dealt with all aspects of aqualung diving. 'Bus' backed me up, as president of the Training sub-committee.

Back in the UK, our liaison with the Fisheries Committees was getting better and they agreed that legislation was not the answer to problems in the South-West. I had met the Devon Sea Fisheries committee for an open discussion. Our 'war' with them seemed to be ending and I persuaded the Club to arrange for all BSAC diving boats to be marked for easy identification. Kendall McDonald, retiring as Chairman of the Club, thanked us all for our efforts. My team at HQ was now 16 strong and included my new personal assistant, Sally Melville of London Branch. The Sports Council paid our rent and most of the salaries.

The Club was beginning to suffer from bureaucracy. It first arrived in the shape of the new Health and Safety Regulations which were originally designed to apply to all diving operations, whether for profit, or not. They insisted that there should be a recompression chamber at every dive site, which would have made most branch dives illegal. Parliament had always decided that the Club's own safety rules were excellent and that they were all that was needed to keep the sport safe. There would always be accidents, but they were few and far between. Adventurous sports were accepted as part of young people's lives.

The *Mary Rose* project was gaining pace and it was now clear that the ship lay on her starboard side with a good deal of her internal structure intact and a mass of objects to be recovered. It had been decided that it would be completely excavated from the seabed and then lifted in one of the greatest underwater operations of all time. Margaret Rule, the Archaeological Director estimated that 30 amateur divers would be needed each day during the summers of 1979 and 1980 to help the excavations. I was a member of the Mary Rose Fund Raising Committee and became more and more interested in the project.

In February 1978, I received another invitation to take a party of ten divers of my choice to dive in the Red Sea with the Scandinavian Tjareborg organisation. Besides Janie and friends from London branch like Annie O'Dell, I decided to invite the Club part-time coaches who did such sterling work for us. Gordon Ridley, David Swales, Bill Burdett and John Page jumped at the chance. We were warned that the limited accommodation available might entail separating males and females, but Janie was happy to accept this to be able to get back in the warmth of the Red Sea. When we arrived at the hotel in Sharm, the receptionist took me aside.

'We have a small problem with the accommodation of your party'.

'Don't worry', I said, 'Jane and I can be separated.'

'No', she answered, 'that won't be necessary, but would you both share a room with Annie O'Dell and the Tjareborg courier?'

The courier was a tall, slim English girl. We all settled into the large 4-bedded apartment and Annie opened a bottle of gin. It wasn't long before our laughter was interrupted by tapping on the door by curious coaches.

The diving boat was a 60-foot ketch, *Colona II*, run by a crew of Scandinavians who, when away from the shore, operated in the nude. Jane and Annie made no complaint.

It was wonderful to anchor off the famous drop-off at Ras Muhammad without having the long swim to get there from the shore. The chief diver, Simon Corper, and I decided that we would cruise along the reef edge above the deep water and put the girls on the 'outside' so that they had a better chance of seeing big fish. They later accused us of putting them there as 'shark bait'. He held Jane's hand and I followed with Annie who had less experience of tropical diving. She jumped when she first saw the large amberjacks and then again when a white-tipped shark glided into view.

Then we all froze as a large Tiger shark appeared ahead and turned towards us. It passed effortlessly close by and must have measured 15 feet from nose to tail. Annie's eyes widened, but her training with London branch ensured she was under control. The next thing we knew, the shark had returned from behind us and passed even closer. I knew that they had a very bad reputation, but it disappeared into the distance ahead of us, not to be seen again. Afterwards I asked Janie if she had been scared. 'No', she answered blithely, 'as Simon wasn't wearing anything on his bottom half, I felt that he would be the first thing a hungry shark would be attracted to.'

* * *

The South African Underwater Union were members of CMAS, but at that time the Russians frequently tried to veto their membership and activities. The South Africans invited several of us to visit, so that they could demonstrate that there was no discrimination in their diving organisation. I went and they arranged for me to stay with a different family nearly every day, starting with the Union's President, Owen Bryns in Jo'burg. My first dive was with 'the grand old man' of South African diving, Darroll Smith. Unfortunately the visibility was bad on the day we dived east of Durban with lionfish tumbling in the surf next to us.

I then travelled on to Cape Town and stayed with a couple of young newly weds, Chris and Jill van Niekerk. Chris had just qualified as a Doctor and was a member of the university air squadron. He flew me around Table Mountain in a tiny plane, but declined to go into any clouds that appeared as he was only qualified to fly in good visibility. I dived with him on the wreck of the *Rock Eater* off Cape Point. It was impressive and we swam along companionways and through sea bream and 'pajama' sharks down to 35 metres.

I spoke at their conference and then dived with Jill in False Bay with the sea lions, who played around us, showing off their agility. There was mercifully no sign of the Great Whites that prey on them here. My last dive was at Vulcan Rock, off the Atlantic coast. We arrived late and it was already dusk when we left in a fast launch for the isolated site. The rock looked sinister in breaking seas. Underwater our torches illuminated a wreck with hundreds of crawfish antennae waving from it.

The South Africans showed me a game park and a wine chateau and then asked if there was anything else I wanted to see. I mentioned that I had relations in Zulu-land at a place rejoicing in the name of 'Post Office Ntambanana'. They flew me up through a thunderstorm in a small plane. The relatives were not Zulus, but proved to be in the sugar business. They asked how many servants I had back in London, and seemed disappointed when I replied that I had none.

Back home, the SOS import business was still operating although my friend Jim had long since given it up. The day-to-day work was done by Fred Pite, a friend of my brother's, who had his offices in the City. In July, I visited the SOS works in Turin and then stopped off for a few days on the Italian Riviera. I dived at Portofino and at nearby San Fruttuoso where the Italians had erected an underwater statue of Christ on the bottom at 17 metres. I snorkelled down to pose for photos taken by Otto Honeggar, a Swiss underwater photographer who I had met there.

My friend, Peter Dick and I had been commissioned to write a book on the history of diving for which Peter was doing most of the research. We became interested in the story of John Day, who disappeared in Plymouth Sound while trying to become the deepest and longest surviving man underwater, back in 1774.

John Day was a dockyard labourer from Yarmouth with big ideas. His patron, a Dr Falck, described him as 'gloomy, reserved and peevish … but obstinate in his opinions and jealous of his fame.' Around 1772, Day had gone down in an enclosed tub to a depth of 30 feet in a pool in Norwich, but he sought sponsorship for greater things.

He found a backer who provided him with £340 to buy and convert a fifty-ton sloop, the *Maria* which he painted red and announced that he was going down to 300 feet for 24 hours in a large reinforced living chamber on board. It measured twelve feet by nine, by eight. He had the vessel towed out into Plymouth Sound in 130 feet of water. He equipped her with coloured buoys that he could release to inform the surface as to how he was faring. He also had access to huge weights that he could discard when he wanted to come up. He knew little or nothing about water pressure and its effects on empty sealed containers.

He waved to the crowds lining the shore and finally entered the chamber with a candle, a bible, biscuits and water. Dr Falck writes: 'He was sunk at two o'clock on the afternoon of the 20th June 1774 and descended into perpetual night.'

Some time later, not surprisingly, there was an 'irruption of air' on the surface, which was probably the result of the box collapsing. The learned Dr Falck gave his opinion that Day had died of cold. We only hoped that he had gone quickly, as the water gushed in upon him. The watchers waited a day before taking further action and then dragged the ship towards Drake's Island to try to recover it. The advent of winter gales soon prevented any further efforts.

Peter and I had done an exploratory dive in the area in February 1975. At 42 metres, it was freezing cold and black. We returned to get torches and returned to the rock and shingle bottom. A powerful tide moved us as we clung tightly to our line to the surface. There was nothing to be seen except a few surprised crabs. Alan Bax, who acted as our archaeological adviser took sextant bearings and then dived on a line, also without success.

By 1978 I decided that the search would provide an excellent winter project for London branch, of which I was now President. Dr Falck had provided illustrations in his book, not only of the boat, but also of the area where it had disappeared. We soon realised that we had dived in the wrong place in 1975 and, if what we now called 'The Red Maria' was to be found, it would be in the shallower waters off Drake's Island.

Alan provided special charts designed to record 'fixes' and Alan Harper-Smith, the branch diving officer asked for volunteers and was given 18 names. It was not until November, however, that Malcolm Jobling and a new committee member, Tony Smith, took up the organisation.

Tony and I briefed the first group at our home in Sheen. The group now included Peter Edmead, Richard Grayson and my PA, Sally Melville. Malcolm and Richard were unable to make the first weekend but the rest of us did and listened to Alan's plans that we should set up a rectangular search area and then tow divers into it, plotting their position on his waterproof chart. He had also unearthed an old chart dated 1779 showing many contemporary features which helped to estimate the probable position of the wreck. Our excitement rose.

The weather was bad on our first day in the Sound, and, although it had not improved, we dived the next day. We obtained permission from the Long Room, home of the Queen's Harbourmaster and launched our inflatable into the waves at the bottom of the 'Bovi' slip for the bumpy journey across the Sound.

Sally and Peter bottomed at 15 metres and then went on down to 30. The water was clear, but very cold and pitch black. Torches were a necessity. I dived with Tony on to a bottom of slates, pebbles and stones. We crept along in the darkness. I couldn't help thinking of Mr Day and how he must have felt down there. Had the water slowly risen around him? Had he tried to release the weights? Most likely the end was very quick.

The project continued during the following weeks with Malcolm, Tony, Caesar Kamieniecki, Ginny Ashton and our French diver, Philippe Dumortier, who worked for Shell. Philippe located a large ring in the bottom that was attached to something beneath. We had an agreement with the RN harbourmaster under which we could pull divers up at once if large vessels approached. I dived again with Philippe in murky and dark conditions and began to believe that the heavy tidal flow might have removed evidence during the many years that the ship had been down. The search continued in subsequent seasons, but, sadly, we still found nothing. Anything that remains of Mr Day and his ship still lies somewhere beneath the Sound.

CHAPTER THIRTEEN

Red Spiders, Hans Hass
& a Master Dive on the Hermes

WITH HELP FROM THE SPORTS COUNCIL, we organised the first 'Sub-Aqua Exhibition' at their centre at Crystal Palace. There were demonstrations, competitions, branch stands and films. It was a huge success with 6,000 members of the public visiting and participating.

The membership had increased by 2,000 during the year and there were new branches in New York, New Zealand and Malawi. Others were being formed by universities, police, fire brigades, commandos and lifeguards. There was even one on the Great Barrier Reef. A junior section, which I had set up under Lionel Blandford, an enthusiast from London branch, already had no less than 233 branches of young snorkellers throughout the country. All was going well except that, very sadly, Jane and I had now separated after much soul searching.

In July I was again diving with London branch, this time from Penzance, and organised a day for them, out at the Wolf Rock lighthouse. Robert Louis Stephenson, the author and one of the famous 'lighthouse Stephensons', had once landed on the rock, which lay some 10 miles off Land's End and declared that it would be possible to build a lighthouse there. It was finally built by James Douglass and the light was first lit on 1st January 1870.

It took us two hours to get there in a shark boat called *Hustler*. The weather was overcast and there was a strong tide running, but we managed to get down to 27 metres among many crabs and lobsters.

In August, I was off to Lundy again, staying at the Old Light with Don and Jeannie Shiers and family, and marine biologists, David and Jennie George. We saw a shark and seals, before taking part in an investigation of the fresh water ponds of Lundy. Jennie had got a grant to research them and it seemed that they had never been dived before. Most were shallow but Quarry Pond was said to be 'bottomless'. I persuaded her to let me dive there first, to check the depth and, if possible, take bottom samples.

I kitted up and slowly walked into the pond. The water came up to my knees, then my waist, then my neck. Soon it reached eye level. I continued walking and found myself walking up the opposite side. So much for the bottomless pool. Jennie asked me to stand in various parts so that they could estimate the depth and I held a tape to measure the distance from the shore. I did a brief dive to five feet and found red spiders skittering over the bottom.

When we got back to the Old Light and changed, she, and her research assistant Brenda, asked me to lie on the kitchen table so that they could measure the distance from my feet to various body parts that they had seen above the surface. The subsequent research produced a certain amount of unscientific hilarity.

In September, I flew out to Israel again for a few days as the guest of Club Med. I had been invited to act as an expert witness in a case in which the Club was being sued following the loss of a trainee Israeli diver.

The court was convened at Beersheba and the case proved intriguing. The defence lawyer had apparently demolished the prosecution case in the criminal trial, and these subsequent civil proceedings seemed to hinge at one point on the distance that a beginner diver could be expected to swim on the surface in two minutes. The club's instructor had reported on the time he had seen the diver swimming back to shore and the first expert witness had disagreed with his estimate of the time taken.There were three prosecutors firing questions at me and trying to tie me up in knots. The judge demanded that I answered 'Yes' or 'No' to some, despite my insisting that they were not relevant to the case.

I was prepared for the question on the swimming distance but the prosecutors didn't ask it. Our defence Council told the judge that he would ask it, and then a game of bluff ensued. The judge asked the prosecuting Councils if this new line of questioning would extend the case. 'Yes,' they said, 'probably by a week.'

I was very concerned, as I had to be back in my office in a few days time. 'Don't worry', whispered my defence Council. 'It's only a bluff.' I hoped he was right. He asked the question. I gave my reply. There were just three counter questions to me, and the case ended. The prosecutors later apologised for being so rude to me, but I assured them that I didn't think they had. I snatched some dives with Willy Halpert's centre at Eilat, exploring Coral Island and its crusaders castle, before returning full of good Club Med cuisine.

Alex Double was now running an expedition-holiday on a reef off Port Sudan in the Red Sea. I booked a place, together with the London branch Treasurer, a young banker called Fiona Bennett. We flew out on one of the few planes that Sudanair possessed to arrive in Khartoum in the early hours of the morning.

The connecting Sudanair plane to Port Sudan was the dirtiest I had ever travelled in. There were locals preparing food on board and even chickens in the aisles. We hoped the cockpit was in better shape. We arrived in one piece before breakfast and made our way to the Palace Hotel and booked rooms for the night to await Alex's arrival. He appeared at tea time with departing expedition members from Switzerland, Norway, Scotland and England. The Palace Hotel's restaurant seemed to be the only place to eat, but it had the worst selection of food I had ever come across.

The roughly scribbled menu read: 'Sinkit soup – Rost Sinkeet – Custard – Water-mellon.' I can eat most things but some of their 'food' defeated me. At night the corridors in the hotel were full of sleeping locals.

Fiona and I shopped in the heat of Port Sudan the next morning discovering the Red Sea Hotel, which actually provided iced lemon drinks. Port Sudan was a disappointment. There was little water, and beer, which suddenly seemed a necessity, was unobtainable due to 'a strike'. By nightfall, we had located the Red Sea Club, which actually dispensed gin and lime. We looked forward to getting out to the Sanganeb Reef with its solitary lighthouse, where Alex would be doing the cooking as well as leading the dives.

The next morning we took a taxi to the deserted port of Suakin, which had been abandoned when the harbour had silted up. In the afternoon the expedition's work boat *Stormbringer* was ready to take us out to Sanganeb. It was described as a 'diving jeep' being completely square, rather like a packing case, with a rough flying deck built on top.

Two hours later we arrived at the lighthouse twenty miles out. We had brought sleeping bags and Alex walked along the islet's narrow rock reef with us suggesting places we might put them down. We chose a disused concrete emplacement off the Northern jetty. 'Don't worry, it never rains', Alex assured us cheerfully. The boat skipper's wife had cooked the, now welcome, tinned food.

The next morning I opened one eye at daybreak to see a multi-coloured crab running sideways a few inches from my nose. I stretched and went into the shallows, as instructed, to relieve nature. The fish took an extremely close interest, which speeded up my performance no end. After breakfast we left with the skipper for the north end of the reef. I dived with Fiona on to a medley of fishes including huge Napoleon wrasse, lion and unicorn fish. She snapped away happily with her underwater camera. Alex came with us for the afternoon dive through coral trees and circling fish. Our time below was punctuated by Fiona's excited squeals to draw our attention.

The next day Alex expressed amazement when storm clouds piled up and torrential rain began. It continued intermittently for several days. The three lighthouse keepers invited us into the lighthouse where they had numbers of spare bare rooms. They had their own ideas, however, about who slept in which room and with whom.

We dived on, going deeper and now, to my delight, seeing sharks, jacks (*Caranx*) and barracuda. I saw my first manta ray and got close up to photograph it. The manta looped-the-loop, but my photo didn't come out.

The next day we were due to dive the *Umbrea*, one of the most celebrated wrecks in the Red Sea which had featured in Hans Hass's book *Under the Red Sea*.

The *Umbrea* was a huge Italian cargo ship that had been at anchor outside Port Sudan on the day when Italy entered the war against us in 1940. The British soon took it over and the Italian crew were about to leave when it was discovered that she was sinking. They had successfully scuttled her. She settled on the seabed 80 feet down, with her davits still breaking the surface. Her cargo, 7,000 tons of munitions and explosives, had been bound for Eritrea.

In 1949, Hass, the first to dive on her, had found her already covered in coral and swarming with fish. Some of the best underwater photographers, including the Cousteau team, followed him down in the following years.

There were no boats or buoys over the wreck when we arrived and rolled off the side of *Stormbringer* sinking through crystal clear, warm water to join Alex waiting on the deck below. I turned and surveyed the scene. The enormous wreck seemed to stretch forever into the distance. The high davits were circled by butterfly, emperor and queen angel fish. A huge cylindrical object lay across the deck in the distance – a funnel. A shoal of jacks streamed past.

At 15 metres, we followed Alex into the wreck. The first cabin we swam into had a porcelain bath and I manoeuvred into it for a photo. Then we were out and swimming along a series of beautiful companionways studded with coral 'flowers'. Down through the vast interior and a long torch-lit swim through a dark corridor under the hull, to emerge in front of the propellers. Alex stood on one of the blades to demonstrate the size. Its diameter must have been at least fifteen feet.

Back into the ship to see the famous cargo – aircraft bombs lying in great heaps. Then into the ship's restaurant and bar where the remains of tables stuck up from the floor. We sat down and pantomimed an orgy of drinking, letting our mouthpieces float out to cover the ceiling with silver bubbles.

Out to the bridge, magnificently outlined above, and we swam in again to the ship's hospital. It lay at 45 degrees and we swam for 30 feet across it, passed bedpans and the remains of beds. We popped out of another door into the sunlight where, to my surprise, a solitary diver wearing silver air cylinders, hung motionless making notes. Alex made some unintelligible sounds in his direction and then wrote something on his slate.

We carried on into the engine room, always the most impressive part of any large wreck. It stretched down from 50 to 80 feet, with catwalks at 20 feet intervals and huge engines and cylinders below us. Finally we swam up to the top of the bridge and fed queen angels and snappers by hand. It was without doubt, the most magnificent wreck that I had ever seen.

Another surprise was in store. Who was the diver with the silver cylinders who appeared from nowhere? Alex showed me his slate. On it he had written: 'Dr Hass,

I presume'. The other diver had added a tick. Afterwards Hass explained to us that he was back on the *Umbrea* on the 30th anniversary of his first dive on her to record the coral growth in the intervening years. It was wonderful to talk to the only diver I had idolised. We later visited him at his hotel in Port Sudan finding him as enthusiastic as ever.

'I am making a film for German television … I seem to produce a book or film every year.' I talked about his early years and finally about the *Umbrea*. In his book he had imagined what the wreck would look like in 50 years time, with coral covering the hull and beginning to close the doors and hatches. Forty years after the sinking, the doors and hatches were not yet closed, but the corals were luxuriant and growing. Hans had found a copy of his original award-winning film *Red Sea Adventure* and projected it for us one evening at the hotel. He put his signature in my log book against the entry on the *Umbrea* dive.

In the following days we dived deeper looking for sharks at 40 metres. The water temperature was 90 degrees F. at the surface and 88 degrees at depth. Suits were superfluous, except for protection from corals and stings. We did a night dive under the lighthouse where one of the keepers had hung a dead shark that they had caught earlier. I collided in the darkness with a confused globe fish, to our mutual embarrassment.

We saw more white-tipped sharks and dolphins and travelled 15 miles further south to the Sha'ab Rumi atoll where the garage that Cousteau had built for his diving saucer during his underwater living experiment, was still on the bottom. We photographed more very active sharks before returning to Sanganeb.

Diving deeper to 52 metres, we saw sharks again, and a remora or sucker fish detached itself from one of them and stuck itself on to my bare leg. A strange sensation, especially when it rubbed me to try to find a more secure hold. It finally dropped off disappointedly soon after I mounted the diving ladder after the dive.

On our last morning we returned to Port Sudan. As we stood on the quay, the boat that Hans Hass had chartered, swept out passed us. It slowed, and he leaned towards us and shouted, 'Can you help me?' Alex and I ran down like stags. 'Do you have piece of string, zis long? Impossible to find in Port Sudan.' Alex ran back to cut off a length of nylon cord from his store and flung it across. After a brief 'Thankyou', Alex shouted after the disappearing boat:

'One thing, Dr Hass'.

'Yes,' he replied.

'When you make the film, can you put in, "Acknowledgements to Reg Vallintine and Alex Double for provision of piece of string"?'

We heard him laugh as his boat puttered on into the distance.

Fiona and I, sunburnt and happy, waited at Port Sudan airport for our plane. She was happy, that is, until a swarm of bugs the size of bumble bees flew into her hair. She remained calm, a credit to London branch. I was so glad I didn't have hair.

Sadly, 1980 was to be my last year with the BSAC. The new Chairman, an underwater bureaucrat, was obsessed with management techniques and determined that I should go. Even more inexplicably, he and his officers decided to do away with the post of BSAC Director altogether. What the Sports Council felt about this I do not know. They had backed the appointment for eleven years and paid salaries and other costs. Our grant for administration and coaching had reached £90,000 per annum. It was progressively reduced in future years. My last report before I handed in my resignation, recorded that our percentage increase in membership was now 11% per annum. Even the traditional, helmet building firm of Siebe Gorman had its own BSAC branch and others now stretched from the Shetlands to Nigeria and from New Zealand to the Arabian Gulf. It was a tribute to the BSAC system and growing efficiency. I was proud of our record. When I finally left, I held a party for the staff and they presented me with a hairbrush. I should have given it to Fiona.

After resigning, I stood for BSAC Council' the policy-making body, and got more votes than any other candidate. I also continued with my work as Secretary of the CMAS technical committee.

Another change of direction was now a necessity and Alex suggested that we should start a diving school together, not in some exotic part of the world, but in London, where there were millions of potential divers. We could initially teach them in pools and then take them to the sea or abroad for open water training. There were no other schools in London at the time, although there were many clubs, and the idea had enormous potential. We resolved to go ahead as soon as I finished my time with the Club.

Meantime, I continued diving in my spare time with London branch. They had raised some money to support the *Mary Rose* project, and I persuaded Margaret Rule to let a number of us dive on the wreck. The archaeological team had now begun an intense programme of work on the site covering 193 days. I dived with Dave Burden, their Chief Diver. Much more of the wreck was now excavated and I saw the port side of the ship and a beautiful bronze cannon with its muzzle buried in the silt. Many skulls were being found too.

I was back at the site with Don Shiers in June, at Margaret's invitation. The maximum underwater visibility was only three feet. I held my arm out straight in front of me and could not see my hand. We saw a box of Tudor arrows. Over 1,000 had been brought up. Before this there was only one in the Tower of London. ' It knocked the bottom out of the Tudor arrow market', joked my friend, Adrian Barak.

I went off with the branch to Fowey in Cornwall and took in a young Finnish girl called Aija Seppalainen who was to become a great friend. She was a great dancer and became known for the parties she organised. We often danced until we dropped (or I did!). She must have been the fittest girl known to man.

In June Tom Baum was in contact again. He was now freelancing as a design consultant and had acquired a friend in one of the large German companies he worked for. Kurt Haendl had bought land in Sri Lanka and, before building on it, wanted to know if the area was suitable for diving tourism. Tom had suggested that I did a tour and report, and I flew out with the two of them in June 1980.

Kurt knew Rodney Jonklaas, the 'grand-old-man' of diving in Sri Lanka. Rodney had been the star in a number of books on diving written by Arthur C. Clarke and published in the 1950s and 1960s. Rodney described himself as a 'purebred Dutch burgher'. His ancestors had arrived on the island from Amsterdam nearly 200 years before. He was still a fine figure of a man, upright and active, spearfishing or collecting fishes underwater nearly every day of the year. He knew the scientific names of every species, which would be useful for my report.

We visited his house in the jungle that was full of plants, shells, fish tanks and diving books. He soon spoke about the wreck of HMS *Hermes* The *Hermes* was an aircraft carrier that had been sunk by Japanese dive-bombers in 1942, during the last world war, with a loss of 302 sailors. It lay very deep. 'I dived on her for the film *Blue Water, White Death*, he said, 'but don't think I will ever get down to her again unless I do it with you.'

I decided to look at the tourist dive sites first. Rodney drove us across the island to the East coast where Kurt had bought his land. We passed elephants, working and bathing. We came to a huge tree, full of fruit bats, and Rodney got out an elephant gun from his jeep and blasted a shot into the air so that we might photograph them flying.

We had lunch high in the hills on a tea estate, unchanged since the days of the Raj. There were photos of the Queen on the walls and others of local dignitaries after the Coronation, and even older ones taken during the Prince of Wales' visit in 1922. The manager served us a splendid curry before we left for the old city of Kandy where the brake drums on Rodney's machine finally gave out.

We visited the Temple of the Tooth, where pilgrims were praying to the wail of pipes and drums, and then drove on overnight to Batticaloa, passing wild boars and arriving at a beach hotel at 2.30 a.m. The next day we awoke to a temperature of 90 degrees F in the shade. The water temperature was still 85 degrees so we didn't use suits. We went to 'Kurt's Beach' to dive from an outrigger canoe fitted with an outboard motor and sailed by local fishermen. It was so narrow that there was no room to move and our sets were wedged into the narrow slot in front of us. Arriving at the dive site, they threw over a large stone attached to a line. We donned our sets in the water and I dived with Rodney to 31 metres, finding numbers of large trigger, angel and emperor fish. A large grouper played hide-and-seek with us and a white-tipped shark joined in. It finally moved off pursued by Rodney taking pictures. Our air tasted of oil. Rodney's only comment was: 'It was the only oil we could get.'

In the following days we visited 'Rodney's Reef'. I went down with Tom and then took Kurt on his first dive.

It was finally time for Rodney and me to dive the *Hermes*. It lay five miles out, off the edge of the continental shelf in a depth of 190 feet. Rodney spoke of it with awe. 'The fish are enormous', he said. I suggested we used twin-cylinder sets, which Rodney rapidly acquired for us. 'What about decompression?' I asked, 'do you have any tables?' Rodney thought he might have somewhere. 'Don't worry', I said, 'I have some here'. 'We'll need to follow them exactly'. 'I'm so glad you're here' said Rodney.

Our means of transport to the wreck site was a small motor cruiser accompanied by local fishermen in their outriggers. 'They fish there every day', said Rodney. 'Can they guarantee to put a line down the funnel?' I asked. 'I'm sure they can', said Rodney.We set sail over deep blue water until the coast was almost out of sight. Occasional flying fish skimmed the calm surface of the Indian Ocean. Suddenly the fishermen stopped and announced we were over the wreck. How they knew, I have no idea.

The *Hermes* had been the first ship to be built as an aircraft carrier in 1914 and had been equipped with Swordfish biplane torpedo-bombers. They had all been flown off when she was attacked. She had been a powerful ship, 400 feet long, but provided an easy target for the Japanese dive bombers. After 36 strikes she rolled over and disappeared. Amazingly, there were between two and three hundred survivors who paddled ashore on pieces of debris.

Rodney had told me that he thought we needed a minimum of fifteen minutes on the bottom to do justice to the wreck. I checked the US and RN tables I had with me and calculated that we should be all right if we did stops of five minutes at ten metres, and ten or fifteen at five. I made the fishermen hang two spare cylinders with breathing valves on the lines to the bottom, to give us enough air for the stops. As things turned out, we were not going to be able to use them.

We jumped in and swam across to the line, which snaked down into the blueness below. We swam down, clutching our noses to clear our ears. The descent seemed to go on forever. Suddenly our heavy stone 'anchor' was in sight below. It was on the sand. There was no sign of a wreck, but a few pieces of wreckage were in the distance.Rodney signalled the way along the bottom. We moved on and the pieces of wreckage became bigger.

I had misgivings, and tried to memorise the way back to the line. We were at 56 metres, and it was difficult to think coherently. Suddenly a huge shadow loomed ahead, the side of the *Hermes* herself. A five-foot barracuda hovered overcome with curiosity. Thousands of fish turned above us on the wreck. Once in the wreck, two huge groupers peered up at us, rolling their eyes. I sank down towards them, tapping my mask, to encourage them to pose for a photo.

It seemed no time at all when I noticed the minute hand of my watch creeping towards the 10 minute mark on the bezel. The wreck was now dark and sinister, infested with shadowy forms. When the hand reached 10, I tapped Rodney and suggest we moved closer to our line. He nodded and we moved off across the wreck. More and more fish appeared. A 'waterfall' of snappers seemed to pour out of the wreck. Enormous groupers were everywhere. Hundreds of barracuda hovered in the current.

At the edge of the wreck, I imagined I recognised a clump of wreckage. We had already reached our 15 minute mark and I was now anxious. I indicated a direction to Rodney and he nodded. A few seconds later and I was completely lost. I signalled urgently to Rodney, 'Which way?' He pointed in a direction along the bottom. Nothing appeared, but more sand.

I finally indicated 'Go up', realising with apprehension that we still had all our decompression stops to do at the surface and it would now be without the comfort of the line to the boat and the spare cylinders. My decompression meter was well into the red, potential danger area. I hurried on upwards to 30 metres with Rodney dutifully following. I slowed down towards 20 and then crept slowly upwards through the blueness. He followed and I adjusted my buoyancy, letting air out of my jacket and hanging at 10 metres under the surface for the first stop. Rodney stopped dutifully.

The five minutes seemed like an age when there was nothing to look at except blueness all around, and the sinister streaks of foam which stained the water ceiling above.

Were we anywhere near our boat? I concentrated on the dials of my instruments and tried not to worry. My watch was reading 25 minutes elapsed time on the bezel. I calculated that we would have to stop at 5 metres for 15 minutes. Would the air last? We gently rose, adjusting buoyancy again, so that we would hover at the shallow depth. There was no sign of a boat hull on the surface in any direction. Were we drifting in a current? There was no point of reference to tell us. I tried not to remember that we were 5 miles out into the open ocean. If we went the wrong way, the next land was Sumatra, 1,000 miles to the east. After seven minutes, Rodney was anxious to surface and did so to check on the boat. I watched, with sinking heart, as he turned on the surface, rearing up to scan the horizon.

To my enormous delight, I saw him waving into the waves, which had built up since the dive began.

He started to swim along the surface and I followed him below. Every so often, he stopped and threshed upright to shout and wave. I heard his shouts from underwater. After 14 minutes the noise of a boat approaches. A feeling of great relief overcame me as Rodney disappeared up over the side. I decided to do some extra decompression to be on the safe side. I felt completely alone but, glancing up, could see craning faces through the surface above. I was now warm and comfortable in the 85 degree water. After 20 minutes I surfaced into the sunlight. The drama was finished and I had no aches or pains.

The next day, after diving with Kurt on a shallow wreck, we left for Trincomalee via the ancient city of Polonnaruwa. Huge stone monuments are surrounded by Buddhist pilgrims and we pass many lorries stuffed to overflowing, with others of all ages. Further along the road, two wild elephants throw sand and dust over their backs as monkeys run across in front. We arrive in 'Trinco', the biggest natural harbour in Asia, and stay at a half-completed, bungalow hotel belonging to a friend of Kurt's. I dived with a small outfit run by Harry Logan-Smith, a Singalese, married to a Swiss lady. His assistant, Nihal, took us down, off Pigeon Island.

Nihal had previously instructed in the Maldives, but had been 'banished' to a tiny island after being found 'in flagrante' with a Maldivian girl. The local court had also 'banished' some Germans and an Italian for the same offence. Nihal had solved the problem by converting to Buddhism, which apparently provided grounds for immediate release. I made notes of every type of fish seen for my report and Rodney later confirmed the Latin names.

A few days later, I was dropped off at the Ceylon Sea Angler's Club. It was a survival from the days of the Raj. The bar was surrounded by ship's crests and photos of English anglers with record catches. I seemed to be the only occupant. Rodney was due to arrive in the evening, and I spent the afternoon looking through the Club's bookshelf which included the magnificent old volume of Day's *Fishes of India*. At tea time, a dutiful waiter appeared with a white napkin draped over his arm. 'Tea and muffins, Sir?' I nodded gratefully.

The next morning, I talked to Rodney about the many underwater discoveries he had made. These included wartime aircraft – Japanese 'Zeros', Fairey Fulmars and old Portugese cannon too. I dived on one of them, a small single-engined plane with the remains of a long canopy. Possibly a Fairey Fulmar.

Rodney drove me back through the jungle to a hotel north of Batticaloa, through wild peacocks, snakes and innumerable monkeys. As it got dark, it was difficult to see anything except the track ahead in the headlights. I saw a small turning ahead and Rodney suddenly stopped his engine, turned out his headlights, and whispered dramatically: 'Be very quiet, get out of your side, and look ahead down the road.' I did as I was told. He switched on his spotlight and to my amazement, I found that

I was standing next to 23 elephants. A magnificent sight as they slowly moved off illuminated by his light.

Rodney and I had planned to dive the *Hermes* again, but time was against us and our plane was due to leave soon from Colombo. Some months after my return, a fat 'Insight' guidebook to Sri Lanka arrived at my home. Rodney had written a chapter on diving in it. He detailed the various areas around the island, and then added:

Fabulous spots for diving … include the unparalled dive to the wreck of the British Carrier, *Hermes* in 180 feet of water. Nowhere else, within just five miles of land, can you visit a wreck of this size with a fish population to boggle the mind. This dive is for the most experienced and best-trained divers; it is dangerously exciting but the dive of a lifetime. Some of the *Hermes* explorers include great divers like Peter Gimbel, Stan Waterman, Ron & Valerie Taylor and Reg Vallintine.

I felt humble in such company and extremely flattered. It was certainly a dive I will never forget.

CHAPTER FOURTEEN

Mary Rose & the Islands of
Fire, Ice and Killers

T HE *MARY ROSE* EXCAVATION had now begun and I wanted to take part in
this unique operation. The wreck had been described as 'the most historically
important yet discovered in European waters' and I took two weeks of my remaining holiday and arrived at the quay in Portsmouth on a grey, rainy morning in
August 1980 to join a team of volunteers. We were marshalled by a smiling young
lady called Alex Hildred and taken off by a tender headed for the *Sleipner* a large
working vessel which was now permanently moored over the remains of the ship.

Besides Margaret Rule as archaeological director, the permanent staff consisted
of Andy Fielding, her deputy and a friendly team that included my quixotic friend,
Adrian Barak as one of the archaeological supervisors.

A metal grid had now been erected over the seabed for accurate measurements
to be taken. The visibility was low and diving was invariably done alone. Andy described the lie of the wreck to me and suggested that I did a tour, travelling across
it and finding 'Area 7' where I would be working.

I went down the line from *Sleipner* into a murky Solent past concrete sinkers. I
then followed scaffold poles across the wreck, 13 metres down, looking for tags to
show my position. Many of them were out of sight, buried in the muddy bottom.
The underwater visibility was now just a few inches and I arrived at a large timber,
clearly marked 'M-60' and began to orientate myself to find the 'slice' through the
wreck at position 7. I occasionally blundered into other divers and a shoal of pol-
lock, breasting the current, watched my slow progress with interest.

Back on board again, I spoke to a tall, slender Norwegian girl called Berit Mortlock who was also an archaeological supervisor. She told me that they had recently
found the barber-surgeon's cabin in the wreck. The 'surgeon', who also cut hair in
1545, had treated his sick and wounded in a small cabin with six square yards of
floor space and a head-room of five foot, six inches. They had found a large wooden
chest and when they lifted the lid, found rows of wooden jars and ceramic jugs,
some still containing ointment and the marks of the finger that had scooped it out.
There were also the remains of amputation saws (the only anaesthetic was a quick
swig of rum) and two large syringes. These, so Margaret informed us, were for use
in injecting sailor's penises to cure VD. I winced.

The next day Adrian was out on *Sleipner* and organising the laying of an electric cable along the starboard line of the wreck. Lesley Runnels, a Concorde hostess who was also a volunteer, took me down after telling me how the suction pump worked. I unravelled Adrian's cable along the bottom following her to where I was to excavate. We sank down into a black trench in the silt. I picked up the big suction pump and started to feed the silt and pieces of wood into the hungry mouth while checking for any valuable objects. The visibility was now down to zero. I carried on, rising out of the dust cloud occasionally to check my watch. After 45 minutes, and still not having heard the promised banging from the timekeeper on the *Sleipner*'s metal ladder , I joined up with Lesley to swim back.

A day later, I was put under the supervision of the elegant Miss Mortlock, as dark, scudding clouds sped across the sky above us. 'If I said: See you at M60, would that be OK? she said, 'or should I take you?'. 'Good practice for me to find it'. I replied, trying to sound confident. She disappeared overboard.

I went down slowly into the increasing blackness, checking the occasional tag that had surfaced. I counted the poles and arrived at M60 again. There was no sign of Berit. After a few moments, I realised that she might be below me in the black hole under the timber. I edged my way down until one of her fins waved alarmingly in my face. She turned and untied a nearby pump, moving back into the murk after beckoning me to follow down. I felt my way along the tube and she took my hand, gently guiding my fingers until I could feel beams and planks that she wanted me to excavate. I gave her fingers a quick squeeze, and she let go suddenly. I could imagine her thoughts.

I was soon utterly alone in the darkness, but strangely happy and satisfied. Time ceased to exist. I thought of my first diving teacher, Trevor Hampton, and what he had said about getting satisfaction from doing a job under difficult circumstances.

After what seemed an eternity, a figure with a lamp, later identified as Adrian, appeared and I momentarily got a glimpse of my watch, which showed that I had been down for 45 minutes. I carried on excavating, wondering what lay around and below me. I felt a strange object pressing against my foot occasionally, and hoped it was another diver. After an hour I re-attached the pump to the scaffolding and felt my way along to what I hoped was the port side of the wreck. I recognised a line heading to the surface. It was now 65 minutes since I had gone down and I decided to do a short decompression stop at 5 metres.

The beating on the ladder just above nearly deafened me and after a few more minutes I surfaced to banter from Adrian and smiles from Miss Mortlock. I was exhilarated to have completed my first satisfactory working dive on the wreck.

The next morning I came across a ring-like object while excavating, and, pulling it out, discovered it was a human bone. I thought of Lance-Corporal Jones of the

Royal Engineers, who finding a body on the *Royal George* nearby over a hundred years before, had refused to touch it. There were other bones, but I decided not to collect them until I knew the policy regarding their removal. The visibility was slightly better although floating clumps of weed obscured the view. My piece of bone was borne off by Berit to the preservation section.

I next did some surveying and measured nail holes in the wooden planks and recorded them on a pad of waterproof paper. I tangled with another volunteer who mistook my suction pump for his.

Alexander McKee, who had originally found the *Mary Rose*, and visited me on Giglio, came aboard one day. The atmosphere between him and the new organisers was frosty, but he dived twice, being shown round the freshly excavated site. I took a photo of him on board which he used for the dust jacket of his new book *How we found the Mary Rose*.

One evening, a party had been organised and the dress theme was 'uniforms'. Berit went as a St Trinian's schoolgirl, and the sight of her long legs in the brief outfit had a lasting effect on a number of supervisors and volunteers. I managed to persuade her to come to dinner with me at a local pub as a break from the spartan food on Sleipner.

Next day she asked me if I would like to spend the night on board with the permanent staff. I jumped at the chance. I had just got changed in the early evening, when she asked me if I would dive again. Any tryst was to be in a trench on the bottom. At least she held my hand again, even if it was only to run it over a number of odd shaped objects to excavate.

Returning after 7 p.m., I ate a primitive dinner and, as there was no one in sight, made for the bunk that had been set aside for me. Someone seemed to have provided a sleeping bag as well. I curled up in it and was soon dead to the world.

Berit had asked me to dive again at 6 a.m, so I was up for an early breakfast at 5.30 to find that I was less than popular with the expedition's Chief Diver, Jonathon Adams. Apparently I had taken over his bunk and sleeping bag while he was diving, in mistake for the one I had been allocated. I was almost glad to get out on the deck into the cold dawn rain for my early dive.

The next evening, Margaret Rule invited me to dinner at her home in Westbourne, a beautiful old house, dating from the fifteenth century, with wood beams and open fire. I drank sherry with her husband, Arthur and met her son Nic and his friend John Walliker, who were both at Cambridge, while Margaret cooked dinner.

I carried on diving, supervised by Adrian and Berit and helping to excavate more ship's timbers and a cannon that was to be lifted on Press Day. On the day, the television crews arrived and the cannon was duly lifted.

I offered to excavate a body, if needed, as others were not so keen. As I recovered another joint bone and the remains of a thigh, I thought of the panic that must have ensued on board as the ship heeled and water came through her gun ports, and returned happy with my collection.

I had arranged to meet up with Mac McKee in the afternoon and drove to his house on Hayling Island, close by the beach. Paintings of war scenes, underwater photographs and ship designs by his children covered the walls. In his study, he showed me his extensive records on the *Mary Rose*. He seemed to have accounts of most of the places that he had visited. One was marked 'Giglio and Giannutri' and contained photos of his holiday there. He generously offered to lend it to me for my projected book. We lunched at a pub overlooking the anchorage.

He was a dedicated researcher and told me that his publishers had told him 'It's no wonder you don't make any money, you spend too long on research.' 'I read a million words before working on my book *Farming the Sea*', he said. His father had been a Navy surgeon and he had been born in Ipswich, spending much of his child-hood in Malta and on the south coast of England. He started to talk about the *Rose* and his eyes gleamed with enthusiasm behind his glasses.

Two days later, Berit took me aside before my dive and said, rather mysteriously, that she would meet me on the bottom and then show me what she wanted done. I found her back in trench 7 and she beckoned me to follow as she breast-stroked along, as she was working without fins. She passed me a bucket and introduced me to a skull. She wrote on her slate: 'When you have recovered him gently into the bucket, clear the surrounding area with the pump.' I took out my mouthpiece and extravagantly kissed her hand.

I had a happy hour of excavating and also found the sole of the sailor's shoe. It was added to the 6,000 objects brought up by the end of the season during 6,000 working dives by volunteers and permanent staff. Sadly it was time to return to London.

* * *

At the end of November, I had to attend the next World Congress of Underwater Activities' It was organised by the Mexican Federation at Cancun, on their Carib-bean coast.

I flew out with Mike 'Bus' for the CMAS General Assembly and we spent the night in Mexico City at the old Grand Hotel that had been built at the turn of the century around a covered courtyard. There were chandeliers and velvet curtains.

We flew on to Cancun and the modern Presidente Hotel that was to host the Congress. The Mexican Federation had organised some dives during the following days and then, before the meetings were finished, I cabled 'Banane', now Club Med's diving supremo, in Paris, asking to be taken on 'au pair' as an instructor at their village at Cancun. It would provide a few weeks good practice, I thought, for running the new school planned by Alex Double and myself. A day later I got my reply from Paris. It just read; 'Cher Reg, Oui. Banane'.

I set off with my suitcase for the Club Med village along the coast. The guard stopped me at the gate. 'Your new diving instructor', I told him. He unwillingly let me in. I went to Administration, They had never heard of me. I produced my cable from Banane. They rolled their eyes, but nodded and allocated me a straw hut.

I was introduced to the 'chef du village', 'chef du sport' and Christian, who was acting 'chef du plongée'. He, in turn, introduced me to a team of macho French diving *moniteurs* who would be my colleagues. They were called Philippe, Yves and Jerôme.

Philippe had the body of a muscle-builder and was said to be able to breath-hold dive to 60 metres. He invited me to go with him freediving. This activity involved him breath-hold diving through a cave complex. As he did not know how far he would have to go to find his next air pocket, it was a form of Russian roulette that resulted in his death some months later.

I did a warm-up scuba dive and met a trainee *moniteur*, André, who would share my hut. The Club village was on the shore, but behind was a river and shallow lagoon. André and I watched an alligator drift by in the lagoon as we talked. A few days later I was back in the lagoon, taking a party of American beginners through their training dives.

Other Americans, already trained in the States, arrived and we had to check them out with tests. Their abilities were very mixed. One very large gent was very incompetent, but finally managed to scrape through my check. He later gave me his card. He worked for a cruise company that had organised diving as one of their activities. After his name on the card were the initials C.M.D. 'What do they stand for?' I asked. 'Certified Master Diver.' he answered confidently. 'We used to do diving a lot but stopped because we lost so many divers.' I thought that he must be joking, but there was no sign of it.

Christian, the chief instructor took me aside one day. 'Rej, zer ees zis bad job we 'ave to do one time each week. Maybe you do eet once for us?' 'What job?' 'You get up early, collect ze group of divers, drive zem to ze airport, take ze morning plane to Cozumel, take ze taxi to 'otel, join ze boat, dive on ze reef. Zen, you go to ze beach, 'ave peecnic, do calculation of times for ze next dive. Do ze seconde dive and check you 'ave enuff time before flying. Catch ze evening plane back 'ere. You will mees dinner in the evening.' 'OK', I said. 'I weel go wiz you first time.' As experienced divers will know, the dangers of decompression sickness increase if one does more than one dive each day and it is necessary to carefully calculate times and depths for each second or subsequent dive. There was also a time that was recommended before flying again, as this lowered the pressure and could result in bubbles of nitrogen forming in the bloodstream.

We took off in a small 3-engined plane with our seven holiday divers. I looked down on jungle until we crossed the coast to the south. We landed on the island at 9.30 a.m., took a waiting taxi and left, as planned for the hotel and the Club Med boat to Palancar Reef. I was now in charge and briefed the divers as Christian looked on and worked out my timings. I jumped in to see an amazing distance. The sea was clearer than at Cancun with an underwater visibility of 30-40 metres. The others joined me and followed me down a vast and splendid vertical reef edge until I stopped at 30 metres and led them slowly up and along the face. There were many beautiful corals, and inquisitive angel fish followed us as we drifted in the strong current.

After the dive, we enjoyed iced beer and barracuda fried on the beach by the skipper, followed by raw conch and cheese and guava jelly! I calculated that we had a 'handicap' of 10 minutes from the first dive before we were down to 20 metres again on the Santa Rosa reef.

I went in first and dropped quickly to the top of the reef at 15 metres. Suddenly two huge black torpedo shapes hurtled towards me from different directions! They were large groupers who had obviously been hand fed regularly by divers. They circled within touching distance and followed us for the whole dive, looking disappointed. I told Christian that I would do the Cozumel trip again at any time. He was delighted, obviously believing that I was completely mad.

The Christmas celebrations at Club Med were extensive. As a diving team, we had to perform sketches, dressed in old-fashioned striped swimming costumes. At dinner we had to jump on to tables and demonstrate how to drink tequila with panache. I had to be sober by Boxing Day, as I was to take my first group back to Cozumel.

They were a mixed bunch from USA, France, Canada and the UK. André, the trainee *moniteur* would act as 'tail-end Charlie'. We arrived at the hotel in Cozumel to find there was no boat. It had not been ordered, but they said that we could go in the same boat with the hotel 'dive guide' who would go to the sites we wanted. The dive guide was a young American called Hank. 'Pleased to have you aboard', he drawled, as he shook my hand.

At Palancar I briefed my group and was surprised to hear him say to his: 'Listen to these Club Med guys briefings – they're the best'. His group listened carefully to what I had to say. Decidedly odd, I thought. We completed the dive and when ferrying beer ashore for the picnic, Hank said:

'Reg, I can see you've dived a lot before, there's somethin' I've never understood.

Could you fill me in?'

'What's that Hank?'

'Decompression'

'Do you mean the repeat dive rules?'

'No, the whole thing.'

I sat with him while we ate.

'Before I begin, I can see your group knows very little, tell me how you organise the two dives for them.'

'Well', he replied, we dive on Palancar to 40 metres in the morning and then on to Santa Rosa to 25 metres.'

'How long for?' I asked.

'I haven't got a watch, is that important?'

I was astonished that his groups had survived and explained the basic theory.

'Where can I get one of those decompression slates?' he asked. A few days later I caught a plane back to England.

* * *

Alex and I finalised the arrangements for our new diving school in London. Through my friend, Jan Curd, who was in the hotel and promotion business, we hired the pool at the King Henry VIII Hotel in Leinster Gardens. I had originally planned to call the school The British Underwater Centre in memory of the school where I had begun, but it seemed that you had to already to be pre-eminent in your field to register the name 'British'. We settled for London Underwater Centre, its initials seeming to be a good omen, and set about buying the diving equipment and producing a colour brochure. We were established in early 1981 as a 'BSAC Recognised School' and were already teaching our first beginners in January. More soon followed, sent by Mike Bunyan of the Mason's Arms and Trevor Smith of The Diving Locker, which we recommended for diving equipment.

By a strange quirk of fate, I had met up with my old Army friend, Frank Sharratt, who was now Chairman of the British division of an international oil company. Over lunch, he expressed an interest in becoming the first LUC diver to go through our whole course to become a 'BSAC Third Class Diver'.

After successfully teaching him in the pool, we took him with two others to Woolwich Graving Dock, which, following an initiative by Alex, now had an appealing new name, The London Aquatic Centre. It was April and the weather was cold with rain. The dock was uninviting. The water was an unhealthy green colour and the temperature was 9° C. Underwater the visibility was only 3 feet at best, but we sank to the bottom at 7 metres and Frank coped well with the unpleasant conditions.

The next weekend, we were at Bovisand and dived on the remains of an underwater house called 'Glaucus' that had been built by Bournemouth BSAC and was now sunk off the Breakwater Fort. I discussed our new school with Alan Bax, the founder of Bovisand, and took the opportunity to visit Trevor Hampton again after 26 years. He had sold his diving centre some years before and now, at 70 was racing around the countryside on a powerful motor-bike, running a farm. It seemed the new owner of the school had not been too successful, managing to blow up his diving boat during an explosives course. For the final weekend of the Third Class diver course we were in the icy fresh waters of Stoney Cove, and Frank completed his final qualifying dives there.

A few weeks later, I was off again with Mike 'Bus' and other London branch members to dive the wreck of the *Mohegan* off the Manacles in Cornwall and then to the Hebrides again, where they had charted two fishing boats for diving. We dived the *Rondo* and at Canna, before arriving at the Shiants. There we discovered another underwater world north of Garbh Eilean where we were swept down off the basalt cliffs into a shoal of huge pollack, dead-men's fingers and dahlia anemones. The kelp was still growing at down at 25 metres and we peered up through it at the hexagonal basalt cliffs that looked man-made and then swam up through a soup of plankton, jellyfish, comb jellies and strings of eggs in transparent leather pouches.

By now, the BSAC had an organised expedition section run by Gordon Ridley. I had, of course, come across him in the Hebrides back in 1975 and he now had a reputation for energy, persistence and forging on through all weathers to achieve his goals. They said that he had even taken over from terrified skippers, adrift in Force 9 gales and brought their boats back. He was intending to organise a grandiose BSAC North Atlantic Project designed to last over 20 years, diving islands and coastlines as far as the Faroes, Iceland, Greenland, Labrador, Newfoundland and Novaya Zemlya to investigate marine life and geological features.

His 1981 expedition was to Iceland, and I was hooked when I read about his intention to explore Surtsey, the newest island in the world, which had been formed by a gigantic volcanic eruption just 18 years before. It had never been dived and was 25 miles out from the Westman islands that strung out like a chain from South-West Iceland.

We flew North from Glasgow on 10th July, and two hours later were looking down on the Westmans, isolated green-topped islands surrounded by calm blue sea. Gordon was at the airport to meet us, together with Dr Graham Durant, the scientific leader and Dr Andrew Rothersall, the expedition medical officer. They had brought the four expedition Land Rovers and a transit van, and we soon moved off towards our first camp site near Grindavik. New impressions began as the surfaced roads were left behind, and in the distance, a huge column of steam rose into the sky.

Our first night under canvas provided a few hours sleep in the arctic twilight, before leaving for Porlakshofn to catch the car ferry to Heimaey, the largest and only populated island in the group. Our full convoy included a four-ton lorry, carrying the expedition's supplies and recompression chamber. The smaller vehicles each towed a trailer with an inflatable on it.

We bumped along the un-surfaced roads, through lava rock fields that resembled moon landscapes, while sea birds soared above. On arrival our trailers and inflatables were hoisted into the air by the ferry's winch, and our trucks sank into its hold by lift.

Four hours after leaving, pinnacles of rock appeared on the skyline. As we got nearer to Heimaey, more sea birds swooped from above, beating past us up-wind, sitting on the sea and diving – fulmars, puffins, terns and guillemots. We berthed in the shadow of the volcano that had destroyed half of the town when it erupted in January 1973. All the 5,300 inhabitants had been safely evacuated except for one man, who was trying to steal drugs from a deserted chemists. They returned to rebuild the town and clear the six-feet deep ash remains. A long-term bonus was that their island had become a third bigger than it had been. Heimaey now had new straight roads and houses with corrugated iron roofs.

We drove out to the site where we would camp, on the edge of a bay near the southern peninsula of Storhofdi. Straight out to sea was an extraordinary sight. A string of tiny islands with black vertical cliffs and green tops, and, beyond them, the profile of Surtsey – 'child of the mythical fire giant, Surtur,' brooding mysteriously on the horizon. A young diver from Harrogate, Phil Harrison, Mike Audis from Eastbourne and I pitched the tent we were to share for the next two weeks.

The first morning, we motored the inflatables out to the steep cliffs surrounding our bay. Thousands of puffins watched from ledges above us. Gordon and I sank through a bumpy, cold sea to arrive at the top of a beautiful vertical cliff, bright with 'dead-men's fingers'. We swam on down to 30 metres as the water darkened. Among the Alcyoniums were mussels, living in holes in the rock. We could feel the movement of the waves as we swam at 20 metres, and enjoyed being whirled into wave-scoured amphitheatres. Back on the surface, we watched the puffins, fulmars and guillemots above as the air temperature dropped to 10°C.

The wind freshened during the evening and rain squalls swept in. By the morning our tent felt as though it would take-off at any moment. The sea raced in and broke as Gordon and I drove up to the saddle of Storhofdi where the weather instruments on the summit were registering 'wind Force 9'. Meanwhile we could see three inflatable boats leave the camp below, and set out for the lee of the Smaeyjar islets to the North.

We hurried back, changed, and set out with Mick Greenhough and Pete Koke-

71. A new diving school, 1981. Reg with Kristina Ehrenstrale.

72. Longbows from the *Mary Rose*, 1980. L to R: Andrew Fielding, Margaret Rule, Reg, Dave Burden.

73. Sarah Greene at an icy Stoney Cove, March 1982. Alex Double, Reg, Sarah.

74. Jo Yellowlees and Mensun Bound working on Etruscan wreck finds, 1984.

75. Reg and Mensun arriving on the wreck.

76. Using paint brushes to expose delicate artefacts.

77. Quay and boathouse, Montecristo 1985.

78. Monastery walls, Montecristo.

79. During the climb.
L to R: Jo, Luciano, Mensun.

80. Stromboliccio, an ideal dive site in the Aeolians.

81. Vane Ivanovic's launch *Tara* at anchor, Formentor, Majorca 1985.

82, 83 and 84.
LUC reunion, 1988. Anneka Rice,
Mike Portelly and Reg.

83.

84.

85. Mike and Reg (in the blonde 'Anneka' wig) on return to the Red Sea, August 1987.

86. Schooner *Florette*, June 1988.

87. Return to Gibraltar, 1997, 'What was it like then?' Gibraltar TV asked.

88. BSAC President, Prince Charles with a copy of *The Club*, April 2004.

laar, one of our geologists, in the smallest remaining Avon inflatable. As we approached the islet of Haena, the seas increased and we began to ship waves over the stern, which was low in the water with the four of us and our diving equipment on board. I began to bail using the only bucket and we turned to pass between two islets, looking ahead for the others. We bucketed through walls of water and approached a dark cliff in breaking seas. Water continued to slop in and then, suddenly, the engine failed.

A series of waves broke over us and our fuel tanks were now awash. The seas smashed on the cliff, only yards away, as Gordon tried furiously to re-start the engine and Mick and Pete shouted encouragement for my bailing efforts. One of our other inflatables was momentarily in sight and we raised one of our paddles in the agreed distress signal. Suddenly the engine coughed back into life and we were through the pass between the islets and into more sheltered seas beyond.

Although the engine was still 'unpredictable', Gordon and I dived down the cliff face to find many Asterias starfish and an underwater visibility of 20 feet. We returned to camp without further incident.

Back at the campsite, washing was proving a chilly business in the wind, which reduced the temperature to 9°C. We soon found a solution at the local indoor swimming pool, where initial washing and showering were strictly enforced by the staff. After swimming in the pool, we decamped to two hot tubs in the open air which were kept at 45°C and where we sat and talked, or eyed the Icelandic girls who shared the tub with us. The whole operation made me feel cleaner than I'd been for years.

The weather continued overcast with rain and we next dived in the middle of the bay where a sinister breaking wave was said to mark the site of a recent wreck. Dave Lowden and I swam down into the grey twilight of the arctic sea, and landed on huge round rocks populated by strange cold- water sea cucumbers. We found a huge metal cylinder and a chain but no wreck and then the cold got to us and we returned.

After the evening meal, Gordon produced an enormous gas burner that changed the cold and wet atmosphere of our large drying tent into the equivalent of a tropical rain forest within minutes. We sat in the steam and recounted wilder and wilder stories late into the night.

On the 15th of July, we set out on a 'hard boat' we had hired for the first time, bound for Bessi shoal, where we were to make studies of the volcanic bottom for and with our accompanying geologists. The boat was a small, but seaworthy, launch, skippered by Gwuthlyem (an Icelandic William) and was named *Bara*. Twenty metres down we found a huge underwater island covered with Alcyoniums. Suddenly we were in the midst of an enormous shoal of 'coleys' (*Pollachius virens*). They pressed close to us, but finally parted to let us through. Two thousand beady eyes fixed on us, as Gordon's flash bulb lit the scene.

The next day we set out for Surtsey, the newest island in the world. We sailed in *Bara* and planned to dive on a submerged peak called Surtla in an attempt to discover more about how volcanos are formed on the sea bed. A party capable of diving 50 metres was selected, and plans drawn up. As we rolled through the heavy seas, I tried to remember what I had read about Surtsey and its formation.

Iceland forms part of the mid-Atlantic Ridge, a submerged volcanic range that extends from Jan Mayen in the Arctic, across Iceland and the Westmans, down to the Azores, Tristan da Cunha and Bouvet island in the Antarctic. Through its rifts and chasms new volcanic land is formed, spreading the existing sea bed as moving 'tectonic plates' and giving rise to the theory of continental drift. The mid-Atlantic Ridge had been active in the 1940s, 50s and 60s with eruptions in Iceland in 1946 and 1961, the Azores in 1957 and Tristan da Cunha in 1961.

In the early morning of 14th November 1963, the small fishing boat *Isleifur*, out of Heimaey, was paying out her lines in the open sea 15 miles to the south west of her home port. The crew finished doing this at 6.30 a.m. when it was still dark and went into the forecastle for hot coffee. One of them smelt sulphur. The ship's galley was suspected, and the ship's cook accused of burning the toast. Soon after, the sea became rougher and dawn began to break. The cook was now on watch and caught sight of a cloud of black smoke rising from the surface of the sea in the distance. The skipper was roused and guessed that they must be watching the eruption of a submarine volcano. Typically, he sailed his boat up to the rising fumes, although ash, cinders and lava 'bombs' were beginning to fly in all directions to the accompaniment of lightning flashes. The ship's engineer calmly measured the water temperature and found it to be two degrees warmer than usual. They were sitting on top of a 'powder keg', 120 metres below them that was fast building up a cone from the sea bed.

They decided to leave and got away just in time. A few hours later, the smoke clouds had reached a height of eight miles and the explosions had been heard a hundred miles away. A new island burst through the surface amid fire, steam and the explosive effects of molten lava at a temperature of $1,200°$ C jetting into $10°$ C ocean water.

Originally, three islets had been formed, but the seas and gales quickly broke down the two smaller ones, leaving Surtsey with it twin peaks, strong enough to stay above and grow to change the map of the world. At the same time, Surtla nearby, had erupted but had not reached the surface. One school of vulcanologists believed that only molten *magma* could build up a cone from the sea bed because of the immense water pressure at depth. There were others believed that large pieces of solid *tephra* were blown out at the same time. We were soon to find the answer.

As *Bara* bobbed through the rolling sea and flying spray, on course for Surtsey, we clung on to anything solid and were offered slices of dried fish (an Icelandic delicacy) by the crew   It seemed to taste like a mixture of asbestos and cardboard with a faint fish flavouring.

Gradually we got nearer, and finally the island towered above us and a beach of huge, black boulders lay dead ahead. We managed to land using our inflatable, but it was not easy. Expedition members jumped on to rocks, clutching their 'land' cameras. We assembled on the beach for lunch and to get our breath back. I reflected that nothing on this island, so solid beneath our feet, was older than 18 years. It rose 172 metres above us and had an area of two and a half square kilometres. A curious seal watched as we munched peanut butter sandwiches, crisps and biscuits.

I followed Pete, across a lagoon of fine dust where molten magma had swirled just a few years before. The first sign of plant colonisation showed in small, bright green patches of 'sea sandwort' (*Honckenya peploides*). On the other side of the lagoon, was a newly built scientist's hut, but there was no scientist in residence. We climbed on up the side of the main crater, through slippery dust to find a superb view over the Westmans, and then on down into the actual crater, where steam still gushed from crevices and there were views of a red and black interior. We slid further and then picked our way carefully among twisted rocks to look down a crevass into the very heart of the volcano. The rock was becoming unsteady. It was two hours before we were back on the beach, ready to do our dive on Surtla, half a mile further out.

According to the chart, we should find the summit of Surtla 40 metres down, but we guessed that it might be difficult to pinpoint it so were prepared to go deeper. Graham and Gordon set off down our shot line, bottoming at 47 metres. Eric Thompson a geologist and I were following. By 40 metres it was getting dark. At 46 metres, we saw black volcanic sand with occasional cubes of rock – *tephra*. The solidified lava rocks seemed to suggest an answer to the vulcanologist's theories about the formation of volcanos.

Bara rolled back to Heimaey, following the chain of islets – Geirfuglasker, Geldungur, Hellisey, Brandur and Sudurey. At Hellisey, the first gannets joined us, braking in mid-air and craning their necks to watch us below them. A magnificent sight of the largest sea bird in these waters. Then a single black body raced through the flock – an arctic skua. I watched until I was blue with cold.

We hired a light plane from the tiny airport and flew around the islands taking photos. A wild night of rain followed and one tent became completely waterlogged. The friendly assistant harbourmaster called and offered an unused house to the bedraggled occupants and anyone else who preferred to stay within solid walls. Phil,

Mike and I decided to 'stick it out' in our tent. The harbourmaster stayed for a drink and told us how Mediterranean pirates had landed on Heimaey in the early 1600s and massacred part of the population. A progressive Danish governor had then raised the only army in Iceland, consisting of just 100 men. He had also apparently taught the locals 'to wash, sing and drink less'! Most of us later went in to town to drink more, sampling the local firewater called 'brinevin'.

We carried on diving off the more sheltered north and west coasts. One evening Stuart and Yvonne Ward and Phil (who would later become BSAC Chairman) organised a barbecue. We ate hamburgers and steaks under a clear evening sky as a great skua patrolled along the cliff edge and the setting sun picked out the whiteness of breaking waves on the black rocks below. A magnificent sunset developed and the islands on the horizon were outlined, dark and mysterious , leading out to Surtsey, perhaps a symbol of the re-birth of the earth.

On the 21st, I managed to dive with Bernard Picton, our marine biologist, who was one of the three most knowledgeable experts on nudibranchs, the elegant and colourful sea slugs. He was quiet, humorous and dedicated. I watched him find them in unexpected places and then delicately sweep them into plastic bags for further study. He also found a tiny anemone (*Phellia gausapata*) that had not been reported from Iceland before and a cushion star (*Hippasteria phrygiana*) that was rare.

In the evening, we were invited to go with Gwuthlyem to drop off a young deep-sea trawler skipper who spent his holidays hunting puffins with butterfly nets on Brandur. We passed a basking shark and half an hour later, swept into a hidden inlet on the island. We scrambled up the rocky slope and on up over turf, riddled with puffin burrows, to a tiny hut nestling below the summit. Gwuthlyem led us along the crest to a ledge where we could watch and photograph a large gannet colony a few feet below us. We later returned to the hut and drank coffee as the sun set and talked of future expedition plans.

Half way back to Heimaey, Gwuthlyem swung the wheel over and diverted out to sea where a friend was trawling in a 30-foot fishing boat as the moon rose. His friend slowly raised the head of a monstrous fish that he had just brought up from 80 metres. The sight was surreal. We realised that it was a giant halibut and he shouted that it weighed over 60 kilos. Under the huge red moon, the quiet sea was packed with hungry black-backed gulls waiting for spoils.

On the 22nd, the whole expedition set out for Surtsey again. It was 10 miles in the open sea and the outboard motors were pretty unpredictable. Flying icy spray stung our faces as the hours went by. Soon after one in the afternoon we arrived at the islet of Geirfuglasker, an impressive rock that was un-dived and the last place where the Great Auk had nested before it became extinct. We dived down the rock face collecting Dendronotus nudibranchs for Bernard before ploughing on the remaining two miles to Surtsey through 5-foot seas.

As we arrived, a seal was traversing along the shoreline and then, when we landed, actually heaved itself ashore. Very friendly, we thought, but there was another reason. Suddenly I sighted three fins in the distance and shouted 'Dolphins!' Then I saw one spout, and knew that they were whales. The others now stood up to watch. As the whales approached one of the huge bodies rolled out, exposing a clear black and white pattern. Killers! We watched spellbound as they sliced effortlessly through the waves and chased more seals on to the beach.

Mick was the first to act, tugging the smallest inflatable down towards the breaking waves and shouting to Gordon to get his camera. Three more of us jumped aboard and were off through the lumpy seas, getting occasional glimpses of the huge six-foot fins ahead.

Fulmars and gannets swooped low as if to encourage us, and suddenly the pod were only twenty yards away, their great fins rising like huge knives. We held tight as Gordon clicked away. Black and white bodies rolled, one killer momentarily outlined in a vast wave as it rose.

Suddenly they had all disappeared. We cut the engine and rode silently over the waves. Then they were back again, but this time turning purposefully towards us – a sight feared by other great whales since the dawn of time.

I shouted 'You know they've sunk yachts!' and remember Gordon's reply:

'I've only got one thing to say to you guys, if you're going to die, do it with panache and within camera range'!

His camera clicked on. Confused thoughts flashed in my mind. The huge fins roared up to us, and then ...

They dived, and we waited for the worst. Great bodies swung away below us and we breathed again. A few moments more and they had gone for good. It had been a magic ten minutes with the most intelligent and powerful creatures in the ocean.

Back on shore we rested and then reset course for Heimaey, roller-costing down the swells with roaring, cavitating engines under the swooping gannets and rolling fulmars.

A day later we dived off another islet, Einidrangur, where we found rock ridges and Bernard was excited to find a nudibranch that he at first believed was unknown to science. It was a species of *Eubranchus*, but it turned out that it was just unrecorded in the western hemisphere. We felt that the expedition had been of scientific value.

Two days were left to explore the Icelandic mainland and we finally arrived at Reykjavik after an eventful journey during which the 4-ton lorry rolled off the edge of the sodden, unsurfaced road and turned on its side. We righted it using the land rovers. In the evening, we joined an Icelandic party and found out how attractive Icelandic girls could be and, also, the stupefying cost of alcoholic drinks. Our 'grand tour' took us on over more rough country to see water gushing from the earth (Great Geyser), falling over it (Great Waterfall) and frozen to it (Giant Ice Cap). We forded rivers, up to the land-rover's floorboards in water, and felt invincible.

As we flew out, the Westmans slipped away into memory. It had been a land of ice and fire and wild volcanic craters amid a sea of islands, cliffs and a million seabirds. Underwater we had been surrounded by thousands of circling fish, and above, watched the effortless swoop of gannets and the power of killer whales.

I had memories of people too, new friends in adversity and the warmth of an Icelandic welcome. Memories of collecting tiny nudibranchs and setting foot on the newest island in the world. Looking out from a puffin hunter's hut into a red sunset of flying wings, and the moment when our inflatable swamped at the same time as the engine cut out in breaking seas. Above all, the instant when the fins of three killer whales turned purposefully towards our motionless little inflatable and our whole world seemed to hold its breath.

CHAPTER FIFTEEN

Excursions into TV & a Honeymoon shared with Manatees

OUR NEW SCHOOL was beginning to prosper. The only place to learn diving in London before had been with one of the clubs, most of them BSAC branches, who took their time over training, and were not able to do crash courses. As the first school in the capital, we filled an urgent need for those who wanted a quick course before holidays or filming sessions and also for professional people who could not fit in regularly with the branches' regular evening sessions. By November 1981 we were also teaching regularly at an old public pool, Porchester Hall at the top of Queensway.

Among our first students were the financial director of Saatchi & Saatchi, a number of barristers and some girls bound for a Red Sea photo-shoot with Mike Portelly. I had first met Mike when he had come into my office at the BSAC one day and asked if I would introduce him to some underwater photographers. He was then a successful dentist but had the soul of an artist, and had been seduced by the colours and shapes that he had seen underwater. I was to see much more of him in the future.

Viscount Petersham was due to leave on a round-the-world cruise and brought his children, 14-year-old William and 11½-year-old Serena for lessons. Some ten years later Serena was to become Viscountess Linley, after marrying Princess Margaret's son.

In August, I broke off from teaching to join a London branch party on a cheap diving holiday in Malta. I arrived in time to see them do their first dive at night in the Blue Grotto. The Maltese dive shop's organisation was among the most irresponsible that I had ever seen. The dive guide took 14 of them into a cave with only one torch between each pair. His briefing consisted entirely of the dangers of jellyfish that night. I snorkelled above them, watching the ghostly white shapes of jellyfish below, as there was no cylinder available for me. I felt like an anxious parent and was delighted that their branch training ensured their survival.

After that, I planned their week's diving for them and Filfla, the mysterious island was top of the list. I slept on a balcony under the stars and we took part in local fiestas as one of our members, Tony Vella, was Maltese. Another of the party was a chef at the Grosvenor House hotel, so we ate well when he cooked for us.

The next day, we collected our cylinders from the dive shop and drove to Wadi Zurrieq to join the boat we had hired to take us to Filfla. This time the islet appeared low on the horizon below us as we came over the hills. It looked as mysterious as ever. Our boatman set out over a rolling sea and told more tales of the sharks that had been caught there. On arrival, we swam down on to the top of an 'underwater island' at 10 metres and then on down a drop-off to 20 metres. There were impressive arches and then a large cavern with many coral growths. We went on down to another cave at 30 metres, but there was no sign of sharks or any large sea life.

Tony had obtained the use of an old car, and we began to have doubts about his driving ability as he tried to negotiate the narrow streets. The car was now parked at the end of the single road that descended into Wadi Zurrieq and he decided that he had to reverse back up the long slope to turn round. During this manoeuvre, he managed to hit several parked cars and scattered numerous pedestrians.

During the days that followed we had some fine dives round an islet called Feszej and I dived in the caves of Comino with our marine biologist member, Nicki Cropp. Tony's driving continued to amaze us. As he drove us up a two mile incline, it became horrifyingly clear that he would not make the top in the gear he was using. Without hesitation, Ian Doherty sprang out and started to push. The lessened weight and extra impetus made the difference and we were over as Ian sprang back in, as surprised drivers stalled behind us. Another of his manoeuvres involved his reversing into a side road; he then changed gear suddenly and leapt forward driving the bonnet under the middle of a terrified horse. It was unhurt, but disappeared with flattened ears and a hunted look in its eyes. I had to leave before the others as I was due to dive Stoney Cove with beginners and departed after an evening of 'Harvey Wallbangers' at 4.40 a.m.

By September 1981 over 19,000 dives had been made on the *Mary Rose* by the full-time staff and volunteers, and I decided to join them again for another week. We met up again with Alex Hildred outside the Bridge Inn in old Portsmouth to hear the sad news that the previous night's gale had broken part of the ship's diving platform. When we arrived on board, it was clear that due to the damage and current water conditions, there would be no diving for the next few days. We were given lectures by Jon Adams, Margaret, Chris Dobbs and Nic Rule. I was eventually 'checked out' by Doug Barnet and managed to find a variety of locations as ordered. Conditions were still so bad that Chris was not happy sending volunteers in but let me go after two hours. I did some work with my suction pump in nil visibility.

In October, I had a phone call from Rob Benfield, the director of *Blue Peter*, the BBC children's programme. He wanted us to teach Sarah Greene, one of their presenters. Some of the lessons would be televised and it was hoped that she would then be competent to dive on the *Mary Rose* before the ship was raised.

Sarah arrived at one of our regular pool sessions at Porchester Hall on Guy Fawkes night. She was a delightful girl and found diving tremendous fun. The BBC soon began to televise her lessons and she took to diving like a fish to water. Her boy friend, Mike Smith of Capital Radio also learnt at the same time though had to keep a low profile as he was a star of the other channel, Thames TV. She passed her pool training course with flying colours, shouting 'Brill!' at the camera as she surfaced.

Her open water dives were more spartan, involving freezing days in the Woolwich dock and then at Stoney Cove where the water temperature was only 3°C. She survived 30 minutes in her inadequate wet suit until her hands were completely numb, and came ashore to recover under a hot shower.

There was a certain amount of opposition from the regular BBC team filming the *Mary Rose* to the idea of Sarah diving on the wreck. After discussion, Margaret stressed that she did not question my standard of teaching, but in Sarah's case would ask for more than the Third Class certificate that was required of club volunteers. She would need to have a Part IV commercial diving certificate and experience on three historical wrecks. Rob was in despair, but I assured him that we could fix everything.

Biddy Baxter, the Editor of *Blue Peter* and not a lady to be trifled with, arranged a meeting with Margaret, together with the Executive Director, Development Director and Director of Recovery of the *Mary Rose*. The two ladies sat eye to eye at the top of a long table and Rob and I were at the bottom. I had planned for Sarah to complete dives on an archaeological wreck near Bovisand with Alan Bax and with John Bingeman on his excavation off the Isle of Wight. A Part IV exemption was also arranged. All obstacles were in the process of being overcome and Margaret finally agreed to the dive going ahead.

Sarah continued with her experience dives on the *James Egan Layne* wreck in Cornwall and then Alan Bax took us on an ancient wreck, believed to be the *Coronation*, where Sarah helped him to take measurements. For her final archaeological dive, we were under the control of underwater archaeologist and RN Commander, John Bingeman. We did a 'drift' dive to collect Victorian artefacts.

The underwater visibility varied from 9 inches to 2 feet! Sarah and I held hands to maintain contact. At one point, peering ahead into the murk, I was startled as a wildly struggling body appeared immediately in front of my mask. I soon saw that it was a crab and was puzzled that it seemed to have come down from above. I checked that Sarah was OK, and saw bubbles coming out from around her mask. I gradually realised that she was laughing, and then guessed that she must have picked up the crab with her other hand and purposely dropped it just above my head. 'She'll make a diver all right', I said to myself.

Sarah was finally considered qualified to dive on the *Mary Rose* and I left with the *Blue Peter* television team, meeting up with the *Chronicle* filming team at Portsmouth. Margaret discussed the route with Sarah and the rest of us. It was decided that we could dive the next day and I walked up to Southsea Castle where I looked out from the battlements towards the *Mary Rose* as King Henry VIII had some 400 years before. He had heard the cries of the drowning men across the calm sea.

Sarah dived with Margaret and was, as usual, ecstatic. Margaret said: 'Reg, you've trained a really good diver there'. I was given a quick tour of the wreck afterwards and saw the remains of the recently found brick oven on board It was to be my last dive before the wreck was raised and the *Blue Peter* TV programmes were a nice souvenir.

Back in London we continued with our beginners and soon hired an attractive little pool at the Hogarth Club in Chiswick for our day-time sessions. A number of 'tycoons rushed through our hands, together with stock-brokers and the Chairman of the West Indies Development Board. Janie had now met a London branch member, a mechanical engineer who was also a commercial pilot. His name was John Selby and he was to become a close friend and adviser. He sent numbers of his friends to learn with us. Those who wanted to go on to Third Class standard, we made BSAC members through the General Branch, but soon started our own BSAC branch, LUC or number 1301. In mid-summer 1982, young Julia Hines, who had been recommended to us by Col John Blashford-Snell, became our first branch member. Our branch eventually provided the Club with over 1,000 new members. We taught a charming Swedish model, Kristina Ehrenstrale, who later featured in our publicity photos. We also taught BBC presenter Peter McCann of *Tomorrow's World* TV, John Greenwood of Independent Radio News and *Daily Express* reporter, Peter Mason. Others included archaeological conservators, police officers and a minister of the Church of England who proved particularly adept at kneeling on the bottom of the pool to do his mask and tube exercises. As my MGB was unsuitable for carrying all the cylinders for our open water dives, Alex had acquired an ancient hatchback, which we christened 'Horace'. Unfortunately, it was unable to manage some of the steeper Devon hills, and on one occasion, we were reduced to reversing up to the amazement of oncoming traffic.

My first book had been published in the summer of 1981 in the Blandford Colour Series under the title *Divers and Diving*. It was a survey of diving history and current amateur, commercial, scientific and military diving. John Selby had now joined our SOS equipment importation business and we launched out and imported one of the first variable volume dry suits from America. John, Janie and I dived together off Portland early in 1982 to try them out and after that Alex and I were very busy teaching at Stoney Cove, Bovisand, Swanage and Weymouth.

In August I took several beginners to the south of France to join Bob and Daphne Page's charter boat the *Brielle* based at Beaulieu-sur-Mer. John and Janie took the two remaining places and we spent an evening in Monaco watching new owners drinking gins and tonics on the deck of Hans Hass's magnificent yacht *Xarifa*. Bob and Daphne's son, Steve, helped out with the dive marshalling and I enjoyed my first experience of wind surfing although overshadowed by John and Jane. We discovered red coral in caves off Villefranche at a depth of only 20 metres and chased an octopus through the shadows at twilight. A week later I was back on Giglio.

A month or so earlier, I had been phoned by an Oxford University researcher called Mensun Bound who had heard about the Giglio wreck from Alexander Mc-Kee. Over the previous few years I had tried to get some of the leading diving archaeologists interested in excavating the wreck, but they were all busy – Margaret on the *Mary Rose* and Peter Throckmorton on an ancient Turkish ship.

Mensun was a specialist in ancient pottery and came to see me in Sheen. He looked a typically unkempt student, but soon convinced me of his enthusiasm, especially after I showed him photos of what we had found off the Secca i Pignocchi. He said that our finds had been very significant and soon decided to mount an expedition from Oxford University to examine the remains of the wreck. He asked if I would take them there and show them where it was. I agreed.

Dates were provisionally fixed, but then cancelled, as the expedition was not yet ready. I had almost forgotten about the project when Mensun phoned again to say that they were leaving with a large van in a few days time. I pointed out that it was difficult for me to just down tools immediately as I was running a business; but realised that without me they would have little chance of finding the site. They intended to take several days to trundle through Europe with the van full of Oxford student divers and equipment and so I booked a plane scheduled to arrive at the same time as they did. Alex would hold the fort for the few days I expected it would take for me to re-find the remains again after so many years.

Arriving in Rome, I took the train to Orbetello and then the bus to the Giglio ferry. On the crossing, I noticed a young Italian crew member watching me. Eventually he asked nervously 'Are you Valentino?' I nodded. 'I remember you when I was a little boy'. I looked at his prematurely bald head and realised how time flew.

After some happy reunions with the islanders, I met the small advanced party, mainly students who were languidly occupying cheap rooms in the Porto. It seemed that Mensun were still somewhere in the middle of Europe. I booked in with Filippo and Wally at the Bahamas. The *Sea Laird* was now owned by Nilo, who had built an Italian style canopy to cover the deck. As I only had four days before my return, I told the startled students that they would have to dive with me immediately, in case Mensun did not arrive in time.

Filippo offered to take us the next morning with his small fishing boat and lent me one of his twin-sets of cylinders. Two of the youngsters were available to dive with me. One of them, Hamish Hay, explained that he had no deep diving experience as he had only been working on an ancient wreck in Sicily that was only a few feet below the surface. I reassured him that I would bring him back alive.

He, Mike Wright and I did our first dive on the secca the next day. The water was crystal clear. I relocated the cleft where 'my' grouper had once lived. There was no sign of him now. The place where I had found the ingots was nearby. I took pity on Hamish and did not go deeper than 25 metres. There were lots of fish about and I felt as at home here as I had back on the surface.

In the afternoon I walked out to Cannelle and sadly examined the few stones that remained of Victor's house. Now there were a series of tourist bungalows and a beach bar being built. The next evening the van arrived with Mensun, Alexander McKee and more students. I dived with Mensun for the first time on the 4th September, still trying to relocate the actual site which I remembered was out from the grouper cleft over rocks to deep sand. There was a vaguely familiar rock and a sand gulley running out to deeper water. We returned from 35 metres. I was now staying with the others on the campsite on the coast opposite the Secca i Pignocchi, and had only two days left to find the wreck.

On the 5th, Mensun and I were down at 45 metres and things began to come back to me, although the actual site was still elusive. On my last day, I tried an 'into the blue' dive direct from the surface above the grouper hole. I set course steeply downwards and a few minutes later became aware of a very familiar isolated rock below. At last I recognised it as marking the site of the wreck. We swam down to the sand at 50 metres and prospected for amphoras. Mensun and I both found fragments and returned delighted to the surface. He had left a light buoy on the site, so I knew that my job was now done. I left next morning on the 6 a.m. ferry.

Back in London, many beginners were arriving for lessons and it was not long before I was diving again at Bovisand, Stoney Cove and Swanage. A few weekends later, John, Jane and I took time off to watch the *Mary Rose* being lifted and then, at the end of the year, they got married in California and then flew to Miami to meet me for a week's diving in the Keys. We visited the conservationist and turtle expert, Noreen Rouse at West Palm Beach and dived from her centre after meeting up with Roger Hale, who now lived nearby, having married an American lady. A large diving launch took us out into the Gulf Stream where we were wafted along over the bottom 20 metres down, encountering sting rays and nurse sharks. It was like being in a great warm river and we soon saw our first turtle and then morays. Before the dive ended we came upon a huge leatherback turtle that, we were later told, Noreen had named Robert.

John, Janie and I hired a car and drove southwards to the Keys, passed mangrove swamps and huge white herons, storks and pelicans that watched us from the side of the road. Then on over long causeways through shallow blue sea to Marathon and on Christmas day to Key West, the southernmost point of USA. We dived from *Reef Raiders* launch with 10 Americans. Bad weather had reduced the underwater visibility and we jumped in and nearly broke our knees on the shallow bottom. The dive organiser, who did not go with us, responded 'I didn't say it was deep'. It was a disappointing dive over a flat bottom. On the return, he ran out of fuel, put on his fins, and tried to tow the dive boat the last few hundred yards with his teeth! Not an impressive performance.

We met up with Sarah Greene and Mike at Key West They were having a break from filming but the weather was too bad to dive there. We flew up to Tampa and then drove north to the Crystal river.

This was the home of the manatees, the slow friendly, weed-eating, sea cows whose only relations were the dugongs of south-east Asia. We hired a pram dinghy to tour the river. We stopped at Banana Island and slipped overboard with snorkels. Only fish were in sight until I duck-dived and in the low visibility was confronted on the bottom by a huge flat round tail – our first manatee. It must have been eight feet long and was lying peacefully on its stomach, with its head in the weed. After a while it rose slowly to the surface to breathe and John managed to scratch its stomach, causing the manatee to roll in ecstasy and show its small front flippers. Then it crapped and went back down again. We were suitably impressed.

The next day we scuba dived at King's Spring in 30 feet visibility and water temperature of 23° C. Near Banana Island a four-foot alligator gar swept past followed by two jacks (*Caranx*). Then another smooth bulbous and motionless back came in sight. I stroked its rough leathery skin gently and it peered at me above its moustaches. It rolled over and small bubbles came out of an orifice. We were convulsed with laughter. It must be all that weed they ate we decided. Then it started rubbing its front flippers together and dived again. After a while it seemed to tire of us and put its head into a patch of weed. Rather like an ostrich. We took the hint and returned to the boat.

Manatees are an endangered species and protected by American law. They suffered back injuries from the propellers of outboards on the many tourist boats searching for a sight of them in the river. We visited the local dive shop where a girl assistant told us that female manatees 'have their tits under their armpits and that's why they like to be rubbed there.' Fascinating …

During the last days in December we drove on southwards to Clearwater on Florida's west coast to sample diving in the Gulf of Mexico. Mac's local dive shop insisted that we all had octopus rigs on our regulators and then took us out on the

Gulf Explorer. There was a lot of talk about 'the Great Break', where apparently the bottom had 'fallen out of the ocean'. The young macho skipper, who spoke only to his two dolly-bird assistants, anchored over the feature in 15 metres of water. We went down expecting great things. It turned out that the 'great break' was only a fault line, just one foot high along the flat bottom where we found pygmy file fish, grunts and a few nudibranchs. The next day we tried again and watched while the skipper dived first with a huge harpoon gun, surfacing twenty minutes later with two conch shells.

1983 was to be the first year when the LUC took off, teaching 158 pupils including dentists, film producers, actors, cameramen, journalists, stunt men, lawyers and photographers. The daughter of the Lebanese ambassador was enthusiastic as were two schoolboys from Eton bound for a Royal Society expedition on Aldabra. Dr Martha Holmes, a young zoologist, came to brush up her diving skills in the 5°C water of Stoney Cove. She later became the star of the BBC's 24-hour Red Sea coverage *Reef Watch* and another series, *Sea Trek*. Sadly my partner, Alex Double also took off to run a diving holiday in Safaga with his girl friend, Tamara. I decided not to replace him, but continue with help from part-time instructors.

One of the most distinguished wild life cinematographers from Anglia TV, Dieter Plage, took lessons to get his qualification. He had shot amazing films of gorillas and flown over Everest in a light plane while filming. He was quiet, unflappable and fearless. Later he sent me wonderful letters from the Galapagos telling of his underwater encounter with sperm whales 'enjoying a social event.' Sadly he was killed falling from a balloon while filming in Indonesia in 1993.

In April, Jimmy Saville's TV programme, *Jim Will Fix It* were in contact and we taught 13-year-old Kerry Palmer, before she left to 'live her dream' of diving on coral reefs in the West Indies. I appeared on the show to present her with certificates and part of her training with us was shown.

'Cindy' Buxton and Annie Price were well-known TV natural history film makers and photographers, having become famous after being marooned on South Georgia when the Argentinians invaded. They learnt to dive before leaving again to film and photograph penguins on Ascension.

John Smith, the MP for Westminster, and Chairman of the Landmark Trust that now administered Lundy for the nation, sent his son and daughter to learn. His daughter, Serena later became the wife of Nicholas Soames, a Minister in Conservative governments.

Sarah Greene was due to leave the *Blue Peter* programme and they arranged a surprise 'on-air' party for her. Margaret Rule and I gave her presents to celebrate her successful dives.

The BBC history programme *Chronicle* contacted me as they wanted to make a film on the 'Giglio wreck'. Mensun and his volunteers were now bringing up small terracotta flasks or *aryballoi*, some marked with animal motifs. The programme's producer, Roy Davis, came to learn, so that he could direct the underwater sequences.

At the end of June, it was time for the filming to begin and I arrived on Giglio to discover that Mensun and his team had suffered a serious theft of recovered artefacts which had been left out on the seabed awaiting the film makers. Italian divers had visited the site at midnight and made off with nearly everything! Mensun, however, already had many finds ashore being preserved. The expedition seemed to be short of experienced divers and I went in at once to help with the work of deep excavation. Roy arrived from London and I alternated my dives between working the wreck and supervising his first shallower sea dives.

I worked on the wreck with Mike Russell, who had a dive shop near Oxford, and we found the remains of wood planks. We excavated another two *aryballoi*, which had contained body cleansing oil, one with a leaf pattern and the other with a drawing of a goat. One of the portions of an amphora recovered had the drawing of a young man dancing while being slapped on the buttocks – the Etrusans obviously had fun. They had also recovered ancient arrow heads.

A day or so later, I took Roy to 30 metres where he had no problems, and his two underwater cameramen, John Beck and David Swann arrived in Campese. I suggested they chartered *Sea Laird* for a week for the film and sound crew and they negotiated a price with Nilo.

John and David tracked me with their cameras as I swam into the 'grouper hole'. On 5th July, Ric Wharton, who was an expedition sponsor, arrived to dive the wreck with us. He had also sponsored our *X-5* expedition back in 1974. Alexander McKee was also on site as an expedition member. Ric was pushing Mensun for results and, in view of the danger of pirate divers removing finds, the project became one of rescue archaeology, in which everything possible was recovered before the winter started and the Oxford team returned to Britain.

I had a month or so back in the cool British sea, before I made yet another sortie to Giglio, this time with a party of my closest friends. It proved a rather explosive mixture. Keith and Jean Nicholson and I began by assembling equipment and driving a hired caravanette to Giglio. On the island, we stayed with Filippo and Wally. Ginnie Ashton arrived first and joined us on our first dive at Giannutri in the Grottoni. I was surprised to find that there was now a restaurant there and some partly built tourist bungalows.

Three days later John and Janie flew in with John and Annie Bevan, John and Sue Stubbs and one of my pupils, Sarah McDermott from 'Operation Raleigh' who had decided to do her qualifying dives with us. We dived off the northern point of

Giglio and Sarah, doing her first sea dive, declared that she was sure that her teeth had changed shape. An unknown pressure symptom as far as we knew. Gigi, Trudi's husband had now opened a small cocktail bar above the port and we enjoyed his creations, while discussing malt whiskies and John Stubbs's concept of 'the perfect martini'.

A week later, some disagreements began about the diving programme but we enjoyed a lively visit to the Fiesta of San Mamiliano at Castello. Vernon Knapper arrived like a breath of fresh air and finally Tom and Elfie Baum. Vernon had survived an accident in England in which he had accidentally stepped backwards off the top of a three storey building. His fall had been broken by a bush and he had been lucky to only break a leg. When he dived though, an impressive stream of bubbles emerged from his ears and it was clear that both eardrums were broken. That was the end of his diving on Giglio. Ian Forster, the BSAC coach for Germany sailed in with a red ex-fishing boat called *Ettore Fieramosca*. It was owned and run by a stern, bearded skipper called Rudi de Belgeonne from Belgium. Ian had organised a charter diving holiday for RAF divers stationed in Germany and we dived with them at Giannutri.

On 22nd September everyone else left on the ferry to Santo Stefano. I relaxed for the first time, walked to Caldane and swam in clear, blue and warm water. Alan and Rudy returned from Giannutri with their group and invited me dive with them on the Formiche di Grosseto islets to the north-east of Giglio.

On my final day, I caught a bus to Castello and then walked south along the backbone of the island on the route that Barbarossa had taken, in the opposite direction, when he took Giglio by storm by landing secretly on the southern point and walking his pirates overnight to descend on Castello at day break. It took me 1½ hours to walk to Punta Capel Rosso along tracks and paths, passing occasional lizards and vineyards. I sunbathed and swam at the isolated cove Cala Saranesca, ate a solitary picnic and thought how much I loved this island.

On the flight back we went right over Montecristo, 40 miles to the north of Giglio. It was an astonishing sight – great steep crags seemed to leap straight out of the sea. It looked like half a huge walnut below us and I resolved to dive there again one day, although diving was currently forbidden as it had been declared an Italian reserve.

CHAPTER SIXTEEN

Montecristo, Isle of Treasure, Saints & Pirates

OUR LONDON SCHOOL was busy as ever. I began to call in other instructors to help. Andy Pappacosta, who was later to run his own school, Mike Seares, whose ambition was to work in films, Keith Morris, an expert underwater photographer, Peter Farrell, an ex-actor and 'Buff' Norgren from London branch, all helped, usually taking groups during the evening sessions.

Soon Anne Henderson, a lively young lady, became our 100th LUC branch member. I was still secretary of the CMAS technical committee and a member of BSAC Council, receiving the most votes from members in the 1984 election. SOS, our import agency was broadening its lines under John and Janie, and *Chronicle's* Giglio film was shown on BBC television.

We taught Julian Pettifer, presenter of ITV's *Nature Watch*, Jim Cellan-Jones, director of the series *Jewel in the Crown* and Simon Groome, a colleague of Sarah's at *Blue Peter* who was due to film seals off Lundy.

Bryan Murphy and Nigel Learmond, who ran a steel company arrived and were in the middle of their third class training on a murky, cold day at Weymouth, when Bryan took me aside. 'Reg, why don't we continue somewhere warmer?' I told him that the Med's wet season was beginning . 'Tell us what your "fat fee" would be for continuing on individual tuition, and we'll take you to the Maldives to do it.' We flew out in March to arrive on these miniscule islands in the middle of the Indian Ocean. Nigel warned me on the plane that he had a horror of touching live fish and I assured him that wasn't part of the course.

From Male airport we took a small boat to the island of Baros. It took two hours over a calm sea escorted by dolphins. Baros was small, tree-covered and beautiful. It was surrounded by a lagoon and beaches of white coral sand, and took half an hour to walk round. There was a central restaurant, bar and shop, and a series of commodious, thatched huts each with a shower and central fan.

Although it was forbidden to bring alcohol into the Maldives, the bar was reasonably well stocked. Bryan asked if they had any champagne and after much searching in the drinks cupboard, they managed to produce a bottle. The cost seemed astronomical to me. 'Put it on ice for us to drink tonight', ordered Brian, 'and prepare a bottle for us every evening.' They were generosity itself.

I organised a first dive in the lagoon. There were fish everywhere, grunts, wrasse, grouper, sweetlips, butterfly fish, trumpet fish, box fish and, in the distance, jacks. There was even a baby white-tip shark that played around us. The water temperature was a very warm 29°C.

The next day, we joined the island *dhoni* or sail boat for a dive with their dive guide, a Dutch girl who rejoiced in the name of Riet Wubbs, and saw more sharks. The currents were occasionally very strong and we drifted with them as she pointed out rare black frogfish. We photographed sharks that circled us and even occasionally swam in our direction. I was more concerned about the tiny territorial reef fish that nibbled at the back of my bare knees for kneeling on their patch.

We dived at a number of different locations and watched manta rays. Then Riet announced that we could watch the chief instructor feeding sharks underwater if we wished. We jumped at the chance and she briefed us about not waving our hands and, if the sharks became aggressive, to hit or kick them on their noses.

The chief instructor was away filming on the day and his younger brother arranged the session and carried a large bag full of dead fish into the water. The sharks, knowing what to expect, began to circle hungrily. We knelt on the reef edge and watched.

As the youngster waved the first fish, the sharks got rapidly closer. Then one ran in and took it as the others continued to circle hungrily. They seemed to have worked out some sort of priority between them as a different shark came in each time. Then things went wrong.

A shark that had been lurking behind us suddenly swept passed over our shoulders and took the bait before the next 'designated' shark arrived. The disappointed shark started a zig-zag swimming movement and its pectoral fins dropped, a sign of aggression. The others began to change posture too. 'This could be interesting', I thought. Meanwhile extra fish were being hastily proffered. Slowly things slowed down again until the supply of fish was exhausted. It was a demonstration of how easily things could get out of control when humans interact with animals.

The next day we were down surrounded by batfish that also expected to be fed. I had to literally punch them away to watch the circling white tips further out. Many remoras swam around detached from their host sharks. We had bare legs, just using jackets, as the water was so warm. They seemed particularly attracted to Nigel's legs which were pink with the first flush of sun. To his horror they began to stick on to him. Definitely a new experience. He remained cool, doubtless thinking of England.

That evening we celebrated his deliverance with 'bucks fizz' and a fresh lobster dinner.

A few days before, I had been stung on one of my fingers as I pulled myself along a reef against the current. The finger grew in size and did not heal. Back in Colombo for a day on our return, Bryan and Nigel insisted on summoning a local doctor to look at it. A small dark man in a white coat arrived with a girl in nurse's uniform. Without any introduction, he instructed me to remove my trousers and lie on my bed, face down. I indicated that it was my finger that was the problem. He repeated his order and produced a large syringe which he waved in the air. Nigel and Bryan cheered enthusiastically as the deed was done. I had difficulty sitting during the connecting flight to London, but my finger got better.

A few weeks later, I was on my way again, this time to Hurghada on the Egyptian Red Sea coast with Chris and Roger Chadwick, English agents for a diving holiday based there. I took a small party of our trainees, including Annie Henderson, and her boyfriend Steve. Other places were filled by Gill Lythgoe and Sarah McDermot who wanted to sample the diving there. Hurghada was a lot more primitive than the Maldives. Egypt Air started by serving gristly lamb, and our subsequent night journey by coach from Cairo and Hurghada involved our driver nodding off and driving into the desert where the coach was deposited on its side and we were surrounded by broken bottles of duty-free and dodged falling suitcases. A sterling group of north-country divers who were aboard soon righted the coach, and we were on our way again.

Hurghada's Red Sea Dive Centre was run by Rudi Kneip, a German, and it was clear that it provided a cheap holiday for German divers. We were shown to a peeling stucco house where the beds were unmade and dirty and the loos in need of cleaning. Chris organised a better alternative and we dropped our bags in another small house, outside which a notice prominently proclaimed 'Shakespeers Home'.

We returned for breakfast amid the debris left by the departing Germans. Rudi was married to a local lady who was in charge of the domestic arrangements. She sported a silver wet suit and was unimpressed by our suggestions for improvements.

The next day I took my students diving while Gill and Sarah departed elsewhere with Rudi. The fish life and visibility were fine but I was amazed to find that it felt quite cold (23°C) after the Maldives. Chris organised an evening at the local Club Med village with its wonderful cuisine, and we had another at the local Sheriton Hotel, which provided a welcome break from the dive centre's food. At the end of a week, we took taxis back to Cairo, only losing a wing mirror to an oncoming lorry.

In July it was back to the Med with another party of trainees. We were to live aboard the *Fieramosca*, run by the other Rudy and were joined by my new secretary, Moura Williams.

From Talamone, the little Italian coastal town where *Fieramosca* was based, we sailed south to the Argentario peninsula opposite Giglio. After diving there, we left for Giannutri and after another two days diving, made a night passage to Giglio under a full moon. We visited Mensun and the expedition who were now continuing the excavation of the Etruscan wreck. One of the expedition's sponsors was Prince Hans-Adam of Lichtenstein, and he had been diving on the wreck. He was staying at the Demos Hotel and we shared a pizza with him in the Porto.

After my group had left, I returned to help with the excavation. Paul Arbiter, a professional photographer, took shots of Mensun and me fanning sand from the wreck site at 45 metres for an article in the *Sunday Express* colour supplement which appeared soon after. Before I left, Mensun, Joanna and I visited Ruby in Talamone to discuss chartering his boat again to look for an ancient wreck off Montecristo that he had told Mensun about.

Back in London, a Saudi-Arabian prince arrived for lessons. He was accompanied by several armed bodyguards. We persuaded them to cover their guns up when we went for a drink in the Daniel Gooch after the session.

At that time, Porchester Hall, a Victorian institution, had a series of wooden changing cubicles around the pool. They were infested with small fast-moving beetles called silver fish. The staff made valiant attempts to get rid of them, even setting elaborate traps of various kinds with little effect. One night, after the training session, I got to the Daniel Gooch early to try to reserve a large table for the others. The only suitable table had one occupant, a staid-looking local with a cap and pipe. I got a beer, sat down and waited for the others. Suddenly I felt a silver fish running across my back. I reached round and managed to hit the spot. The local took his pipe out.'Are you OK?' he asked curiously. I explained the situation. He said nothing but then quietly moved to another table.

I had been chairman of the BSAC's Schools Association since 1983 and Don Collier and his wife Cheryl, who had helped me with my pool teaching, now set up a shop, school and dive boat at Poole in Dorset. I went down with some of my clients and we dived on a seventeenth-century wreck that had an improbable cargo of antlers, a last war wreck inhabited by crabs, and on a Valentine tank that housed a large conger.

In November I organised our first Red Sea live aboard course on a steam yacht called the *Lady Jenny V*. It had once belonged to Hitler and based on the Rhine, but was now owned by an Englishman, Tony Turner. We flew to Israel this time and travelled by minibus to Sharm where she was based. She had a friendly crew of six plus an underwater photographer called Lawson Wood. My diving party numbered ten, and I took out Mike Seares to help me. The ship's captain, Jeremy also acted as a dive guide for the more experienced divers.

Jeremy had an interesting scar down through his lower lip and chin as he had been, somewhat recklessly, feeding a moray eel using his mouth. The moray usually took a gentle grip on the dead fish he held there, but this time had slipped on the fish scales, and, moving forward to get a better grip, had caught his lip as well. It tore a piece out of his face. As there was no surgeon near, he managed to stem the blood, bound it up and let it heal naturally over several weeks, resulting in the impressive scar.

Our evenings on board were spent watching Lawson's underwater slides and David Attenborough films through a haze of gin and wine. We sang songs, played games and Jim Cellin-Jones wrote sonnets. After a dive on Jackson Reef, we went to visit the wreck of the *Lara*, a cargo ship that was sitting upright on top of the reef. She had been run aground there in 1981 and by this time had been pretty well sacked by locals. We managed the high climb up a rickety rope ladder to get to the deck and explore.

At Ras Mohammed, the great vertical reef, Lawson and I swam out 'into the blue' and into a rising stream of amberjacks with shoals of barracuda behind them. A marvellous sight. From there Bob Johnson, one of the crew, guided us back via the Shark islands to the wreck of the *Jolanda*, then in one piece, in only ten metres of water with her bow above the surface. She later split in half during a storm and the bow section disappeared down the cliff, beyond diving range.

A day or so later Jeremy managed to find another wreck, the *Dunraven* that had sunk, miles from anywhere, in 1876. There were only three rocks, just a few inches above the surface to mark the spot. We swam through the whole length of the ship, passed hovering lion fish and shoals of silver small fry illuminated in bands of sunlight.

We were still busy teaching in 1985 and the variation in the kinds of people taking up the sport constantly amazed me. We taught models (who supplied us with free gin from their stand at the Boat Show), TV writers (stories featuring underwater crimes), actors, tree surgeons, policemen, ex-jail birds and even one unfortunate who was murdered on Clapham Common soon after his first lesson. We were now also using John and Janie's pool at their new home in Mill Hill, and PR millionaire, Brian Basham, was sent to us there by the new Chairman of BSAC, Ian Irvine, something of a tycoon himself.

Eryl Davies, an ex-lodger of mine and a great drinker and *bon-viveur* took time out from the Science Museum to learn, as did a self-effacing young lady who was one of the only five stunt women in the country. She exhibited some interesting scars from her work. By the end of the year we had also taught TV comics (Jim Davidson) and another TV presenter, Anneka Rice who I would get to know well in future years.

Anneka was then the star of *Treasure Hunt* in which she helicoptered around the country and then ran everywhere to collect clues against the clock. Although she didn't know it at the time, the producer intended to place one at the bottom of the dolphin tank in the aquarium in Miami, hence her diving course.

Mike Seares begged me to let him teach her and I agreed, though reserving the final lesson and test to myself. She was initially daunted by the pool exercises, but persisted and graduated to Stoney Cove for open water experience. She wrote an article in *Diver*, part of which read:

I set off with Reg, Mike and a troop of lunatics at 6am on a bleak and wet April morning. On arrival, the Arctic temperatures served to heighten my growing apprehension. Climbing into a full head-to-toe wet suit, the breathing apparatus and clumsy weights almost sealed my diving career. All I wanted to do was sit in the pub and sulk. But, I couldn't let the side down, so off we went into what resembled a large bowl of vegetable soup. Visibility was nil, the water was cold, dark and murky.

She survived and even enjoyed the après-dive camaraderie. Sadly when she eventually arrived in Miami, the aquarium authorities declined to allow them into their tank. Her training was to stand her in good stead later though.

My second book, *The Pocket Guide to Underwater Diving,* was published and we now had 200 members in our LUC branch, which was becoming one of the largest in the BSAC. We were also the proud possessors of a freshly painted Ford Transit van bearing our tropical motif and the legend, 'Underwater courses, holidays and equipment'. It managed the hills better than 'Horace', the hatch-back.

Mike and I taught the new owner of a small island in the Scillies called The Gugh and he asked if we would do a survey and report on its suitability as a dive school and centre. We made our own way to the island, eventually crossing a sand bar that was covered at high tide, on foot. The only inhabited house had once been a barn. We walked around the small island, being bombed by swooping black-backed gulls.

We dived off a small sand beach and assessed it as suitable for beginners and visited the second house on the island, which they were busy repairing and building a conservatory. We crossed the sand bar again to St Agnes to investigate the local pub where we watched two youngsters caught by the tide as they rowed back to St Marys. The friendly publican alerted the coastguard and HMS *Beaver* sent their inflatable to pick them up before they reached America.

We decided to check out the boat diving for our report and used Jim Heslin, a well-known operator. He took us to the wrecks of the *Brinkburn* (1898) and *Zelda* (1874). They were beautiful sites with cannons, corals and anemones. We had a long swim through the tide back to his anchored boat though. I prepared a comprehensive report on my return and sent it with our account, which was never paid.

By June I was out at the Eddystone again, this time in the powerful rigid inflatable owned by John Parker, the London coach, who was helping me teach two young business ladies, Helen Brierley and Mary Platt. We found we could see underwater for 20 metres and enjoyed exploring gulleys populated with cuckoo wrasse, breadcrumb sponges and bushes of gorgonians. The under-surfaces of the rocks were covered in a blanket of mauve, green, blue and pink cup corals.

For many months, Mensun had been working to obtain permission to dive off the 'forbidden' island of Montecristo with Rudy and the Fieramosca. Unfortunately both Rudy's boats were now impounded by the tax authorities in the harbour at Talamone, so he had arranged to hire another motor yacht owned by a friend of Rudy's and which Rudy would skipper to take us to the wreck site. I arranged to hire the same vessel the week before so that I could take some of my students who were keen to come to Montecristo, and give them some deep diving experience before we arrived. They were Anne Henderson, Steve Gentry and Barbara Duckett.

We arrived in Talamone and stayed the night on *Fieramosca II*, lying in harbour with plants and window boxes demonstrating its 'immobility' to the Guardia di Finanza. Dario, an ageing Italian arrived, and we sailed out on his yacht, *Antalea* to dive the Grottoni at Giannutri and then the wreck of an Italian cargo ship, sunk just a few years before in the Cala Ischiaola. A day or so later, after some deep dives, we motored across to Giglio, the students having proved that they were happy down at 52 metres.

As always, it was good to see Filippo and Wally again, together with both their sons, Luca and Paolo, plus a little grand-daughter who had been christened Valentina. Later Trudi and Gigi opened a bottle of spumanti and showed me a report in a recent Italian daily on the Campese wreck and its discovery by Raig (*sic!*) Valentine. Mensun and Jo were now in Campese with the other expedition members and had finally got permission for us to dive on Montecristo, providing we agreed not to try to live ashore. Mensun, Jo, Dick Hill and Angus Butler settled aboard and we sailed out westwards for the island.

Montecristo had been a nature reserve since 1971. It was a high granite mountain with an area of 10 sq. km and had 16 km of coastline. The resident *guardiano* and his family inhabited the remains of a Royal shooting lodge, which was surrounded by gardens. The island had been known to the Greeks as Okrasia and to the Romans as Oglasa. The name probably originated with the Liguri, early sailors and pirates active in these waters. By the 7th century, it boasted a temple dedicated to Jupiter and the name changed to Montegiove and finally Montecristo.

The story of the island really begins with the arrival in 455 AD of an ex-bishop of Palermo called Mamiliano who was to live and die there as a hermit. After his death friars and monks came to follow in his footsteps. They built a monastery in his honour on the summit of the island which was inhabited from the 6th to the 10th centuries. In the 10th century, donations of money were made by the Counts and Marquises of Corsica. It became obligatory to give alms to the island and the funds were swelled by the crusaders whose route took them past on their way to the Holy Land.

In 1553 the corsair, Dragut, who had been a lieutenant of the famous Barbarossa, arrived on the island with a small fleet of ships of the sultan Suliman II. He sacked the monastery, searching for the treasure it contained and enslaved the few inhabitants. The treasure was said to have been buried under the altar, but whether the pirates found it or not was never recorded.

In 1850 a Frenchman, who was a friend of Alexandre Dumas bought the island and tried to cultivate it with little success. Dumas wrote his novel *The Count of Montecristo* soon after. After being in the ownership of the Grand Duke of Tuscany, it was sold to an Englishman, Lord Taylor, who proceeded with a plan for 'recolonisation and revegetation'. Most of the trees around the lodge, which he built at Cala Maestra were planted by him and many strange foreign species introduced.

In 1889 a gentleman from Florence acquired Montecristo and tried to make it a centre for forestry. He finished off the shooting lodge to accommodate his friends who hunted on the island and it later became known as The Royal Palace when it was used by the Italian kings.

In 1899, the ownership passed to the Italian Royal family and it gradually deteriorated until 1954 when a private society re-established it as a hunting reserve. They introduced more foreign species to hunt. It was finally declared an Italian national state reserve in 1971 and access was forbidden.

We sailed the 40 miles through gently rolling seas until we caught sight of the sinister scarp, high above the clouds surrounding the island. As we approached, huge rocks and cliffs broke through the mist We sailed along the coast with Rudy pointing out the position of the wreck off the Punta Diavolo and turned into Cala Maestra, the only good anchorage on the island. I led a landing party ashore but before we even arrived, we were intercepted by a Guardia di Finanza launch. They were initially hostile, but calmed down after examining our permit.

We sailed out again to Devil's Point and I dived with Angus, then chief diver of the expedition and an ex-commercial diver, to locate the wreck. At 40 metres, we came in sight of clefts and ravines running along the bottom and out to seaward There was a chain lying across a low rock, but no sign of ancient wreck. We returned with a strong impression that there would be an awful lot of bottom to cover, and that locating the site would not be as easy as Rudy had promised.

There were several yachts anchored in the bay when we returned and their crews watched jealously as we went ashore and met the island *guardiano* who promised his help. Angus went snorkelling in the bay and the other yachtsmen complained, as they were not allowed to do so. The guardian went through the motions of recording our *contravensione* for their benefit. He later happily tore it up.

In the evening, Giovanni, the guardian invited us ashore. We walked up from the small quay, through a boathouse and up a wide path shaded by trees planted by 'the English Lord'. Beyond his house was a small museum with displays on the local Monk seals, the island's birds and animals, including some dangerous snakes. It was sad to think that it was only very occasionally seen, by visiting parties of students who had obtained the necessary permits.

The Montecristo viper was among the most dangerous species in the world. 'Without the serum, you last 10 minutes', said Giovanni, 'and with it, two hours'. Enough time apparently to get you flown out to hospital. They always carried the serum when venturing into the interior of the island. He believed that the monks had introduced the viper as a weapon against Saracen invaders. There was excellent drinking water on the island and he had fountains and wells in his garden.

We spent a slightly uncomfortable night at anchor as a *mistral* (*maestrale*) blew in to the bay. The next day it slowly settled down and Mensun dived with Angus. Rudy, although he was allegedly a diver, declined to go down. After his dive, Mensun said that he thought he had seen the outline of a wreck in the distance. I dived at the spot with Annie and Steve and found no sign of it. Rudy's young son, Alexandre, was on board As he could not swim, his father would tie him to the mast in rough weather! We decided to teach him and by the time we left, he was enthusiastically practising his new strokes. Back in Cala Maestra, Giovanni and his son Luciano visited us and invited us to use their shower on the beach. We gratefully accepted and afterwards he broke open a couple of bottles of vino for us at his home. We looked at the many strange plants and trees in his garden.

Luciano offered to take us up to see the ruins of the monastery and the next day we climbed up out of the fertile valley above Cala Maestra, passed rocks and shrubs until *Antalea* was just a tiny blob below. Luciano took the serum with him. We went through a long moss-covered tunnel among the trees and arrived at an open area where the Germans had established a small observation point during the war. There were pieces of shrapnel and bullets still scattered around.

After an hour's climb, the monastery was in sight above us. I thought about the saint and the treasure. The earliest known recording of the treasure was in a document dated 11th June 1277. Three centuries later Cosimo I of the Medici became interested in recovering it, but Dragut got there just before him. More researches were undertaken by the Prince of Piombino in 1613 and a monastic document preserved in Pisa, records that in April 1670, 15 men set out from Corsica in a gondola with an old book which gave details of the position of the treasure. After working for 15 days they returned empty handed, without finding any trace of the treasure.

Mamiliano had been bishop of Palermo in the fifth century. The vandal king, Genserico advanced southwards and took him prisoner, deporting him and his followers to Africa. They escaped and lived for a time on Sardinia and then Elba. He finally set sail to the 'unknown and untouched' isle of Montecristo, inspite of legends about a huge dragon that lived there.

The story goes that he climbed the mountain when he arrived and slew the dragon. On the spot a fresh water spring appeared. During the following years many tried to reach the island to be blessed or cured by him. He chose a cave at the top of the mountain by the spring to live in and after some years as a hermit, died there. Before his death, he had told the inhabitants of the surrounding islands that there would be a sign when he died. 'When you see a cloud rise like smoke from the summit, you will know that I have departed this life.'

The Gigliesi were the first to see the sign on the horizon and at once rowed out the 40 miles to collect the body of the saint for their church. It was said to have been safely embarked, together with three monks singing soulful dirges. The story goes that the people from Elba and Santo Stefano arrived later, delayed by storms and then chased the Gigliesi back to Allume beach on Giglio where a fight over the remains ensued. The body of the saint was conserved on Giglio until 1110 AD when, because of pirate incursions, it was moved to safety in Civitavecchia, near Rome. The arms of the saint were conserved separately and one is held to this day in the church at Giglio Castello of which Mamilliano is the patron saint. It is celebrated each year at the town's *festa* on 15th September.

We climbed higher and arrived at the ruins of the monastery. It was built on steep slopes, but still had habitable rooms. There were carvings at the top of a wall that looked about to crash into the valley below. The main gate still showed the holes that were made for great wooden bolts. We visited the small fresh water spring still bubbling up nearby. On the way down, Luciano showed us how to extract rubber from a tree and we examined the burrows of 'mice that act like squirrels' and collected laurel to garnish our dinner.

After the heat of the climb, it was good to dive again, down through clear, cool water and continue the search for the missing galley. Barbara and I covered a different area of bottom, but there was still no sign of wreckage. We waited on our shot line for 10 minutes decompressing and I took out my mouthpiece to sing:

My father was the keeper of the Eddystone light,
He slept with a mermaid one fine night – *and after a pause,*
And from that union there came three,
A porgy and a porpoise and the other was me.

The next day Steve and Annie found an amphora neck which encouraged us, but sadly we found little else. A large motor launch passed us while we were still in the water after the dive. Filippo was on board it, obviously taking supplies for Giovanni and his family. On our return to the bay, I walked up to the house where they were having a picnic lunch. I was welcomed by Filippo, Pepe Rhum and also Georgio, who had become Mayor of Giglio again. Others included Filippo's son, Luca and the Giglio police chief. There was also a smartly dressed young man whom I did not recognise.

It was my birthday, and they toasted me in wine while I spoke to Georgio about the museum of the sea we had planned on Giglio many years before. He was enthusiastic to make a fresh start but, to my surprise, the unknown youngster interrupted to say 'Rubbish'.

'Who is he?', I whispered to Filippo.

'Oh, he's the local judge from Grosseto'.

'You look very young for a judge', I ventured.

'Yes,' he replied, 'we have young judges in Italy.'

'Why did you say 'rubbish'?'

'Well, this country is full of museums and half of them are shut most of the time. You want to open another? It would be a waste of space.'

In honour of my birthday, they presented me with several cases of wine to take back to Antalea. They were enthusiastically received as we had run out of alcohol some days before. The party continued.

After a short siesta, we went ashore for a shower and I borrowed the island's only telephone to ring John and Janie in London. It was the first call ever to be made from Montecristo to England. In the evening, we lay at anchor celebrating and drinking our wine as we watched the moon rise over the cliffs. There was another legend, that the monk seals would come ashore on Montecristo on moonlit nights to steal the fruit and become drunk on wine. We talked of the many facets of the island – a strange mixture – treasure, saints, pirates, wild goats, vipers and monk seals.

CHAPTER SEVENTEEN

A Film Epic &
More Underwater Volcanoes

As a book collector and ex-spearfisherman, I was delighted to hear from one of the founding fathers of the sport, Vane Ivanović, whose first book on the new underwater sport had been published in English in 1951. He was a Jugoslav, and an ex-Olympic hurdler who had been educated in England. He was currently in his seventies and the Consul for Monaco in London. Vane was an elegant and sophisticated figure and invited me for opulent lunches during which he explained that he wanted his grandsons to gain diving certificates. He had a villa in Majorca that was patronised by royalty and members of the House of Lords and was still diving there every morning from his own launch during the summer months. However, he also needed some proof of his own diving ability to show the Spanish maritime police who visited his boat from time to time.

He invited me as a house guest to his villa which was on the rocky coast of Formentor in the north of the island, but meantime, asked if I would check out his regular diving companion, an American called Jack. Jack phoned me a few days later from a castle in Scotland and I made an appointment for him at the pool in the Hogarth Club and checked his details.

'How do you spell your name, Jack? Is it H-I-N-D-S?

'No', he replied, 'H-E-I-N-Z', then added quietly,' President of the Board'.

I resisted any attempt to ask him to bring '57 varieties'.

Jack, or H.J. Heinz III, as he was usually known, was, I discovered, a well-respected philanthropist and anglophile and an Honorary KBE. His 75th birthday party had been held at Ascot and was attended by the Queen and the Duke of Edinburgh.

After checking his diving ability in the pool, I gave him a theory test. At one point he asked for clarification.

'You say that, if you go down 100 feet for 20 minutes and then come back, you need to wait on the surface to get rid of the nitrogen?'

'Yes, otherwise, you'd probably get the bends.'

'But', he continued, 'Vane and I go down 100 feet for that time then come up, get more bottles and go straight down there again for another 20 minutes.'

'You're lucky to be alive, Jack'.

'What d'ya mean? We've bin doin' it for 20 years.'

I flew out to Majorca at the beginning of August 1985. The plane chased a yellow full moon from France to Spain and then a taxi whisked me through the night and down a private tree lined lane to a wrought iron gate inscribed Villa Ivanovic. Vane welcomed me in and we drank gin and tonics. After breakfast the next morning, I met June, Vane's English wife, and Richard Sender, an engineering student from Southampton University who was helping with Vane's boats and filling the diving cylinders in his vacation.

We motored out to Polensa Bay in Vane's vessel *Taro* and dived. Vane never wore a suit and seemed impervious to the cold thermocline as we arrived at 28 metres.

The next morning, I did a deeper dive with him as part of his course, and persuaded him (with some difficulty) to do a decompression stop, and then took Richard on his first open water dive. We enjoyed an excellent breakfast on board consisting of Spanish omelette, tomatoes, onions, sardines and red wine all prepared by Vane as the sun rose.

The next evening more house guests arrived. Lord and Lady Mancroft, Moira Fraser, the ballerina, Lady 'Patsi' Fisher and Jack Heinz. Lord Mancroft was witty and self-effacing. He had been a barrister, Colonel in the gunners, Punch columnist and many other things. 'I'm the son of a Jewish tailor', y' know', he told me, then added 'all men are born equal, but quite a few get over it.' In fact, his father had risen to be Financial Secretary to the Treasury and he himself had been a member of Churchill's government.

The next day, Jack dived with us. He reminded me of a small, round Sancho Panza to Vane's tall, slim Don Quixote, carrying no less than three Hawaiian slings for him to use on unfortunate fishes. I mentioned to Vane that I now had friends living on the island, as Tom and Elfie had bought a house near Calvia, further south. He immediately invited them for lunch and then took Tom, and his son Marc, out to dive with us from *Taro*.

During the following days, I tried to impress on Vane and Jack how important it was to follow the rules regarding underwater times and depths. It was an uphill struggle. The days passed in a routine of early morning diving and breakfast on board On our return each day, we changed, and champagne was served to the assembled company at eleven, followed by lunch under a canopy in the garden and a siesta before dinner. A sybaritic life. After we had completed the training dives, Vane dived mainly with Jack and I took Richard on his 3rd Class course. Both Vane and Richard took the theory paper and passed with flying colours. After I left, Vane continued to dive in Majorca and around the world with the new CMAS 2 star diver card I had sent him, but three years later, I had a letter from him telling that he had had to 'hang up his fins' after a serious decompression accident.

I had returned to England in time to drive up to Oban to join a new schooner-rigged sailing yacht that had been built in France and named *Jean de la Lune*. She was run by Dave Burton, his wife Kay and their girl friend Stella. We were joined by Nigel, Ginnie Ashton and a small group of my pupils. *Jean de la Lune* was 91-feet long and very seaworthy. They also had a diving deckhand called Wayne who developed a lasting attachment to Ginnie.

After a warm-up dive, we travelled north into the Sound of Mull and dived the *Rondo* in a fearsome current. We sailed in to Tobermory where Bert Hall, landlord of the McDonald Arms gave me the news that Boyd, our first Hebridean skipper, was currently in Barlinnie jail for skippering a boat that was smuggling drugs into Malta.

We sailed across to Barra in a following wind and sea and dived there collecting scallops for tea. The wind freshened and Dave navigated in darkness to spend the night in Castle Bay. We dived the wreck of the *Seniority* with Nigel, Kay and Stella. She was a large ship that had been sunk in 1950.

To my surprise, Dave suggested a night passage to St Kilda although the sea was anything but calm and the wind gusting to Force 6. We rolled our way through the night, but I was by now confident of his navigation and skippering skills. Just after seven the next morning we approached St Kilda, having covered the 80 miles from Barra. It was now calmer, and we dived Glen Bay, site of prehistoric settlements among a bevy of seals. Back in Village Bay, Dave organised us into 'anchor watches' because the weather had changed again but the next morning dawned bright and calm.

We sailed out to the Stacs under squadrons of gannets, flying in V formation, and swooping fat fulmars. I decided to dive a very impressive underwater grotto off Boreray called Sgarbhstac. The vast arch came into view 30 metres down and the vertical rock faces were covered in coloured corals and anemones.

After the dive, we climbed from Village Bay up to the ridge between the peaks of Conachair and Oiseval and looked out over Boreray and the Stacs below. Another night passage, and we were through the Sound of Barra and down into the Sound of Mull to dive the *Hispania*. Another splendid diving cruise with a first class skipper and crew.

LUC was now teaching at several new pools, and I was helped by Ron Bendall while Karin Abay became our book-keeper. Reporting on behalf of schools at the DO's Conference, I announced that there were now 56 BSAC schools and that they were the fastest growing section of the Club with an accident-free record

Mensun had created an Oxford Trust called MARE (Marine Archaeological Research for Europe) and I was invited to be a member of its advisory board. Our meetings were chaired by Lord Bullock, the University Vice-Chancellor, an unassuming north-country academic and historian. Reunion dinners were organised at Oxford Colleges, the Tower of London and on board the *Cutty Sark* at Greenwich.

When I had met Pepe Rhum again on Montecristo, he had asked me why I no longer brought students to Giglio, and promised that if I did, he could hire me any sized boat I needed. I took him up on the offer and booked three weeks in September 1986. I arrived before my first party of five who then completed a week's Sport Diver Course. They returned happy, and I was joined by another five including Eryl Davies and his new wife, Ruth. I did my 3,000th dive on 9th September off Giglio's most northern point, Fennaio before the last group arrived. After returning, it was off to Scotland again to join another group on the *Jean de la Lune*. The party included Nigel, as chief organiser, Bryan, and Paul Etgart, who had become a keen underwater photographer.

When I got back, I had a call from the producer of a video which would star Anneka Rice. It would be sold through shops, together with a book and would show her learning to dive. She had asked for me to be filmed instructing her and I agreed to do the job in return for the resulting publicity. They planned to shoot it in the Cayman Islands, but as I was due to be on the *Lady Jenny* in the Red Sea in April, I persuaded them to use her instead, so that I could remain in the same location. I gave Janice Broxup, the producer, and her script writer some pool lessons.

I took the first LUC party out to the *Jenny* in early April. There was a new skipper, called Adrian, and Alex and Tamara were now the dive guides on board. Janice came with us to plan underwater sequences and get a little open water experience herself. The week before shooting was due to start, they were still dithering about who would direct the film. I persuaded her to contact Mike Portelly, and he agreed to do it at short notice and for a small fee, because of his friendship with Anneka and me. It was a brilliant decision.

When my second group arrived, the weather turned unexpectedly bad and the *Lady Jenny* crew seemed unable to suggest any alternative sheltered dive sites. This put more pressure on me, but luckily the beginners overcame strong currents and choppy seas. Mike arrived a few days early and when my students left, we worked to completely revise the underwater script and storyline, which were completely unrealistic. The weather calmed and we dived together, planning underwater shots and sites. Finally Anneka arrived with Graham Berry, her above-water cameraman, and the Director of the video company.

Shooting began. Sadly Alex and Tamara were anything but enthusiastic, giving the impression that we were interrupting their serious diving schedule. Alex insisted that any tuition filmed on board should be given by himself or Tamara, rather than by me. I shared a cabin with Mike who quietly re-assured me that films are made on the cutting room floor and not to worry. Mike's enthusiasm soon became infectious and we became increasingly involved, working long hours as we realised that this would be an exceptional film. He did five or six dives a day and a night dive, trying always to get the best underwater footage with his camera. We followed him down day and night.

He started by filming the recovery sequence, one of the last in the film, in which Anneka showed how to recover me from depth on the wall at Ras Muhammed before resuscitating me on the surface. I enjoyed making a theatrical collapse off the vertical wall and she duly took a grip on me and gently inflated my jacket. On the surface, she removed our mouthpieces, and lent over me to perform mouth-to-nose resuscitation. After a suitable period, she gave the emergency wave towards Tamara, who was running the inflatable, and, when she arrived, cheerfully announced: 'One dead body for you, Tamara'. 'Well done', I said, coming back to life, 'blow in my nose and I'll follow you forever.' We had, of course, to repeat the operation innumerable times for Mike to get the best camera angles.

A day later, we moved back to Eilat and then spent several days filming her doing initial training with me in the pool at the luxurious King Solomon's hotel. I lectured to her in 'Coral World', a tower built in the sea with windows through which to watch the fish on a surrounding coral reef. Mike devised a wonderfully imaginative underwater sequence in which he filmed from outside, swimming slowly towards the dark profile of the tower in the distance. He had to be perfectly balanced under the surface as the tower had heavy metal doors above the underwater windows that would slam shut at any vibration from visiting frogmen. Eventually a small light appeared and, as he got closer, materialised into a window, through which I could be seen, and heard, lecturing to Anneka.

In the evening, Mike had another idea. He would film Anneka in bed, reading a book on Red Sea fishes before she went to sleep. He could juxtapose real images of the fish with those in the book. We all crowded into Annie's bedroom and cameras and lights were erected round her bed. It was a hot evening, and the lights made it even hotter. Someone ordered drinks from room service. A waiter knocked and entered. His eyes widened as he saw us all surrounding Annie on the bed. He came to the obvious conclusion about what sort of film we were producing. Early next morning, it was time to drive back to the Jenny through the mountains of the Sinai.

Mike was a true artist and, like all artists, completely dedicated to his work. He was happy, good-natured and excitable but shouted at us constantly to try to get what he wanted. We didn't get upset, as Annie and I had known him for so long, and knew he would return to his happy self as soon as the shot was finished.

At dawn a couple of days later, he decided to film a sequence of Annie talking to camera before rolling in backwards to dive. He did this with the dive boat pulled up

1. Neptune Club and London Underwater Centre brochures, 1963-89.

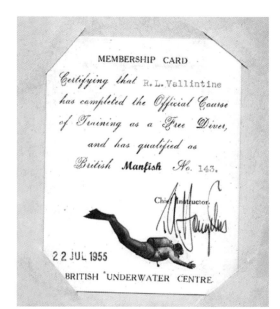

The British Underwater Centre
Warfleet Dartmouth

MEMBERSHIP CARD

Certifying that R.L.Vallintine has completed the Official Course of Training as a Free Diver, and has qualified as British Manfish No. 143.

Chief Instructor.

2 2 JUL 1955

BRITISH UNDERWATER CENTRE

2. First diving certificate, 1955.

3. Breath hold diving to the 'Christ of the Abyss', San Fruttuoso, 1978.

4. Corinthian helmet found on the Etruscan wreck at Campese.

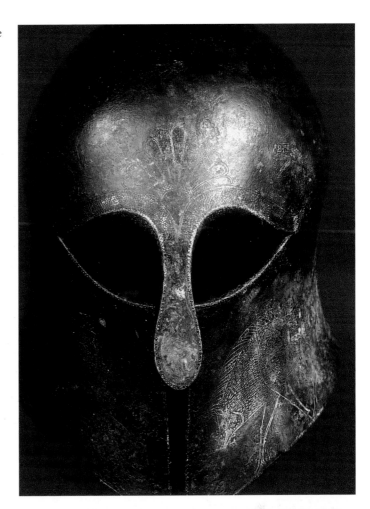

5. The curious Hammerhead Shark, Cocos, mid-Pacific, February 1989.

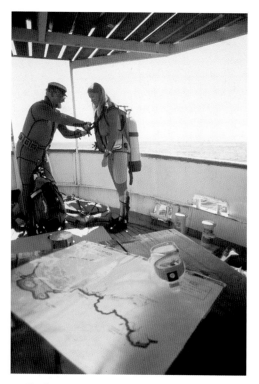

6. Checking Anneka before dive, April 1987.

7. Hungry Napoleon Wrasse approaching.

8. Reg and Anneka logging the encounter.

9. Return to the Red Sea, August 1987. Fleur Knox-Peebles, Jon Nigel, and Bob Johnson on the *Apuhara* with the wreck of the *Lara* in the background.

10. The morning after a surfeit of rum punches. Sandy Bulgin, Reg and Keiran Sykes in Dominica, 1991.

11. Reg with Trevor Jones before the underwater shoot for *Challenge Anneka*, May 1992.

12. Reg checking out the 'dolphin reef' at Eilat before filming began on the Dorling Kindersley shoot 1992.

13. Keiran and Mark with baby Lion fish at 'dolphin reef', 1992.

14. Frozen but happy. 12-year-old Samantha Selby after her first dive, Ibiza, May 1995.

15. Martina with Claus Valentin at Campese, May 1996.

16. Reg before descent in a Heinke Pearler, St Peter Port, Guernsey, 1997.

17. Return to Corvo. Reg and Roger Hale, September 2004.

18. The entrance to the Medici villa at Campese on a calm night.

to the beach so that he could film the close-ups from the shore. He decided that he needed some bubbles breaking the surface just below her to simulate other divers below. Although the depth was only two feet at this spot, he asked me, with a grin, whether I thought I could lie on the bottom, just under the surface and 'make bubbles'. 'I think I might manage that.' 'We'll tell you when to come up' – Don't surface before, or you'll ruin the shot'. I got down and lay on the bottom and started quietly breathing. Time passed. I watched tiny shrimps in front of my mask involved in having adventures with other tiny shrimps. More time passed. I was tempted to rise up to see what was happening, but knew it would result in a furious shout of 'the shot's ruined'. A long time passed and finally, my air pressure started dropping. I knelt up. There was no boat and nobody left on the shore. They had forgotten I was there, and left. I dripped my way back to the hotel and threatened to write a book entitled: 'Dives of less than 2 feet in Egyptian waters with Mike Portelly'.

Annie was filmed feeding a giant Napoleon wrasse that Mike had trained over the years to take hard-boiled eggs. They grew up to 2 metres in size (the fish, not the eggs). She had an experience that was rather similar to that of the shark feeder in the Maldives. A hungry female wrasse came over her shoulder unexpectedly and grabbed the egg she was holding up for a gently approaching male. Annie's hand disappeared inside its mouth. Although the teeth were tiny, it managed to inflict some deep scratches on our star. Mike was unsympathetic, even delighted. 'Can you do that again?' he shouted.

Annie, Mike and I stayed for a few nights on another yacht *Ghibli VI* that was moored close to us in Sharm. It was run by Renzo, a quiet young Italian and his English girl friend, Tanya. They were very helpful, and I promised to hire them for another LUC party when they would be in the Med later in the year.

When the shoot finally finished, Anneka and Janice left and I helped Mike clear up and transport the 27 huge pieces of luggage – cameras, lights, lighting cables and sound equipment to Eilat and we flew from there to Tel Aviv. The Israelis had not charged us for the baggage on internal flights in return for publicity, but on the last leg from Tel Aviv to London, Mike had to reach for his credit card to pay over $2000 in excess weight.

A week or so later, he invited me to his flat in Earl's Court to help him put the video together. He finally assembled 40 minutes worth of good material, but felt it needed a final lift and some long shots as he had not been able to film the wrecks due to the weather. There was no chance of Annie returning as she had a tight filming schedule, but he asked if I would go back with a group of his friends at my own expense. It didn't take long for me to say yes, and he started ringing his friends who were in the film business. Jon Nigel and Steve Smethwick agreed to come as did Mike's girl friend, a stunning model called Caroline Williams and Steve's fiancée,

Fleur. Finally Bob Johnson, who had been dive master on the *Jenny* during my first trip on her in 1984. In the weeks before we left, I put Caroline and Fleur through their Novice Course in the pool, as Mike intended that they should stand in for Anneka in the distance shots he needed. We flew to Sharm via Cairo and I took Caroline and Fleur on their first sea dives.

Caroline had some difficulties as she was obliged to use Anneka's mask and it did not fit her well, and Fleur had ear problems. They survived and eventually both arrived at 10 metres and enjoyed watching the fish. After a couple more shore dives, we boarded the *Apuhara*, a working boat run by a German called Ado. She was nicknamed the 'yellow pig boat'. It was August and extremely hot. I slept on a mattress on the flying bridge.

Mike decided to try to get an exciting sequence, and as we sailed for Tiran, gave me a large plastic bag to take on the dive. It was full of bait to encourage the sharks that he was sure would be there. The others had seemed less enthusiastic about carrying it.

We dived and Mike and Bob went off to the reef edge to sight sharks and a pantomime ensued, during which I scattered hunks of meat and offal, we beat on our cylinders and a fish was harpooned and left dangling on a line. I even managed to cut myself on a piece of coral but not even the surrounding angel fish were interested. There was absolutely no sign of 'the tigers of the deep'.

The heat was now intense and we approached an Italian minesweeper, operating for the United Nations peacekeeping force and asked if they would let us have more drinking water. The sight of Caroline and Fleur sun bathing on the foredeck produced 100 gallons and a case of good Italian wine as well. We promised to meet up with them later in Sharm.

As high winds were again preventing us getting into the Gulf of Suez and to the photogenic wrecks there, Mike decided on filming a closing sequence of me and 'Anneka' apparently swimming down a sunbeam 'into the blue', out of sight of the surface or the bottom. This was rather beyond the capabilities of the beginners, but Mike had thoughtfully brought a long, blonde wig with him to dress one of us up as Anneka if necessary. Jon unwillingly put the wig on and we were instructed to hold hands and swim straight down to 30 metres away from the coast We were not to hesitate or stop. It was difficult to keep direction when out of sight of bottom or surface or even of our own bubbles. Jon also had trouble with his ears, and we were lambasted by Mike for not keeping a straight course downwards. We screamed insults at each other on the surface, but the sixth time we went down, he was finally satisfied.

The 'yellow pig' took us back to Sharm and we offloaded cylinders before running out into the bay for the night. We suffered from the heat, town noise and isolation. It was rather like being in a prison hulk in the eighteenth century. We were due to leave again at 6 a.m.

After dinner, I sat on the prow, listening to the sound of bongo drums coming from a disco at the dive centre in the port. I was up at 5 a.m. to watch dawn break in a red glow over the sea. Sharm was now quiet as a grave. Slowly light increased until the gold globe of the sun rose over the mountains in the distance and, as Swinburne wrote, 'dawn skimmed the sea with flying feet of gold'. By 5.30, a morning chorus of dogs began and Sharm came slowly to life.

The video, like Mike's experimental film, *The Ocean's Daughter* was an enormous success, shown on television, and winning awards at festivals throughout the world. In California it was proclaimed 'best sports training video of the year'. The book, *Scuba Diving with Anneka Rice* that went with it, was jointly written by Anneka and myself. She had kept a hilarious diary of the trip and the book was illustrated with photographs and cartoons by 'Larry'. I hardly had time to catch my breath before leaving again for the Med on a very different assignment.

Vane had been recommending my services to a number of his distinguished friends and acquaintances. The previous year he had put me in touch with Clarissa, Countess of Avon, who was the widow of former prime minister, Anthony Eden. She had visited Vane in Formentor and expressed a desire to dive with him on an expedition he was planning to the Andamans, Maldives and New Guinea. Lady Avon, a distinguished lady of indeterminate age, was also the niece of Winston Churchill and shared some family traits of determination and single-mindedness.

I gave her individual pool lessons and as she needed sea experience, arranged for us to visit my friends the Miltons at 'Divewise' in Malta. During her pool training, she had expressed a strong dislike for our compressed air jackets, complaining of the complications of operating the various buttons, but I assured her that they were absolutely necessary for her safety.

We flew out in the usual cramped charter aircraft. 'Have you been to Malta before?' I asked, brightly. 'Once', she replied, and then added drily, 'but that was in a battleship with my husband.' The Dragonara Hotel was next to Vince Milton's dive centre, and he hired us equipment before I did my first dive with her off his jetty. She complained again about the lifejacket buttons and I arranged another jacket which she was happier with. After a few more dives, she began to enjoy the diving and gained confidence.

I managed to get an ear infection in the shallows which kept us out of the water for a day. We dined with the Miltons and Vince's wife, Sarah, an astonishing lady, recounted some of her exploits, smuggling, being jailed in Italy, and then opening a dress shop in Malta. After a few more dives we returned to London and Lady A. left with Vane for foreign parts.

A week later I was due to keep my promise to hire the *Ghibli VI* from Renzo and Tanya. They were now based in the Aeolian islands, north of Sicily and I took Alison Skye, who was to do Second Class exercises and novices including Barry Smith and Jean Samuels.

After a night in Palermo, we caught the morning hydrofoil to the islands. We swept passed Alicudi at high speed, to stop briefly at Filicudi and were then on, via Salina and Vulcano to Lipari where Tanya met us, and we took taxis to the *Ghibli VI* and settled on board I had not been on Lipari since the World Spearfishing Championship back in 1960.

One of my plans for the cruise was to meet up with Mensun and Jo, who were now working on another ancient Greek wreck off Dattilo, a tiny islet close to the island of Panarea. Panarea had white-washed, cube-like houses and there were no roads. The wreck dated back to classical times and was sunk in 32 metres of water in the crater of what had been an active volcano. The expedition boiled their eggs in the hot silt on the bottom.

We first dived at a spot where we saw volcanic bubbles welling from the bottom. It was covered in a fine white deposit. Afterwards our lips itched from the bubbles of gas which dissolved and formed dilute sulphuric acid. Mensun arrived in the evening and invited us to his headquarters to see what they had found. Miniature bowls, cups and oil lamps – a cargo of 'fineware' dating from the fifth century BC.

The next day we dived off Bottaro, another islet where there were the remains of a Roman harbour, and possibly, fishtanks. There were a number of small walls rising from the bottom.

'Mensun's wreck' was on a flattish bottom surrounded by low rocks. Below 20 metres, the water temperature dropped from 29°C to 20°C. At 35 metres, the bottom was covered with pieces of pot and bowls concreted into the rocks beneath. There were patches of yellow sulphur deposit and the bottom felt hot when you poked your fingers into the soft silt. Back on Panarea we met the Italian who had originally found the wreck. He boasted that he could no longer feel his feet when he walked due to 'bends'.

We sailed on round to the south of Panarea for a BBQ and to visit the remains of a prehistoric village there. We night dived in the bay off the village. The next morning we were off to Stromboli, easily recognisable in the distance from its impressive profile and plume of smoke rising from the summit. Stromboli is one of the most active volcanoes, erupting every fifteen minutes. This is like a safety valve, which makes it potentially less dangerous. The island of Vulcano that we had briefly visited, was a different matter with temperatures of a thousand degrees close to the surface. As we sailed closer over a flat calm sea, a magnificent vertical rock appeared. It was called Strombolicchio, a 'little Stromboli'. It looked an ideal dive site though Renzo found the bottom was too deep to use his anchor. He kept an eye on our bubbles which were clearly visible in the calm water.

Below the surface the huge vertical cliffs plunged straight on down. They were covered in cup corals and many other growths. There were bunches of black gorgonia growing out from them, and clefts and holes that provided homes for crabs and lobsters. After visiting Stromboli itself and enjoying cold beers on a terrace overlooking Strombolicchio, we left to dive the Roman port off Basiluzzo, another island to the North East of Panarea.

Before our last day we managed to locate the isolated Secca del Capo, an underwater island north-east of Salina. Its summit was 10 metres down and we dived on down to 30 metres, discovering caves and a curious sponge, (*Cacospongia cavernosa*). Our last dive was a training one and I was again 'rescued' by Ali and given mouth-to-mouth resuscitation on the surface afterwards. The end of a perfect cruise.

BSAC Schools now made up 10% of the new membership of the Club. The LUC had had a record year teaching 193 clients from the Earl and Countess of Verulam (at their country seat) to a number of Italian waiters and young teenagers in Frinton. One young man baffled me. I had never known anyone who used so much compressed air. 'What do you do for a living?' I finally asked. 'I teach the French Horn'. Then I understood.

Mike Bunyon from the Mason's Arms brought his son and daughter to finish their training with us and Brian Basham sent his wife, Eileen. Ali became Diving Officer of Banstead Branch of the BSAC and sent all her beginners to us for Novice training. She soon became an Advanced Instructor herself and taught for us occasionally. Another of our trainees, Jimmy Clarke went on to qualify as a BSAC instructor and came along to teach regularly. At the end of the year, we held our LUC Reunion party at the Henry the Eighth Hotel and over 100 members came to see Mike preview the video and Annie present the prizes. A wonderful evening.

By April 1988, it was time to take another party to the Red Sea. This time I tried a different vessel, the 65 ft *Colona IV*. She was owned by a Norwegian, and run by a friendly, relaxed and efficient crew from Sweden, Norway and Germany. Steve Reeves, who had been with us at Hurghada and Giglio and Dr Antony Ashe another previous visitor and seven others also came. Mike, the Swedish skipper, happily sailed overnight to arrive off the wreck of the *Dunraven* in the early morning. Yet again, the weather took a hand, and we were prevented from visiting the Gulf of Suez wrecks. After a few more days, we did a final dive at the lighthouse off Taba, which was still unspoilt. Things were rapidly changing though and the peaceful waters would soon be alive with hundreds of divers from the schools that were springing up on the Egyptian and Israeli coasts.

More and more clients wanted to holiday dive with us and we were back on *Colona* a month or so later and then, in June, I decided to try the *Florette*, a 36-metre brigantine sailing ship based at Porto Santo Stefano in Italy. I had been on board previously while cruising with Rudy and met the skipper, a quietly-spoken north- countryman called Ron Haines. This time I had a group of sixteen including one Club instructor, Peter Wingett, to help

Florette's crew consisted of Ron, his Austrian wife Christel and deck hands, Robert and Doris, plus the heir to the Haines fortune, three-year-old Jennifer. We arrived on Giglio, where Wally told me that Filippo had had a heart attack, but was now better after being fitted with a pacemaker. We dived Giannutri and the body recovery site at Corvo. There were two guitars on board so we enjoyed songs from Christel and the crew. My own efforts were also politely tolerated. On the last night on Giglio we celebrated in the new beach restaurant at Canelle. For me though, there were ghosts and memories all around. The trees and the walls had been part of Victor Perrocino's old house. We slept through a calm night and returned to the mainland the next morning.

Back in England, I was soon down diving at Fort Bovisand again. Eryl joined my beginners and we were invited for dinner at the home of Jim Gill, co-founder of the centre. Jim, an engineer and architect, now lived with his wife in a chapel which he had converted. His son, David worked as a commercial diver for one of the largest companies in the North Sea and had just survived a hair-raising dive when his breathing mixture had been cut off 600 feet down.

After dinner Jim told us the story. David and his co-diver, a close friend, were diving out of a bell on umbilicals and had been detailed to perform a routine task of connecting two ends of a pipeline together. This entailed using heavy-lift air bags to manoeuvre the pipes into line. Unfortunately, their new foreign supervisor had insisted on arranging the rigging of the bags and their anchors, in such a way that, as the bags rose, the two diver umbilicals were also dragged upwards and became jammed in a snatch block. This resulted in David's breathing supply, hot water heating, helmet light and communication systems all being cut off. At the same time his friend was trapped with no heating although still able to breathe and to communicate to the surface.

David had only his 'bale-out' emergency bottle, which would last him just three minutes at that depth. He had to get back to the diving bell he had left, which was now 150 feet away through the darkness. He switched over to his emergency set and started back along the bottom 600 feet down. He was colder than he had ever been in his life and breathing oxy-helium made him even colder. When in sight of the bell, he was stopped dead as the slack in his trapped umbilical ran out. He was now seconds away from death as his breathing supply also ran out.

Meantime his friend was trying to tell the surface what was going on, but communication was difficult. The 'bell-man' was inexperienced and unwilling to leave the bell. Surface control sent down its remote operated vehicle to video the situation.

David's friend luckily noticed that David's umbilical was caught and took the decision to cut it free. David felt himself released and, barely conscious, started for the bell again, holding his breath. He was working in heavy boots, and so it was a desperate struggle. He finally reached the bell, his unique fight for life being recorded by the camera of the 'ROV'.

Once in the bell, he took over from the panicking bell-man, and ordered that they moved it back to his friend who was finally recovered, nearly dead from cold. David acquired a new nickname from his fellow divers: 'Cool-hand Luke'. The company refused to release the video. I felt glad that I was just a sports diver.

Marc, Tom and Elfie's son, had come to stay with me while he studied at Imperial College for a degree in chemistry. He stayed for seven years in all, going on to take a PhD, and we became good friends. He spent much of his summers back at his parents' home in Majorca and told me that he and a German friend had found an ancient wreck there. Mensun agreed to assess it, and we flew out at the beginning of September 1988 to be fed, wined and welcomed by Tom and Elfie.

The wreck was right in the middle of a huge bay. It must have been sheer luck to have found it at all. The remains included amphoras and a certain amount of wood from the hull. They had also found a beautiful Roman plate, decorated with dog and flower motifs and an ancient jug. It seemed to be of Roman or Punic origin and Mensun was impressed.

A few weeks later, I took a party back to Jordan. Things had developed since I had written my report on diving there, and there was now a well established Royal Diving Centre near Aqaba run by Allan and Bunny Colclough from the Midlands. We dived from the beaches on to drop-offs, and on to a specially sunk wreck, the *Cedar Pride*. The ship had been sunk three years before and was sitting on its side in 20 metres of crystal clear water. We night dived as Allan took a retired Jordanian General in. He had brought a pipe band with him, who played enthusiastically during the dives.

Finally, at the end of the year, I took a group to the West Indies for the first time. Jim Clarke came to help me with their training. We had to stop overnight in Miami, and Jim fell foul of the immigration department as he had no American visa in his Irish passport. He did have the Irish gift of the gab though and was finally shot out with a stamp in his passport which read 'Paroled on humanitarian grounds – leaving for foreign parts.'

We arrived on Provo, the largest of the Turks and Caicos islands and settled into the ramshackle but comfortable Island Princess' hotel. We ate our way through excellent clam chowder and turtle steaks and then dived with 'Art' of Turtle Bay Divers. I discovered the commonest Christian name on the island was Reginald. I was instantly popular with the locals and when entering the hotel's crowded bar, the barman would shout over the heads of waiting customers 'What you want, Reggie?'

We visited the local conch research station and Jim managed to get stung by a jelly fish while swimming. He was in a lot of pain and suffering palpitations and fever. Luckily we had a lady doctor on course, who produced the necessary pills and sedatives. He survived to dive off French Cay and to explore that islet and also West Caicos. Just a month later I was to dive another Cocos, way out in the Pacific, one of the most exciting places in the world.

CHAPTER EIGHTEEN

Cocos, Isle of Sharks & an 800-foot Dive

FOR MANY MONTHS, I had been planning to get to one of the most exciting islands in the world. It lay some 4,000 miles away in the Pacific, 300 miles southwest of Costa Rica. It was said to be the largest uninhabited island, with a torrential rainfall of 27 feet per annum and over 70 waterfalls. Because of the rain, it was covered in luxuriant tropical forest, and its isolated position had ensured that there was more treasure hidden there by pirates over the centuries than anywhere else. In more recent years it had also gained a reputation as a place where there were always hundreds of sharks, mainly hammerheads, that congregated there in huge shoals.

The new 'live-aboard' dive ships were just beginning to get there and one of the first was the luxurious *Okeanos Agressor*. We were booked to join her in Costa Rica, but first arranged to spend a few days in the country with 'Jungle Trails' who handled safaris.

Most of those who came with me were experienced LUC divers. Tony Kirkby had been on three of our holidays, Peter Collins, Clive Hayley and Andy Leslau on one each, but there were also Sonia Bryan, an old friend, and Adrian Norrman, both from Holborn branch, plus Emma de Pass from the BBC, and Clive's brother Keith, who was one of our beginners.

Costa Rica was a friendly country and we were greeted with welcoming smiles from Debbie Kushner, manager of 'Jungle Trails' and her team of dark-haired girls who included a slender young botanist who introduced herself by saying:

'My name is Mildred.'

'That's a very English name', I countered.

'Si, my grandfather come from Richmond. You know it?' I was astonished as it was only four miles from my home.

The girls drove us off eastwards from the capital, San José, through lush foliage with smoking volcanoes above. We got to know them better when we stopped for beer and *tapas* in a bar that also sold Indian pottery, swords and daggers. Then we were on, climbing through darkening forests of sugar cane and bamboo under a full moon. It felt like bandit country. On the way they told us about the history of Costa Rica which lay between the more volatile republics of Panama and Nicaragua, and how their President had abolished their army and armed police and won the No-

233

bel Peace Prize. We dropped off our bags at an hotel in the valley of Turrealba and climbed on up to a *mirador* to eat beef, rice and beans, while a gentle marimba band 'thrummed a threnody in the dusk'.

The next morning at breakfast we watched vultures watching us from neighbouring rooftops and then were off to explore trees for exotic birds, finally arriving at a bridge over a river where our white-water rafting expedition was due to start. The rafts arrived and turned out to be large inflatable dinghies without engines. We were given life jackets and crash helmets and briefed on when to paddle and what to do if we capsized or fell out ('lie on your back and keep your feet facing down stream').

The drift started slowly but our boat was frequently out of control and then, we were going faster through rapids with great foaming waves and black, shiny rocks. We spent most of our time trvelling backwards. It was fairly hair-raising, but exciting, and our technique eventually improved. We had a sandwich lunch on a bank before the most dangerous stretch, eventually arriving wet-through and exhausted, but happy.

The next day, the *Okeanos* sent a pick-up truck to collect us from San José and we drove east through rolling hills and finally got our first glimpse of the Pacific, calm and blue between distant hills. I was reminded of a wonderful book I had loved when I was young called *The Story of the Pacific* which had quoted Keats's lines;

Or like stout Cortez, when with eagle eyes
He stared at the Pacific – and all his men
Look'd at each other with a wild surmise –
Silent upon a peak in Darien.

We drove on down and along the coast to Punta Arenas, where *Okeanos* lay, large as a cross-channel steamer, waiting for us. Ray and Paula Gates, the dive guides introduced themselves. They were youngish Americans, he with beard and protruding eyes and she somewhat more comfortably rounded. Tbe ship's agent, a friend called Mary Crowley, had also booked three Americans when she had discovered that I only had a handful of divers booked from Britain.

We slipped our moorings at 5.35 p.m. Cocos lay many miles steaming away, over the horizon, as we downed rum punches under the early evening sun. The ship had a crew of seven, all Costa Ricans. The American divers introduced themselves. There was Geoff Trotter, a self-confessed 'shark nut', John from Hawaii and Robert, who went everywhere underwater with a huge 'bang-stick'.

The next day we were out of sight of land travelling over a smooth Pacific as a school of common dolphins passed us bound north-east. I compared charts with the Captain and thought about the treasure and maps of it.

Cocos was alive with legends of the pirate hoards, and every headland (if not re-christened by the Costa Ricans) had been named after a sea brigand of some kind – Dampier, Wafer, Manby, Gissler. The island had frequently disappeared off charts altogether and so provided an ideal hiding place, veiled in mists and showers with its very existence sometimes questioned. It measured some 3½ miles across and 4 miles long with two peaks, one almost 2,800 feet high.

The first buccaneer to bury treasure there may have been Edward Davis. He had originally arrived with William Dampier and Lionel Wafer, his surgeon, in *The Batchelors Delight* in 1684 and later became master of the ship. He raided Spanish ships, burying their treasure on Cocos and, finally forgiven by James II, retired rich to Virginia.

Royal Navy ships sighted the island from time to time, but it was not until the early years of the nineteenth century that Beneto Bonito, an ex-Portugese Navy of-ficer turned pirate, had buried several million dollars worth of treasure that he had sacked from Peru and Mexico. He had even captured a treasure train ashore worth eleven million dollars at the time. It was all buried on Cocos. Afterwards, he had operated successfully in the West Indies until we had sent no less than two frigates and a sloop after him. He escaped round the Horn, but was eventually killed in 1821, allegedly leaving a map giving the whereabouts of the treasure.

The largest buried treasure was, however, the 'Lima Hoard' taken there in the 1820s. The Spanish occupiers of Peru only realised very late that Simon Bolivar was about to liberate Lima, the capital, helped by Lord Cochrane, a heroic Royal Navy captain who now commanded their navy. The Spaniards looked desperately for a way of preventing the treasures they had prepared to send to Spain, plus the gold and jewels in their churches, from falling into his hands. The last non-military ship in the port of Callao was a British sloop, the *Mary Deare*, commanded by a Captain Thompson. They came to an instant agreement with him and loaded her up to the gunwales with gold, silver, emeralds and diamonds. They are also believed to have put aboard an escort of six soldiers and two priests.

It is said that the mate of the *Mary Deare*, an enterprising Scot called Forbes, engineered the killing of the guards and the priests and presented Thompson with a *fait accompli*. They sailed to Cocos and buried the hoard, but some weeks later, the Peruvians caught up with them when they went into Panama. They executed all the ship's crew with the exception of Thompson and Forbes and took them back to Co-cos to show them where the treasure lay. Cocos is thickly carpeted with forest and the two men made a run for it, disappearing into the undergrowth. The Peruvians searched for months with no result. Eventually they had to leave, and the fugitives were later picked up by a visiting whaling ship that called in for water.

Some years later, Thompson was on his way back. On his way to Newfoundland, he made a friend and then became ill and died. His friend, called Keating, was given his map. The story goes on, but it is enough to recall that treasure hunters have been searching ever since. Sir Malcolm Campbell went to look with a friend's yacht, as did Errol Flynn, the actor. Franklin D. Roosevelt, the American President went with the 7th Fleet and Admiral Palliser RN, in a British cruiser. Many other expeditions were there during the early years of the twentieth century and the Costa Rican government began to sell treasure concessions to ambitious searchers. August Gissler, a German, who took Costa Rican nationality, lived on the island for 20 years searching, apparently with little result. The wonderful old naturalist, William Beebe, went there in the yacht *Arcturus* to study the wild life in 1925 and left one of his open diving helmets behind somewhere on the bottom of Chatham Bay.

The only successful attempt in recent years seems to have been by four young Frenchmen who arrived on Cocos after doing extensive research, in 1966. They found a cave on the hillside with two skeletons inside, one clasping the hasp of an axe and the other with a hole in his skull. There were also two boxes, each with 2,000 Spanish gold coins and 30 long gold bars. The French students allegedly smuggled the gold back to France, stitched into their rucksacks and concealed in their diving cylinders. As recently as 1980, the actress Moira Lister who had discovered a map, organised an expedition, but found nothing.

We enjoyed a further day at sea before waking to find Cocos, a long mountainous shape on the horizon. Boobies swooped above us and puffs of white in the distance marked the position of blowing whales. A group of bottle-nosed dolphins led us in as the sun broke through the rain clouds. We prepared to do our first dive off the islet of Manuelita near Chatham Bay (*see front endpaper map*). The water temperature was a warm 25° C, but the water was murky. After sighting a few rock fish and white-tipped reef sharks near the bottom, the first hammerheads appeared, weaving in from the deeper water. They were definitely impressive. On the following dives we managed to get a bit closer through the swirling currents.

We sailed round the island to Wafer Bay where we saw the first high waterfall pouring down. Gissler's old home on the beach was still standing amid the amazing greens of the forest We dived at Boat Rock off the north-east coast and I took Adrian, Sonya and Emma ashore to meet a small group of Costa Rican National Guards, who were very friendly. They had even erected a notice, which read 'welcome' in Spanish. They guided us up the path into the rain forest towards a waterfall. We waded on up the stream, when the path disappeared, through small rapids and warm pools and swam in one before returning to the ship.

No sooner were we back on board than a manta appeared, circling us as we lay at anchor. We grabbed masks and rushed into the water to admire its black and white markings, but had less feeling for the ugly white sucker fish hanging from its back. Getting my fins, I managed to take hold above its mouth and it took me for a ride, swimming in a large circle shallow enough for me to breathe through my snorkel. We changed positions and the manta continued to tow others in circles for several minutes. It was not to be our last time riding mantas. Paired off with Peter off an isolated rock off Cape Dampier, they cruised in above us and we swam hard to catch up with them. Peter held on to one of them while I photographed.

The next afternoon we went ashore to climb up the river, which tumbled on to the beach at the Bay of Hope (*Esperanza*) in the south. Our plan was to find another waterfall and (so I discovered) to look for treasure, as Clive and Andy had smuggled an (illegal) metal detector in their bags. It gave out signals continually as we climbed. After half an hour we stopped to watch large yellow and red crabs and scorpion-like creatures among the river fish. After 50 minutes, the high waterfall came in sight with the river dropping at least several hundred feet over a sheer rock wall. The air became suffused with spray and rainbows.

A day or so later, we went ashore again at Chatham Bay and looked at the ancient carvings on the rocks there which recorded many passing ships. The oldest we could find read , 'HIS BRIT MAG' SCHr LES DEUX-AMIS 1797'. We found a young couple from a yacht in the bay living under an awning where they had been for six weeks, and a large group of overweight Californian treasure hunters excavating the beach with a coffer dam, that was constantly flooded by the sea. A high reading on their metal detector had been enough to start them off. They eventually retired, swamped by the rising tide, having found nothing.

Diving off Boat Rock, the hammerheads suddenly disappeared and we became conscious of the squeaking of pilot whales. On nearly every dive we were seeing the hammerheads, sometimes as many as 50 schooling around and above us. Unfortunately we were always directed to swim out to sea against the prevailing current and found that they then quickly faded away in the distance. When I queried the dive plan, Paula's response was: 'Maybe some of your divers aren't up to it.' Peter and I decided on a plan of our own for the next dive.

The inflatable slowed down as we approached Nuez island and, according to the prior briefing, the Americans rolled over to follow Paula. Peter and I sat still on the gunwale. 'Take us on to where they will finish their drift', we told the boatman. Five minutes later we were in position over a group of rocks 20 metres below. We went over and, sure enough, after a few minutes of quietly waiting, several curious hammerheads appeared.

I held my breath and slowly moved round to crouch in a little amphitheatre of rock where I could even place my Nikonos camera on a rock shelf. I waited patiently and was rewarded. A large hammerhead, overcome with curiosity, slowly passed close by. It was too big to to fit in the photo frame but I was happy with my effort.

All too soon, our week on Cocos was over. We were again surrounded by dolphins – allegedly the souls of ancient mariners – as we left. The island lingered on the horizon for hours. The next morning we were far from land again over a blue, calm, dappled sea. What a beautiful ocean it was! 'Que mare pacifico!' the first explorer to see it is supposed to have exclaimed and the name stayed.

Back home in London w2, we had been persuaded to add the grander Queen Mother Sports Centre to our regular teaching pool at Porchester Centre. The pool there had an adjustable floor so that the depth could be varied down to a depth of 3.3 metres, which made it ideal. I now had a list of 16 instructors available in the evenings and Keith Tuckwell from Devon became my right-hand man. We taught 294 beginners in 1989.

John, Janie and I opened a small dive shop near their home under the name London Diving Centre and I was now driving a more 'sensible' Ford Granada. In June I took John Brown-Squires, one of my regular instructors, out to *Florette* again with a group of 18 divers and, a month later, Brian Basham commissioned me to take his family diving 'anywhere in the world'– no expense spared. This was a temptation. However, Eileen, his wife, whispered in my ear sometime later that the girls would be a bit bored with the family on the yacht that I had suggested in the middle of the Pacific. I finally decided on Grand Cayman where there would be some evening activity for them. The girls, Kate and Victoria, joined up with us at London airport and we flew via Miami to arrive in the evening at the Hyatt Regency Hotel which Brian had booked. This was a different world from that of Jerry Wilcox's happy hospitality at Sea View in 1972. 'If you haven't got a gold or platinum Hyatt passport card, you can't have coffee from there', I was told. We dived with the local dive centre and a few days later, arriving at a dive site, they announced, 'This reef is named after the old Sea View Hotel over there – one of the first hotels on Cayman – now being renovated.'

I arranged for us to go down to 800 feet in one of the 'Perry Cubmarines' of Research Submersibles who were based there. We motored out to the 'sub' that was casually moored to a buoy offshore. She took three people and I scrambled aboard to meet the skipper, Stuart Mailer, a marine biologist and friend of Liz Sides. The 'fish-eye' dome gave an impression of the bottom being only inches away, although it was in fact 30 feet below. I changed places to sit with Stuart in the cabin where the perspective was better. We sank deeper and deeper and eventually, in the gathering gloom, a dramatic shape spread below us –the wreck of the *Kirkpride* on the bottom at 800 feet. It was white and very ghostly as we explored along to the bridge – untouched of course by any diver – with the wheel and engine telegraph intact. A profusion of delicate tracery covered the sides – crinoids, bryozoans, gorgonians, basket stars and sponges. Gobies flipped into holes as we drifted past and a half hour passed like five minutes.

'Would you like me to switch the lights out?' Stuart asked, 'it will give a better impression of the wreck.' I nodded. A minute or so later he asked if I would like him to switch the engines off as we drifted. 'Can you switch them on again?' I asked nervously. 'Even if we couldn't, we'd just drop ballast by mechanical means and float up again'. 'OK'. It was like a dream world or even a visit to outer space.

We toured the island by car, visiting the ancient capital and blow-holes where surf jetted upwards in columns of spray. Far away from the big hotels, we found a ramshackle hut on a beach with a battered blackboard that read:

'CHICKENS – TURTLE'.

The 'restaurant' was run by two large black ladies. I had not had such a delicious turtle stew since the Sicilian fishing boat many years before. As we drank cold beers, I complimented the largest lady and asked:

'Will you marry me?'

'Yes, yes', came a chorus from the girls in the background, 'then we can come and visit'. The lady looked at me carefully.

'You got any money?' she asked.

'Not a lot'

'Not interested', she decided, to my relief.

We drove on, avoiding the crabs running across the road, in the gathering twilight.

The girls and I joined Cayman BSAC branch for a day's diving off the north wall and then at 'Sting Ray City', where the well-fed rays flopped around like demented pancakes. Bored with their antics, I took them along the shallow bottom, looking for a 'great moray' that was said to live nearby. Eventually we found it, and managed to entice it out of its hole and along the bottom. We dived through the 'Devil's Grotto' and came round the corner to surprise a huge silver shape in the tunnel – a tarpon. More of them followed, a beautiful sight with the sun sparkling off their backs.

The Bashams had decided to spend a few more days on the island after finishing their diving, and I had booked in three 15-year-old boys who had trained with me in England. They were all at different public schools and had met for the first time on the plane coming over. There was Brian Murphy's son, Matthew, Vernon's son, Thijs and the grandson of Lord Hailsham, Alex Hoare. They were excited by the diving and enthusiastically finished all the 'Sports Diver' exercises. The weather got hotter with an air temperature of 83 °F and sea at 85 °F. The Basham girls were curious about the young boys, and dived with me again. We finished on a wreck called the *Oro Verde* with horse-eye jacks, tame groupers and hovering barracudas.

Four weeks later Liz Sides joined me to take a party back to the Red Sea. I chartered a new boat, the *Manta Ray*, a twin-screw cabin cruiser owned by a girl called Mandy Blumenthal, whose boyfriend, a mad Israeli instructor called David Hillel, acted as skipper. We sailed through a torrid night from Eilat to Sharm. It was a happy, if hot, boat and we all enjoyed ourselves.

By 1990 our number of trainees had risen to over 400 per annum and I had 17 instructors on my books. We taught doctors and dentists, Earls and hairdressers, violinists and barbers, nine policemen and two young socialites who were soon pursued by a fearsome group of HM Customs police, who warned me of the consequences if I withheld information on their whereabouts abroad. They were later jailed for setting up a false theft of gem stones and collecting the insurance money.

Another *Florette* holiday course followed, and then an invitation to explore the Medas Islands and their famous caves, from the Estartit tourist board in Spain. I took my long- term diving partner, Aija Seppalainen, and we met up with Alan Bax and Jill who were also there. We dived with Tony Murray who ran the local 'Unisub' centre and enjoyed the huge groupers living in the underwater reserve, which had been created only six years before. Then a local took us into the caves with no briefing or torches! I kept a close eye on Aija, remembering that the famous American, Conrad Limbaugh, had died nearby after becoming disorientated.

I had been interested in diving history for many years, and my first book included an account of it. I had also met up with a number of book collectors, such as Adrian Barak and Nigel Phillips over the years and we visited each other's libraries. I was pleased then, when John Bevan contacted me about an idea for starting a new Society devoted to diving history. It was formed as The Historical Diving Society at a meeting in September at the works of Siebe Gorman & Co. in South Wales, where they still built the old diving helmets. John became Chairman and I agreed to be Vice-Chairman. It wasn't long before I was organising an annual conference, book meetings and visits and contributing regularly to a Society newsletter.

A television company phoned me regarding two comedians known as Hale and Pace who had concocted an underwater sketch called *Natural Childbirth*. Gareth Hale and Norman Pace were ex-school teachers who were on television each week with their eponymous programme of lightning sketches. They were extremely funny, knowledgeable and enormous fun to work with. After a couple of pool lessons, they asked me to choose some friends to play parts in the new underwater sketch.

I asked Hattie Davies, an ex-student who was now my PA and Secretary, 'How would you fancy having Gareth Hale laying rude hands upon you in a hospital bed'?

'Yes, please', she answered, and played the 'pregnant mum'.

Norman would be the 'expectant husband', and Janie was an obvious choice for the midwife, as she was qualifed as such. Our friend, Brenda Hall would play a hospital cleaner, Gareth the hospital doctor, and I, a GP. We prepared to shoot in a deep pool at Copthorne near John and Janie's home, where the TV company had built a 'mock-up' hospital. We all wore weight belts under our clothes and no fins or life jackets. Gareth succeeded in executing an amazing run along the bottom. At the last minute, I realised the safety implications. There was no way that we could get back to the surface quickly without assistance. 'Who is going to be responsible for safety?' I asked. Norman and Gareth thought a moment, then said 'I guess it must be you.' My place as the GP was taken by John Bevan.

The shoot began as a car arrives and Hattie, 'a great believer in natural child-birth' is wheeled in on a stretcher as she mutters 'Hurry, hurry'. John and Norman wheeled her straight down a slope into the pool and on underwater to the 'Jacques Cousteau Maternity Unit'.

'Norman is nervous', we are told, and bubbles appear from the back of his wet suit trousers. A phone rings and bubbles next to a sleeping Gareth 'who has been on duty for 18 hours.' He answers, bubbling the words, 'I'll be straight there.' He starts his run. A few moments later Norman removes his mouthpiece to shout 'Push … push'. A doll appears in tiny mask and fins with the caption, 'It's a buoy'. They all remove their mouthpieces and smile broadly.

It was one of their most successful mini-sketches and Norman and Gareth went on to complete their diving course, and then asked me to teach their wives so that they could dive together when they toured Australia, where their programmes were also enormously popular.

In August, I persuaded two groups of friends to come together to visit the Caribbean 'nature island' of Dominica which lay between the French islands of Guadeloupe and Martinique. It was a beautiful, mountainous island that boasted rain forests, cloud forests, waterfalls, hot and cold springs and a unique parrot. I took a talented novice with me to do her Sports Diver and Dive Leader courses.

Keiran Sykes was an elegant, young lady who was 'something in commodities' in the City. We met up with John and Sue Stubbs and their friends George and Jane Rowing. On arrival we were driven for over an hour through the unique rain forest amid the croaking of frogs and singing of unseen birds. We looked down on the windward east coast as Atlantic rollers pounded in. We arrived at Castle Comfort, the homely, family-run Caribbean hotel of Derek Perryman from Grenada, an ex-Captain on the local LIAT airlines, and his Dominican wife, Jeanette, and joined up with Bob and Sandy Bulgin and David and Carol Rayner, and the rum punches began to flow.

The next morning the hotel's two dive launches took us off to dive at Scott's

241

Head, a paradise for sponges. At a site called 'champagne' curtains of bubbles rose from the sea bed and I felt a familiar burning sensation on my face and fingers. A black-spotted snake eel (*Quassiremus productus*) advanced towards us and had its photo taken.

We shared a minibus into Roseau, the little capital and ate at Fort Young, which was complete with battlements, eighteenth-century cannons, and a pool. Walking back late at night, we found a large political meeting blocking the road. An organiser with megaphone was complaining about Chinese workers being imported to build new hotels for Americans. We sidled by, trying not to look Chinese or American as the crowd murmured around us.

Derek dived with us off the south coast in a heavy current. 'If you miss the boat', he said, with a smile, 'head for Scott's Head, or the next land you reach will be Nicaragua'. Luckily, Keiran was very fit and a strong swimmer and we managed to catch the boat's dive ladder as she ran out of air. Decompressing on another dive, I tried tangoing with her on the bottom. In the evening we played truant from the hotel and she gave me lessons in *lambarda*, the sensuous 'forbidden' Brazilian dance. She also taught a young Canadian we met who was immediately overcome, and offered to drive us anywhere on the island whenever we liked. We decided to go to the Trafalgar Falls with him the next day.

Keiran, now nicknamed 'Tiger', and I sat in the garden of Castle Comfort drinking rum punches and surrounded with butterflies and a stalking heron while I prepared to lecture to her.

'Today's lecture is on the use of the compass', I began, 'I don't suppose you have used one before?'

'Only once', she replied modestly.

'Where was that?' I queried.

'Navigating my yacht across the Atlantic to Antigua twice last summer.'

'Oh, I see, well perhaps you'd like to give *me* a lecture on the compass then!'

A few days later, we were due to practice the underwater compass swim.

'Couldn't we do it at night?' she asked.

'Well, I don't see why not, if you think you can manage it.'

It was a dark night as she navigated us, without the slightest hesitation, through the blackness and back to our anchor line. I was extremely impressed.

Before leaving Dominica, we took the express ferry to spend a couple of days on neighbouring Martinique. It was large, green and a Departement of France, so the wine was good and the food expensive and French. Before returning, we sailed close by the high (176 metres) Diamond Rock just off the coast.

During the Napoleonic wars, Admiral Hood had winched five cannons plus a Royal Navy Lieutenant and 20 men and boys on to the bare summit, together with powder, shot, victuals and water. They defied and harassed the French Navy and merchant ships for 17 consecutive months. Only when they had no powder left, did they surrender to a French squadron, which they had severely mauled. In the annals of the Royal Navy, it is always known as HMS *Diamond Rock*.

Back in England, I decided to add a conference on to the AGM of our Historical Diving Society that was held in Weymouth in November. We also planned an annual dinner on the lines of those held in the 'glory days' of the BSAC.

In January 1992 I joined the Bulgins and their friends back on the *Lady Jenny*, taking Rowena Barnes, one of the pioneers of diving in the UK and a pupil called Joss Woolf. Alex was now acting as skipper and Tamara as dive guide. Joss enjoyed the wreck of the *Dunraven* and her first night dive. She discovered a crocodile fish (*Cociella sp.*) and navigated us from one wreck to another off Gubal. We went ashore on one of the bleak, uninhabited islets that was covered with broken shells and sand, with a magnificent osprey nesting on a huge nest on the higher ground. We also managed a dive on the *Carnatic*, the wreck that Mike had tried so hard to reach during our filming with him. She was an old Bombay mail steamer also equipped with sails and had struck the reef in 1869. She had been worked by two helmet divers from Whitstable in Kent, recovering a precious cargo worth £40,000 at the time. She had a splendid stern with square ports. We dived an impressive modern wreck nearby called the *Giannis D*, exploring the bridge, engine room and a number of cabins. At Ras Muhammed, a shoal of dog-toothed tuna shot passed us and we discovered that Napoleon wrasse do not like grapefruit.

My next visit to the Red Sea was to provide a challenge of a very different kind.

CHAPTER NINETEEN

More Challenges & Celebrations

I N MAY 1992, I got another call from Anneka. 'Do you think that you could teach eight non-diving paraplegics and two tetraplegics up to a standard where they are diving on a coral reef with clown fish? 'I'm sure we could' 'But, we've got only three days to do it, starting from now, OK?'

She was now the star of a new television series called *Challenge Anneka* in which she was seen persuading various experts to complete almost impossible tasks against the clock for charity. They had rebuilt and re-equipped a Roman orphanage and held a floating symphony concert on the Thames. Our task was, of course, more of a challenge for me, as the actual shooting date was four days away. I agreed to do it.

Although I had dived with a paraplegic called Bob Head many years before at London branch, my experience of teaching them was small. The challenge had come to the programme from Trevor Jones who had broken his neck in a skiing accident and afterwards started a Trust to help those with spinal injuries caused by sports.

Just twenty minutes later I met up with Anneka at Trevor's home in Fulham where the doors swung open by remote control, and I found myself surrounded by television cameras. I gave her my first suggestions and a list of Red Sea travel operators to contact. She disappeared to do so, and soon phoned us to say that she had persuaded one of them to provide the travel, and had also got a local public school to provide their pool for a day's training the next day.

I rang my instructors, and John Brown-Squires, Peter Wingett and Jeremy Smith said they would help with the first day of training. I also spoke to David Royston, the BSAC advisor on diving for the disabled, who agreed to advise us.

The next day, we started training at the school in Barnes and I met the group of paralysed youngsters for the first time, and gave them a concentrated lecture, frequently interrupted by the demands of director and cameraman – 'Can you say that again and laugh a bit louder', and so on.

Our two tetraplegics who were paralysed from the neck down, were Trevor and Shaun Parry-Jones. Shaun, a young antiques dealer, had suffered a rugger injury. There were three paraplegic girls in wheel chairs: Rita Maretha, a victim of meningitis and Linda Williams and Joanna Horsburgh from Scotland, both paralysed from traffic accidents. Joanna had never even seen the sea in her life and so was decidedly apprehensive. The others who had volunteered to take part were Peter Ellison, 15, and Brian Hucker, both from Oxford with car and parachute injuries, Peter Byrne from Sussex (sledging), Mark Casey from Nottingham (biking) and a splendid character called Lorne Williams who had been 'accidentally shot outside a London night club'.

We started the first pool lesson and they adapted quickly. We had to send for extra ankle weights to keep their feet below the surface. After an hour, Joanna was taking out her mouthpiece underwater and clearing her mask twelve feet below the surface. All the paraplegics were doing well, breast-stroking along using their arms, but the 'tetra's' needed help to move at all. Three hours later we were all 'waterlogged' but satisfied with the progress. We would check in for our flight at 5 a.m. the next morning.

We arrived bleary-eyed in the sunshine at Eilat in Israel. At the Red Sea Sports Club, I introduced Annie to Benny and Schmulik, the two principal instructors there, who would help us for the next two days. Benny organised a team of his other instructors for our next pool session and then we discussed how we would get the handicapped divers out to the nearest coral head the next day. We lectured them on the sea conditions and what to expect and then I checked-out the dive location with Benny. Unfortunately, the underwater visibility was bad at only 5 metres, and the nearest coral head was 80 metres offshore. We decided to lay a line along the bottom directly to it.

The next morning we got started. All the students assembled in their wheel chairs on the beach facing the sea. The sun shone, but the sea was covered in small waves and there was a rising wind. Joanna's eyes widened at the sight.

We made a start with the 'tetra's'. We took Trevor down, and Benny and I pulled him along the line. As he was vertical in the water some of the time, it was hard work. Rope burns formed on my fingers and the palm of my hand. Finally we arrived at the coral head and the clown fish reacted splendidly, attacking Trevor with their tiny mouths as he delved into the fronds of their anemone. Shaun was also successful, and then it was time for the others.

I took Joanna. She told me that she was now mainly worried about seeing big fish and I assured her that this was highly unlikely. She breast-stroked strongly along the line, and began to admire the small fish she passed. Enthusiasm grew on her face as she confronted the clown fish. The others followed on, accompanied by the Israelis. The filming finished and the beginners told how much they had enjoyed it. Young Peter Ellison, the youngest and a keen sportsman, had thought that he would never take part in sport again, and his parents later told us that the experience had changed his life.

The televising was finished, but for some of us the best was yet to come: a dive in a fenced off arm of the sea which held 'rescued' dolphins from Japan and Russia. The dolphins surrounded us and were obviously intrigued by the problems of the paraplegics. Soon Joanna and I were stroking 'the biggest fish' she had ever seen – a wonderful end to the challenge begun just five days before.

Back again in London we taught Steve Merson, a violinist in the Royal Philharmonic Orchestra and a number of his friends from the 'band'. I was envious of their foreign tours and the diving they would be able to do. I was also busy organising the Historical Diving Society Annual conference at Charlestown in Cornwall where I got Bill Braithwaite, Alex Hildred, Dick Larn and Daniel David as our speakers. I had been contacted by the publishers Dorling Kindersley regarding a new book on diving in their *Learn in a Weekend* series. It was to be in colour throughout and they would commission the photographs to be specially taken in the Red Sea. They asked if I could suggest a young couple to act the part of beginners in the book and I suggested Keiran, and she brought a young friend of hers, Mark Stanton. We all left early in August, together with a team of editors and designers who all looked as though they might be my daughters, and Brian Pitkin, the underwater photographer, who definitely did not!

After a few dives off Coral Beach at Eilat, we went off to film the dolphins again in their sea enclosure. We were fascinated to watch two of them copulating, while a third used gentle pressure to keep the female in position. Another female swam close by with her tiny offspring. We stroked them as they passed by. Unbeknown to me, one of the other dolphins, known as 'Hindoo', was thought to be 'neurotic'. After a few minutes he headed purposefully toward me and I held up my hand ready to stroke him as he passed above. At the last moment he opened his mouth exposing a healthy line of teeth and nipped my right index finger as he swept by! I was unhurt, but shocked, as I knew that dolphins would be quite capable of taking a hand off if they really tried. I presumed it might be a warning or some kind, or a dolphin joke.

Most of the shots needed for the book involved demonstrating techniques in shallow water, and Brian photographed us from all angles. We dived night and day and were also photographed on the beach, in the dive centre and leaving and returning from and to, various boats.

On one dive we came across a large trigger fish guarding its eggs and Brian mischievously indicated that he wanted me to approach it while he photographed. I knew enough about trigger fish behaviour not to do so, and so avoided being bitten again.

Three days after our return, I had a new experience. My arm suddenly became sore and when I spoke to Janie about the symptoms, which were getting worse, she suggested I contact my GP at once. 'Sounds like a heart attack', she said on the phone, 'Is there anyone who can take you to hospital?' Kate Peters, my lodger, offered to drive my car, but, as it was an automatic, went off in it for some practice first. The arm became more painful and I began to sweat. Arriving in casualty, I was eventually asked what I was there for. My response, 'Suspected heart attack' generated a lot of sudden action. After a subsequent angiogram, some 'tender loving care' and reduction in weight I was passed as fit to dive again.

1993 was the 50th anniversary of the birth of sports diving, and the 40th of the creation of the BSAC. We celebrated at the Guildhall with the Club's President, Prince Charles and his favourite goon, Harry Secombe.

I spoke about Cousteau at a later event in Weymouth, which celebrated the anniversary of his development of the aqualung. For our annual conference I arranged talks from the HDS President, Vice-Admiral Sir John Rawlins on his development of underwater escape apparatus for Navy pilots. We also heard from Professor David Elliott on deep diving, Peter Dick on the history of compressed air and Ray Sutcliffe on his *Discoveries Underwater* television series.

The new book *Learn to Scuba Dive in a Weekend* was published and became very successful. The publishers arranged its translation into a dozen languages and thirteen years later, it was still selling in the tens of thousands in Poland.

Cilla Black's TV series *Surprise! Surprise!* gave chosen members of the public the unexpected chance to fulfil their dreams. One lady dreamt of diving with dolphins. Thanks to their PR, Eileen Basham, I provided the tuition and then arranged the dive. It was off to the dolphins again! I had suggested that they used Peter Scoones to film in the absence of Mike elsewhere, and took the lady, called Pauline, on her first dive off the beach at Eilat, before we were in with the dolphins again. I 'made friends' with several of them before feeling a thump on my right side. Hindoo was in action again! The shoot went well, over the following two days, but every time Hindoo caught sight of me, he clicked his teeth together and rolled his eyes. I kept my hands to myself, and concentrated on manoeuvering Pauline close to dolphins and into camera range.

After the filming was finished, I dived briefly with Peter while he did some macrophotography. On our last evening in Eilat, I was told that Hindoo had died, apparently trapped under one of the jetties in their enclosure. The keepers told us that he was not liked by the other dolphins. Was it an accident, or suicide? I felt a strange sense of loss and began to question whether this was a suitable environment for 'rescued' dolphins.

A few weeks later I was off to Majorca with John, Jane and their children Samantha and Paul. The kids snorkelled and we dived with John Bantin at his new centre at Cala Conils.

In September we had our CMAS meetings in Rome and afterwards, I was picked up by Gilly Lythgoe in her Land Rover Discovery. We drove north and joined up with Bjorn Thorsen and Christina to dive on Giglio. Bjorn was an old friend and currently President of the CMAS Technical Committee of which I was General Secretary. When we arrived, Valdivio, the ex-crewman of *Sea Laird*, offered to get us a boat to take us to the Secca della Croce and we dived there very successfully. We enjoyed the fiesta at Castello and then Gilly and I left to return to England via her pied-a-tierre, an ex-shepherd's house in the middle of a forest in France. We lit candles, as electricity had not yet been fixed, and Gill cooked spaghetti. We later finished our wine sitting on the steps of the house, listening to the noises of the forest under a sky full of stars.

In 1994 our conference was at Whitstable and nearby Tankerton, and I persuaded my heroes, Hans and Lotte Hass, to talk. We also had one of the almost mythical figures of submarine escape, Commander Matthew Todd MBE. The Canterbury Council hosted a civic reception and the dinner was held at a recreated Dominican priory nearby. I was proud to present my new Historical Achievement award to Hans and the next day, after all the pomp and ceremony, enjoyed being wedged into the tiny original Wheeler's Oyster Bar listening to his tales and those of Sir John.

Early in 1996, I had taught my 11-year-old God-daughter Sam to dive, and we left with the rest of the family for a stay in Ibiza with their friend Mike Feasey, who I had also taught and who had a large flat there. He also had a Fairline 'Sports Fury' motor cruiser which made 30 knots, so there was no difficulty in reaching dive sites and the next island of Formentera. I took Sam on her first dive and she did well in the chilly (20°C) water in her short 'pool' suit.

By February, I was diving again off Provo, in the Turks and Caicos islands with Bob and Sandy Bulgin and their 11-year old grand daughter, a recent pupil. We stayed on Bob Gascoine's boat, the *Aquanaut*. He was now producing charts of the area and after a few day's diving with him, we took a tiny aircraft northwards to Salt Cay. We swept in to land among huts and cows, and were then driven by the only island taxi to the Mount Pleasant Guest House, run by an eccentric American called Brian who was a pillar of the small community.

We planned to dive the wreck of HMS *Endymion* which had been wrecked in 1790. She had been a 44-gun 'fifth rater' with a crew of 300 men. On the way out, we watched humpback whales 'topping and tailing'. The wreck lay in 13 metres of water and we dived there in a strong current.

Salt Cay had a population of only 80 and, as the guest house was now fully booked, we stayed with a cheerful local lady called Mrs Bean. She had been married three times: to a Scottish professional footballer, a Chinese businessman and to a local islander, producing a large family in a variety of colours.

We changed planes at Miami on the return and I encountered that rare phenomenon, a friendly American immigration official. I passed up my passport.

'Hey, man', he interrupted, 'look at dat girl walkin'. Ain't dat poetry in motion?'

I looked across and agreed, before he studied my passport photo, that had been taken underwater.

'You Jacques Cousteau?'

'Nope, but the photo's taken underwater'.

Then he looked at the passport again.

'You want de good news or de bad, man?'

'I'll take the bad'.

'De US visa's out of date'.

'What's the good?'

'You just need to fill in a 'visa waiver' form'. 'But', he went on, 'de bad news is you can't do it here'.

Then added, 'But de good news is y'can do it over der'.

I eventually passed through smiling.

The LUC was now one of 85 BSAC Schools and the American PADI organisation with its emphasis on individual commercially operating instructors was beginning to arrive in the UK. I split my time between LUC teaching sessions, helping Mike Portelly with his 'commercials', and endless meetings and conferences.

In April I was summoned to the 'Our World Underwater' conference in Chicago to be presented with the Leonard Greenstone Diving Safety Award and a cheque for $1,000, and met up again with Art Bachrach and Glen Egstrom. Afterwards I flew down to Nassau for a few days diving break in the Bahamas. Back at the school we were now teaching publicans, actors, tube drivers, bankers and film directors. I got a phone call from Bernard Eaton of *Triton* magazine.

'Reg, you remember that you told me that you would be happy to be sent out to do any overseas diving holiday article for us?'

'Yes, but I've given up hope'.

'Well, there's something that might suit you'. 'They say it's based on an unknown island in the Med'. He laughed.

'Sounds interesting, what's the island called?'

He laughed again.

'Giglio'.

'Do you know who runs the dive centre there now?'

'No'

'A Dr Claus Valentin'.

This German school and marine biological centre was now based at Campese on the west coast Dr Claus proved to be a very civilized professor with an interesting background. He had studied in England, had been an aquanaut in the Heligoland underwater house and had even had a brief spell as a coral diver to raise money. We got on well. Unfortunately, I shared a small flat with two young German students who, like many others, were completing their university field work there.

They were friendly but distant until I realised we were there on a self-catering basis. We discussed the organisation necessary.

'I vil do ze cooking', said one quickly.

'And I vil do ze wash up', said the second.

They looked at me expectantly.

'And I will buy the food and wine'.

They cheered enthusiastically and became very friendly.

Claus had an assistant diving biologist called Martina, something of an expert on malt whisky. They had a magnificently equipped laboratory with innumerable proton microscopes and lectured there every day. Martina gave a memorable malt whisky party before I left.

In July I was off to Turkey with the Selby family where we met up with Peter Dick and Jeni. I took Sam, now 14, down again with a friend of hers, Hattie Jordan, a youthful violinist My old friend Stan also came and dived. Sam's brother, Paul (now 10) also did a trial dive with me and afterwards, we explored Bodrum castle and the excavated remains of a wreck from 1200 AD held there. The next village, Gumusluk, had a beautiful little harbour with the remains of ancient jetties. We ate sea food and drank cold white wine at a table on the beach as the sun went down into the sea.

Cousteau had died in June '97 and I was invited to BBC TV Centre to answer questions about him after an 'appreciation' on their international news. It was some-what daunting as they gave me no prior warning of what they intended to ask.

In all my years of diving, I had only used an old 'standard' diving helmet once, back in 1967, when London branch had visited the Siebe Gorman works, and so I was pleased to have the opportunity again some 30 years later when I organised an HDS visit to Guernsey and Mick Peters dressed me in his Heinke 'Pearler' and I gingerly carried my 187 lbs of weight down a long series of stone steps into Guern-sey Harbour. The first divers from the Channel Islands had descended at the same place in 1833. Minnows flashed passed my face plate, reminding me of my first dive in the Dart Estuary.

Gary Potter of the HDS had been researching the life of a famous old helmet diver called William Walker. Walker had spent many months in the very early years of the twentieth century in a black pit filled with murky water, below Winchester Cathedral. The cathedral had originally been built on marsh land and each time they dug holes to shore it up, they filled with water so the diver was called in. The cathedral was saved by his efforts, and he was presented with a medal by King George V who famously said 'You saved the cathedral with your own two hands.' Fifty years later it had been decided to erect a small statue of the diver in the cathedral, but due to a mistake by the sculptor, when it was unveiled, the face was that of the resident engineer, Sir Francis Fox! William's relatives were horrified, but the Dean was too embarrassed to change it, as it had been paid for by the Lord Lieutenant of the county. Successive Deans had taken the same line, but, as a new Dean had just been appointed in 1997, I determined to have another try, especially as Gary had discovered a beautiful original statue of the diver, made at the time by another sculptor, Norman Pierce, whose widow was still active and would support our efforts.

I wrote to the new Dean, the Very Reverend Michael Till, for the first time in August and he agreed to meet us. Gary and I argued that it was time for the statue to be replaced and, to our delight, the Dean agreed that 'something should be done'. He warned us though, that the proposal would have to pass through numerous committees and national heritage bodies and progress would inevitably be slow.

I continued to check each month and finally the good news came through three years later, that a new statue would be erected inside and an original bust by Norman Pierce would also be erected in the grounds of the cathedral. On the occasion we invited over 60 of William Walker's descendents and, with numerous Society members, organised a celebration lunch during which Gary and I outlined the work of Walker and our successful efforts in 'righting a wrong'.

I decided to revisit Gibraltar after a 44 year absence when my friends, John and Annie Bevan would be in the vicinity on holiday. I stayed with Fred Short and his wife Chris who now ran Rock Marine the BSAC school there. They had a home in San Roque, across the border in Spain, which was no easier to cross than it had been back in 1953. On the return journey to Gib, cars were often delayed to dissuade tourists from visiting the colony. Fred, however, had found the answer. I travelled on the back of his high-powered motor bike, and we merely had to wave our passports as we sped through.

We dived on wrecks off the South Mole and I then walked up Engineer Lane to where my father had had his Command Pay Office in 1952 and then on to our old house in Town Range which now had a shiny plate outside, on which was engraved 'Attorney General's Office'.

John Bevan came over with his son, Tom, who I had taught, and we dived at the Seven Sisters which had been our favourite spearfishing spot years ago.

By the end of the year, I had decided to give up the LUC. There were now very many PADI instructors working in the London area and profit margins were small. I was also enjoying organising the HDS events although they did not, of course, provide an income. Seth Sethna, who had worked with me and now had his own school, took over the LUC and continued at the Queen Mother Sports Centre in Victoria.

I taught my last pupils in 1998. They were John and Janie's son Paul (aged 12) and Anne Hibbert, the most attractive and appreciative vicar I had ever met. A few months later I took Paul on his first shallow dive in Barbados where the Selbys and I were on holiday. To my consternation, he disappeared like a rabbit into the engine room of the first wreck I showed him. I was relieved that he came out again soon afterwards, or there would have been hell to pay from his mother who was diving nearby!

Barbados was one of the friendliest islands in the West Indies with policemen wearing English type helmets and statues of Nelson among the hibiscus. In spite of this, the dive centre was robbed at gunpoint while we were on the island but, as the charming local girl behind the counter hastened to hand over the diving watches, no one was hurt.

We visited Julian Marryshaw, a friend of John Rawlins's whose father had been a leading figure in the history of the island of Grenada. Julian was tall and patrician and had been one of the few black Spitfire pilots in the RAF during the Battle of Britain. His wife Rhondda was an ex-concert pianist. Julian prepared a Chinese meal for us at his home. I was on the island for my 68th birthday and, over rum punches, gave thanks that I was still in reasonable physical shape in spite of more 'ups and downs' with my heart. My childhood years in the West Indies now seemed like another life altogether.

Our next conference was in Bristol with dinner on board Brunel's great steamship the *Great Britain*. Stan Waterman, the famous film-maker agreed to come and we listened, enthralled by his stories and films.

I became good friends with Seth who had bought the LUC, and we visited the tropical island of Madeira together in December 1998, exploring the old whaling village of Canical, and Camara de Lobos, where Churchill painted and monk seals visited. We jumped off a 15-foot deep water jetty to get down into a rolling sea at Porto Novo and stroked big groupers that followed us through the underwater reserve.

A few months later 'the elastic' that was said to connect me to Giglio was at work again and I took Seth there and we dived with Claus and his students. He enjoyed it so much that we were back there again in September!

In August I had visited Trevor Hampton, my old diving teacher, at Warfleet Creek and interviewed him. He was now a sprightly 87 and had recently bought a new Swedish motor cruiser in which he toured us around the Sound to show us where I would have done my original dives.

During one of the mini-conferences I organised, John Lowe showed a slide from a rare publication of 1730 by Captain Jacob Rowe, one of the first 'barrel divers'. It was the first publication in English on diving and one of the very few copies was owned by the National Maritime Museum. I suggested to the Society that we should contact them to arrange a joint re-publication of it. I set up a Society publications committee consisting of Nigel Phillips, Mike Fardell and myself. The new museum publications officer agreed to a joint publication and we had a series of meetings to iron out the details. The monograph was finally published, with an introduction by Mike and Nigel, in 2000 and became the first in a series.

I visited Turkey again with Peter and Jeni who were now well established there. Bodrum was dusty and infested with cars, but with cheap and good food and they got me a room for the equivalent of £5 per night. I met Joby and Kenan who were now local dive operators. They arrived on the quayside, where their dive boat *Nimets* was berthed, on a couple of powerful motor bikes. Joby had managed a pub in Brighton until she met Kenan, a Turk, and they set up house in Bodrum. I dived with her mother, Margot, who was intent on becoming an underwater archaeologist and helped them out with numbers of beginners in the days that followed.

After yet another visit to Giglio with Seth, I was there again, this time with the Bulgins and a party of their Italian friends who had booked the large villa in Campese with its 'Saracen' tower overlooking the sea. It had been originally constructed by Ferdinando de Medici in 1600. We dived with Claus and another set of young biologists.

Early in 2001, Graham Gourlay, the publisher of *Dive* magazine asked me to write a history of the BSAC in time for their 50th anniversary. It was to be a celebration of the Club's achievements in a substantial book of some 100,000 words.

I was contacted by Faith Warn, an expatriate writer, now living on the island of Kalymnos in the Greek Dodecanese. She had written a book on the nineteenth-century Greek sponge diving industry and wanted to quote from *Divers and Diving*. She told me that the Kalymnians were planning an annual diving festival that would include demonstrations of their traditional ways of diving, and I decided to visit the island to find out more and perhaps find a suitable speaker on Greek sponge diving for a future conference. Bill Braithwaite was interested in going too, and we set off in September. Faith, and her partner Al, acted as our guides and arranged meetings with various local businessmen and dignitaries, including the Mayor, who made a long speech to us about the value of tourism in the future. We enjoyed Telendos, a small island off the coast with its Roman remains and an excellent restaurant and I swam each morning before breakfast The diving was good and I promised to try to organise a visit from the Society.

My cardiac specialist, Jonathon Clague reported that my heart had gone into a 'bubbly rhythm' and took me in to administer some electric shocks to it. Mike Fardell, our HDS Secretary, asked if he could come and watch, as he said the smell of burning flesh would give him an appetite for dinner. Jonathon was not so keen, but performed the operation with his usual panache and it was pronounced successful. He later fitted me with a pacemaker, which would prevent me taking up an arc-welding career, but would not stop my diving.

In August I had a flight in a 'Tiger Moth'. I had not been up in one of these tiny machines since my father had taken me up at an air show when I was five. The flight took off from Redhill and we got airborne at 70 mph and rolled around Godstone on a beautiful day. The particular machine I was in had been built in 1929 – one year before me.

Some time later, I flew out to Antigua with British Airways and my friend Rowena. From there we flew on to Dominica and were driven up through a darkening forest before descending again to Roseau and a welcome from Castle Comfort. A day or so later, two small sailing boats arrived in the bay. They held Bob and Sandy Bulgin and eleven of their friends who had sailed in from Martinique.

I dived with Dave Hurley off Derek Perryman's new catamaran and then again with the whole party before we left to go whale watching. The Sperm whales looked like huge mobile tree-trunks when they surfaced. A day later a Carib Indian rowed us up the Indian River to drink 'Dynamite Punch' from a shack in the forest. 'It makes you want to fly', they told us.

Rowena and I changed places with one of the couples on board and we sailed in formation northwards, bound for the Saintes, off which Admiral Rodney successfully battled the French some centuries before. Then it was on to Guadeloupe where we dived in a fearsome current before coming ashore for the return journey.

My book on the history of BSAC was published in 2003 in time for the Club's 50th Anniversary party at the Waldorf Hotel in central London where it had been originally formed. I was asked to present a copy to the BSAC President, Prince Charles, some time later when he was touring the city and seeing a junior snorkelling club in action. He told us that he still had an excellent pair of shoes made from the leather recovered from the 'leather wreck' in Plymouth Sound.

The Kalymnians organised their first festival in 2004 and I joined up with Bill, John Bevan, Mike Fardell and John and Una Smillie to participate. Our first dive was from an old sponge boat, with a 'modern' sponge diver who used primitive 'hookah gear' connected by what looked very like an old garden hose. The Kalymnians now had a Scuba diving operation, known as 'Pegasus' and we aqualung dived with their chief instructor Michael Genevrakis and a young Finnish girl assistant who rejoiced in the name of Tiia Porri. Tiia and I had a mutual fascination with octopi and spent some time trying to coax them out of their holes. We visited the impressive 'museum' of an old diver, Stavros Valsamides, which held an astonishing collection of amphoras, sponges, miscellaneous sea life and old photographs of the Kalymnian divers.

Roger Hale who had helped me during my second season at Giglio now lived in the United States and was keen to return to Giglio and show the island to his young son and daughter who were both now divers. John Towse, who had originally found the *Mary Rose* with Alex McKee came too. We enjoyed many happy reunions and dinners with Filippo and Wally and Trudy and Gigi besides meeting up with the elusive Costantino again.

Roger and I dived together again after 43 years, and had a nostalgic dive at the Scoglio del Corvo where we had made the 'body recoveries' back in 1961. Barracudas glistened in the sun as we flew down the rock walls, but we kept our young charges a good deal shallower than the recovery site.

In 2005 I met up with another of my early instructors Vernon Knapper. Vernon had been one of my closest friends and supporters ever since his arrival in Zembra in 1966. He now had a *pied-à-terre* in Antigua and I joined him and Christina there to enjoy a little diving and a three-day circumnavigation of the island in a 50-foot sailing schooner. I survived wine tastings, belly dancing, crab racing and a promise of 'seven years bad sex' from a dusky couturière friend called Noreen

John and Janie organised a splendid party to celebrate my 75th and I was presented with some interesting mementos and presents. It was exactly 50 years since my first dive at Dartmouth and I felt so lucky to have been in at the beginning of the great aqualung adventure. I now wonder how long the beauty I have seen below the surface will remain to be seen by the youngsters of tomorrow.

My memories stretch back to those first youthful spear-fishing days in Spain, where we first explored the

> Sand-strewn caverns, cool and deep,
> Where the winds are all asleep.

Then on to the years taking 'my' beginners on their first dives, and watching their delight in their first experiences underwater. Walt Whitman's lines seem strangely applicable:

> Sail forth, steer for the deep waters only,
> Reckless O Soul, exploring, I with thee, and thou with me,
> For we are bound where mariner has not yet dared to go.

I hope that new adventures still lie ahead.

ILLUSTRATION ACKNOWLEDGEMENTS

BLACK AND WHITE

11, Sigi Koster; 12, 21, 27, Roger Hale; 13, 14, 26, Tim Glover; 16, 17, Maurizio Sarra; 18, Victor de Sanctis; 20, Helga Traschler; 22, Claudio Ripa; 25, Bruce Fraser; 28, Angus Loch; 32, Stan Hayward; 33, Bill Smith; 36, Wendy Lloyd-Kirk; 39, Geoff Harwood; 40, Susan Telling; 46, Zarah Amadouny; 48,49, Ken Hay; 56, 57, Stuart Usher; 59, 60 Hannes Zimmerman; 66, Alex Double; 72, Jerry Amos; 74, 76, Paul Arbiter; 75, David Swann.

COLOUR

2, Sigi Koster; 3, Otto Honneggar; 4, Mensun Bound; 6, 7, 8, Robson Books; 9, Mike Portelly; 10, Robert Bulgin; 12, 13, Brian Pitkin; 16, John Bevan; 17, John Towse; 18, Michael Seydell.

CARTOON SKETCH

Page 10 and front of binding, by Dick Williams

INDEX

Illustration numbers are given in bold, those in colour are prefixed **C**.